Better Homes and Gardens®

Christmas from the Heart®

Holiday Magic

Better Homes and Gardens® Books
Des Moines, Iowa

Better Homes and Gardens® Books
An imprint of Meredith® Books

Christmas from the Heart: Holiday Magic
Editor: Carol Field Dahlstrom
Technical Editor: Susan Banker
Graphic Designer: Gayle Schadendorf
Technical Illustrator: Chris Neubauer Graphics
Photographers: Hopkins Associates and Scott Little
Copy Chief: Angela K. Renkoski
Editorial and Design Assistants: Judy Bailey, Jennifer Norris
Electronic Production Coordinator: Paula Forest
Production Director: Douglas Johnston
Production Manager: Pam Kvitne
Prepress Coordinator: Marjorie J. Schenkelberg

Meredith® Books
Editor in Chief: James D. Blume
Design Director: Matt Strelecki
Managing Editor: Gregory H. Kayko
Director, New Product Development: Ray Wolf

Vice President, General Manager: Jamie L. Martin

***Better Homes and Gardens®* Magazine**
Editor in Chief: Jean LemMon

Meredith Publishing Group
President, Publishing Group: Christopher M. Little
Vice President and Publishing Director: John P. Loughlin

Meredith Corporation
Chairman of the Board: Jack D. Rehm
President and Chief Executive Officer: William T. Kerr

Chairman of the Executive Committee: E. T. Meredith III

Cover photograph: Hopkins Associates

All of us at Better Homes and Gardens® Books are dedicated to providing you with the information and ideas you need to create beautiful and useful projects. We guarantee your satisfaction with this book for as long as you own it. We welcome your questions, comments, and suggestions. Please write to us at: Better Homes and Gardens Books, Crafts, RW–240, 1716 Locust Street, Des Moines, IA 50309–3023.

First Edition. Printing Number and Year: 5 4 3 2 1 01 00 99 98 97

ISBN: 0-696-20653-6
ISSN: 1081-4698

Our seal assures you that every recipe in *Christmas from the Heart: Holiday Magic* has been tested in the Better Homes and Gardens® Test Kitchen. This means that each recipe is practical and reliable, and meets our high standards of taste appeal. We guarantee your satisfaction with this book for as long as you own it.

If you would like to order additional copies of this book, call 800/439-7159.

How does it happen year after year? Sometimes in those wintry days before Christmas, it seems like it will take a miracle to create the kind of holiday you envision for your family. But each year, almost like magic, the gifts are wrapped in printed paper and shiny ribbons, the cards are addressed with special notes inside, dear friends come to call, and you've made just the perfect cookies to serve. Your home sparkles with the excitement of the season, and you are ready to celebrate once again. Amid the bustling crowds, the last-minute party rush, and the gifts that took so long to make—you always seem to do it all, and your family loves you for it. We hope this book will help you keep those traditions that you hold dear and will inspire you with gift ideas, decorations, and trims so you can continue, year after year, to create your own

Holiday Magic

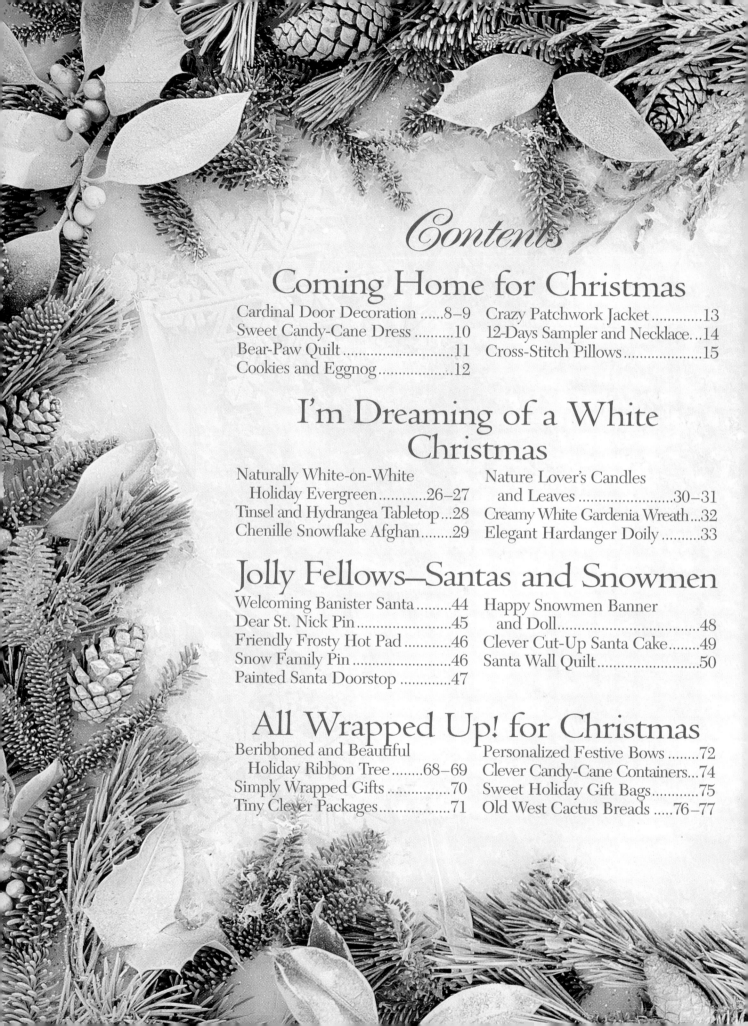

Contents

Coming Home for Christmas

Cardinal Door Decoration 8–9
Sweet Candy-Cane Dress 10
Bear-Paw Quilt 11
Cookies and Eggnog 12
Crazy Patchwork Jacket 13
12-Days Sampler and Necklace...14
Cross-Stitch Pillows 15

I'm Dreaming of a White Christmas

Naturally White-on-White Holiday Evergreen............26–27
Tinsel and Hydrangea Tabletop...28
Chenille Snowflake Afghan........29
Nature Lover's Candles and Leaves 30–31
Creamy White Gardenia Wreath...32
Elegant Hardanger Doily 33

Jolly Fellows–Santas and Snowmen

Welcoming Banister Santa 44
Dear St. Nick Pin 45
Friendly Frosty Hot Pad 46
Snow Family Pin 46
Painted Santa Doorstop 47
Happy Snowmen Banner and Doll....................................48
Clever Cut-Up Santa Cake........49
Santa Wall Quilt..........................50

All Wrapped Up! for Christmas

Beribboned and Beautiful Holiday Ribbon Tree........68–69
Simply Wrapped Gifts 70
Tiny Clever Packages..................71
Personalized Festive Bows 72
Clever Candy-Cane Containers...74
Sweet Holiday Gift Bags............75
Old West Cactus Breads 76–77

For Unto Us a Child Is Born

Cross-Stitched Nativity........88–89
Folk Art Pillow 90
Sweet Advent Angel....................91
Sparkling Chrismons 92
A Child Is Born Card and Bookmark................................93

The Stockings Were Hung by the Chimney

The Enchantment of Christmas Stockings.......104–105
Felt St. Nick Stocking..............106
Country Patchwork Stocking...107
Festive Hardanger Stocking....108
Nutcracker Ballet Stocking......109
Crochet Candy-Cane Stocking...110
Tiny Felt Stockings..................110

All I Want for Christmas

Goodies and Giggles Tree...126–127
Faux Gingerbread Friends.......128
Christmas Twins.......................128
Freddy the Frog Prince...........129
Tiny Carolers............................130

The Glorious Evergreen

Button-Tree Trims 146
Gift-Giving Mittens 146
Flannel Tree Quilt 147
Hankie Tree...............................148
Holiday Yule Log......................149
Country Homespun Trims 150
Christmas Collection Tree.......151
Index and Abbreviations...158–159

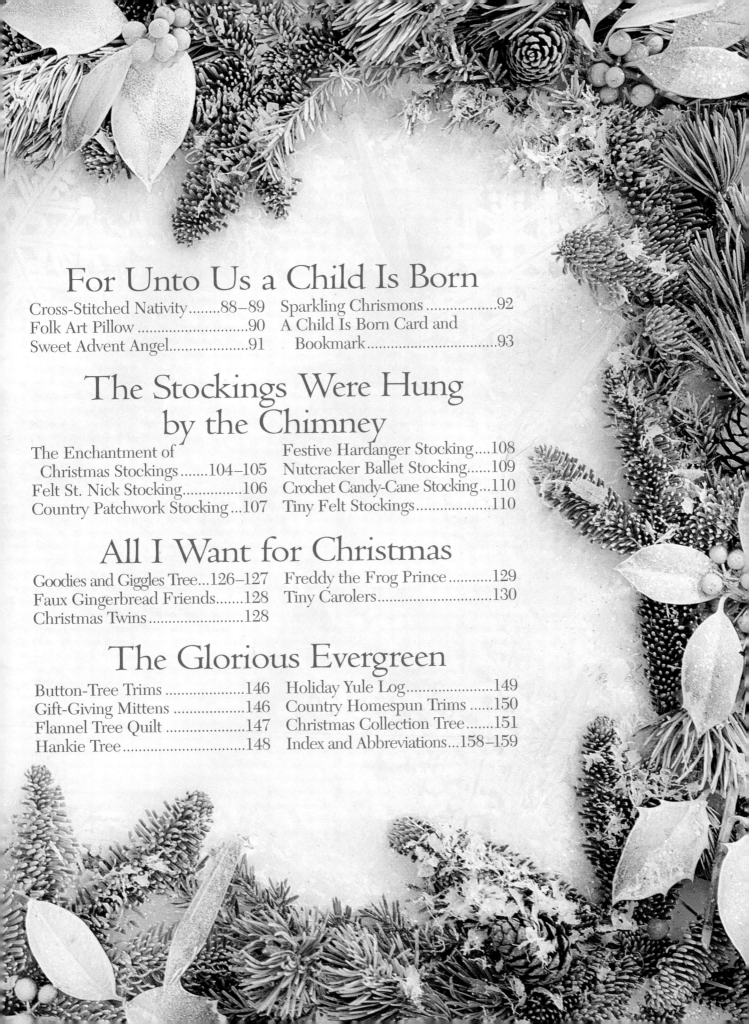

Coming Home for Christmas

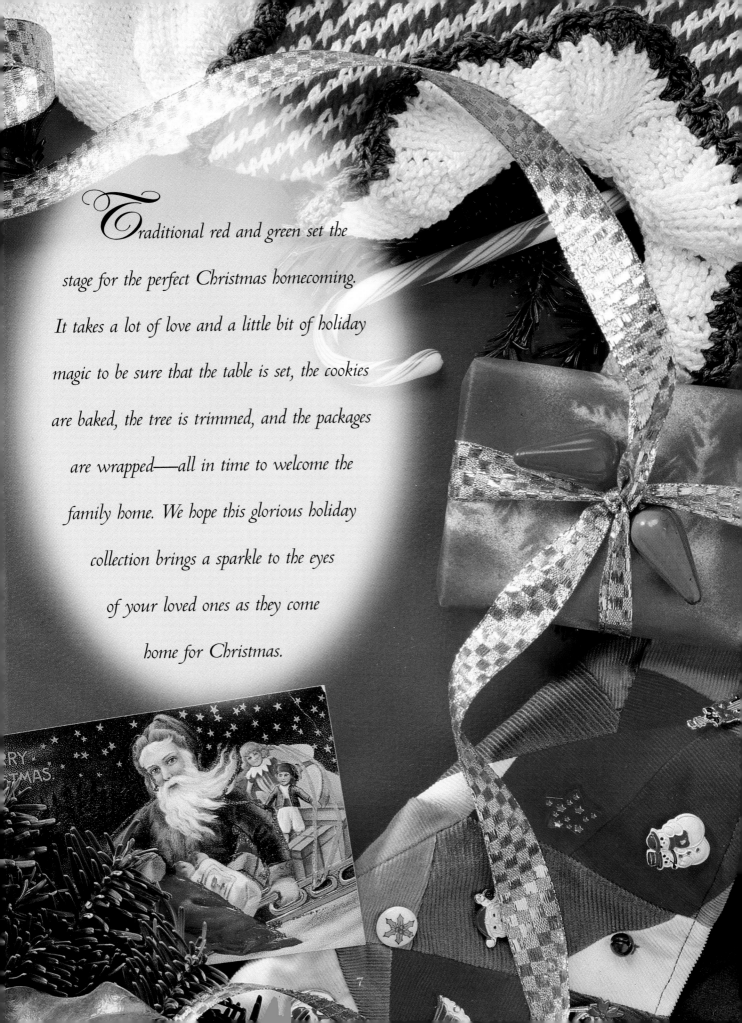

Traditional red and green set the stage for the perfect Christmas homecoming. It takes a lot of love and a little bit of holiday magic to be sure that the table is set, the cookies are baked, the tree is trimmed, and the packages are wrapped—all in time to welcome the family home. We hope this glorious holiday collection brings a sparkle to the eyes of your loved ones as they come home for Christmas.

Cardinal Door Decoration

Good old Santa himself waits at the door, seemingly framed by our stunning door decoration, ready to greet our little one for the big day. The simple yet festive door piece is fashioned from straight twigs bundled together and embellished with purchased red cardinals and berries. The entire display is then lovingly sprayed with white snow for a wintry touch. Instructions for making the door decoration are on page 16.

Design: Donna Chesnut

Sweet Candy-Cane *Dress*

Our sweet toddler is dressed for that special day in her bright and cheery holiday dress. Knit with sport yarn, the dress has a striped yoke and white cable skirt. Instructions for the dress begin on page 16.

Design: Ann Smith

Bear-Paw *Quilt*

Cuddle under your very own Christmas bear-paw quilt and read some favorite holiday stories to the ones you love. This classic design complements the season with its bright red and white color. Complete instructions to make this favorite quilt using our full-size templates are found on pages 17-18.

Design: Antique

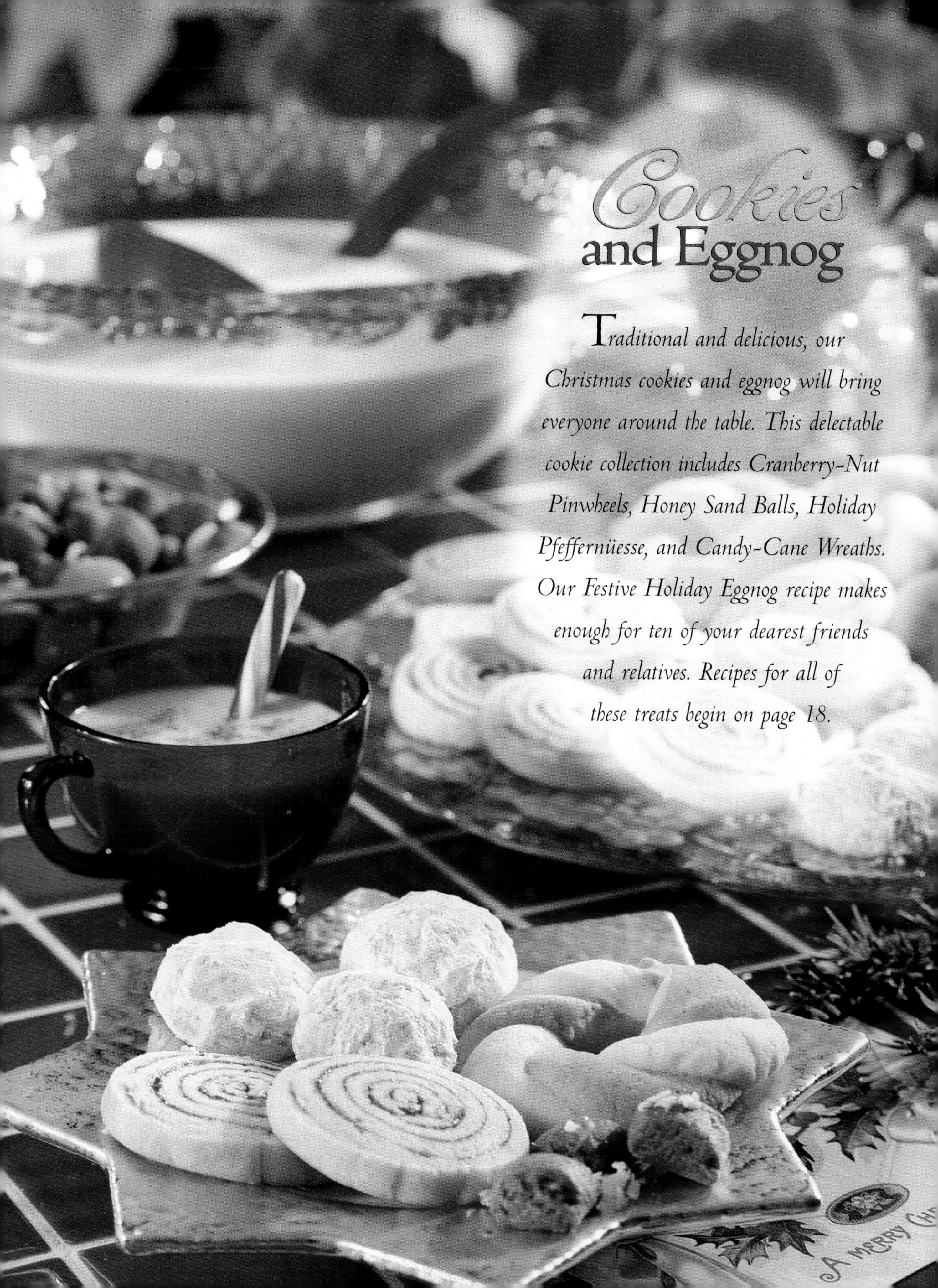

Cookies and Eggnog

Traditional and delicious, our Christmas cookies and eggnog will bring everyone around the table. This delectable cookie collection includes Cranberry-Nut Pinwheels, Honey Sand Balls, Holiday Pfeffernüesse, and Candy-Cane Wreaths. Our Festive Holiday Eggnog recipe makes enough for ten of your dearest friends and relatives. Recipes for all of these treats begin on page 18.

Crazy Patchwork *Jacket*

You'll look simply charming in our crazy patchwork jacket trimmed with clever charms and buttons. The lapels are worked in colorful corduroy patchwork, making a happy holiday statement. Instructions for the jacket begin on page 20.

Design: Margaret Sindelar

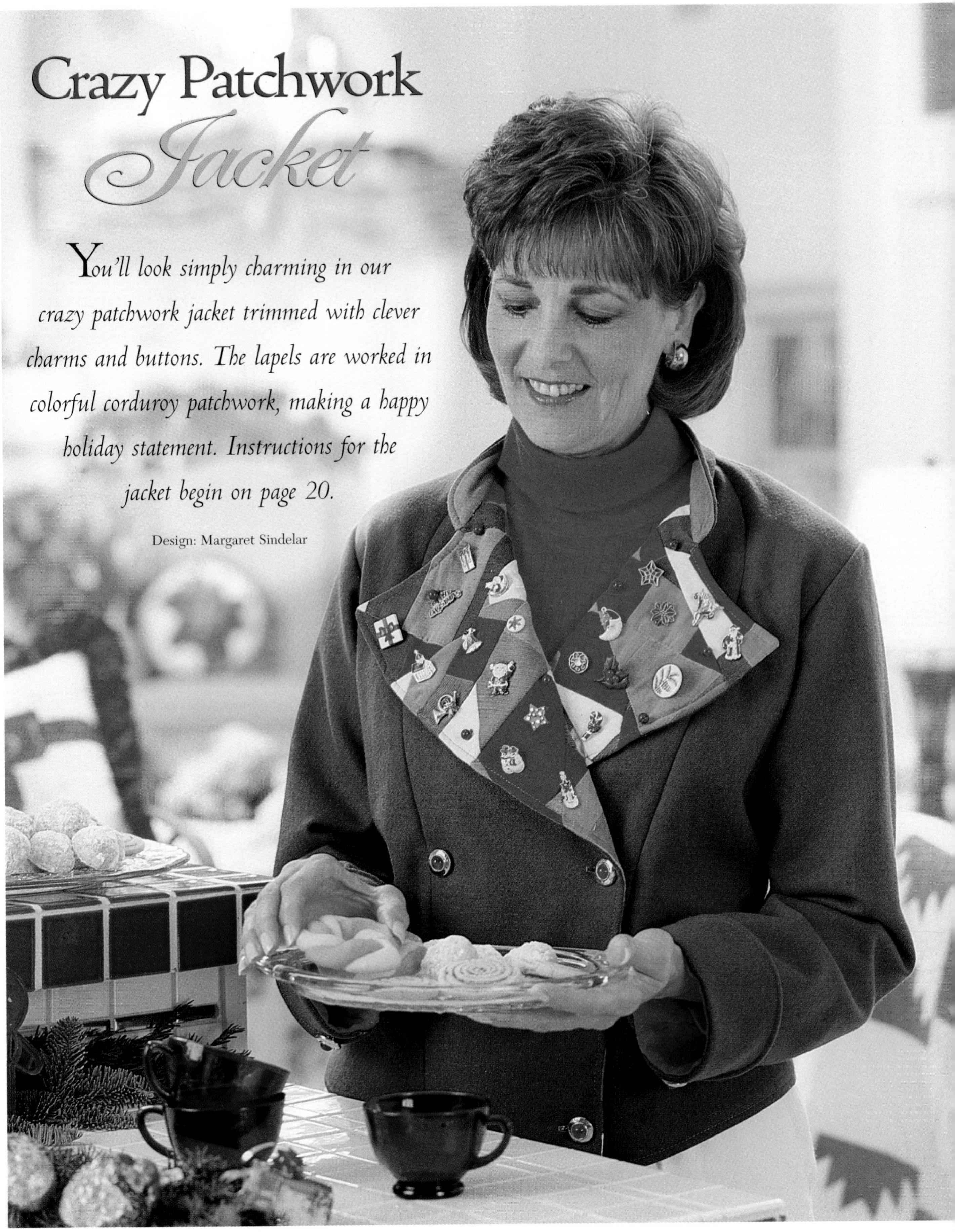

12-Days Sampler and Necklace

Your true love will adore our 12-days sampler stitched just in time for Christmas. Each day of the song is represented in colorful cross-stitch that you lovingly create. We've simplified the symbols and framed them in purchased gold charms for a clever necklace that will keep you singing as you wear it during the season. Charts and instructions for both projects begin on page 20.

Design: Carole Rodgers

Cross-Stitch Pillows

In the wink of an eye you can cross-stitch our pretty package and poinsettia pillows. Worked on seven-count Klostern fabric, the pillows stitch up quickly to accent your holiday home (or to give as a special gift). We have added beads for a sparkling touch.

Charts and instructions begin on page 20.

Design: Jim Williams

Cardinal Door Decoration

Pictured on page 9.

MATERIALS

Twigs, gathered or purchased
Craft wire
Hot-glue gun; glue sticks
Artificial berries
Decorative moss
Artificial feathered cardinals
Artificial spray snow

INSTRUCTIONS

Measure width and height of door to be decorated. On a flat surface, arrange the twigs in a rectangular shape slightly larger than the door measurements, intersecting the twigs at the corners. Wire the twigs together.

Arrange bunches of berries around the twig frame as desired, concealing the wire. Glue the berries in place.

Shape small portions of the decorative moss into nest shapes. Secure nest shapes to frame at each corner with glue.

Wire the cardinals to the twig frame as desired. Hang the twig decoration around the door. Spray as desired using purchased snow.

Candy-Cane Dress

Pictured on page 10.

Directions are for size 2. Changes for sizes 4 and 6 follow in parentheses. Finished chest size = 23(25, 27) inches. Skill Level: For the intermediate knitter.

MATERIALS

Reynold's Saucy Sport (50-gram or 123-yard skein): 6(7, 7) skeins of white (800); and for all sizes, 1 skein each of red (361) and green (604)
Size 3 and 4 circular knitting needles, 24-inch length or size needed to obtain gauge recommended below
Size 3 straight knitting needles
Size D crochet hook
Tapestry needle
Five ⅝-inch-diameter buttons
Stitch holders

GAUGE: In Stockinette Stitch (st st) with larger needle, 31 sts = 5 inches and 9 rows = 1 inch. In two-color st st with larger needle, 15 sts = 2 inches and 7 rows = 1 inch.

INSTRUCTIONS

Note: To work the diagonally striped st st bodice, carry strands loosely across WS of fabric. To change color, bring new strand from under previous strand for a twist to prevent holes.

SKIRT: Beginning at the hem, using white and with the larger needle, cast on 199(211, 223) sts. Beginning with a k row, work 4 rows st st. For the eyelet row, k 1, * yo, k 2 tog; rep from * across. Beginning with a p row, work 4 rows st st.

For skirt pattern: * K 1 row on the WS of fabric, work 11 rows of st st, beginning with a k row; rep from * for pat to about 13(15, 17) inches from beginning, ending with a WS row.

WAISTBAND: Change to smaller needle and green and k across, dec 34(30, 26) sts evenly spaced = 165(181, 197) sts.

Ribbing, Row 1 (WS): P 1, * k 1, p 1; rep from * across.

Row 2: K 1, * p 1, k 1; rep from * across rep rows 1 and 2 once more, then rep Row 1 again.

BODICE: Break off green and change to larger needle. To est the diagonally striped bodice, work as follows:

Row 1 (RS): * K 2 red, k 2 white; rep from * across, ending k 1 red.

Row 2: * P 2 red, p 2 white; rep from * across, ending p 1 red.

Row 3: * K 2 white, k 2 red; rep from * across the first 40(44, 48) sts for left back. Place remaining sts onto holders for later.

For left back armhole shaping: In est striped pat, bind off 6 sts at the beg of the next row, then dec 1 st at armhole edge every other row 5 times = 29(33, 37) sts rem. Work even to 5½(6, 6½) inches from first Waistband row. Bind off all sts.

For front: Return center 85(93, 101) sts to larger needle, leaving remaining 40(44, 48) sts on a holder for right back; rejoin strands. Beginning with a RS row and working in est striped pat, bind off 6 sts at beg of the next 2 rows; then, dec 1 st each edge every other row 5 times = 63(71, 79) sts rem. Work even to 4(4½, 5) inches from first Waistband row, ending with a WS row.

Neck shaping: Work est pat on first 25(28, 30) sts; join new strands and bind off the center 13(15, 19) sts for front neck; work rem sts. Working sides separately and at the same time, dec 1 st at each neck edge every other row 5 times = 20(23, 25) sts rem for each shoulder. Work to same length as left back. Bind off all sts.

For right back: With the RS facing, join new strands and bind off the first 6 sts for armhole, then dec 1 st at armhole edge every other row 5 times. Cont as for left back.

SLEEVES (make two): With smaller needle and green, cast on 37(41, 45) sts. Work ribbing rows 2 and 1 as for Waistband. Change to larger needle and white and k across next row, inc 27 sts evenly spaced = 64(68, 72) sts. Working in st st, inc 1 st each edge every other row 3 times = 70(74, 78) sts. Work even to about

1½ inches from beginning. Shape armholes as for front bodice = 48(52, 56) sts.

Work even to 3(3½, 4) inches from beginning of armhole shaping. Bind off 3 sts at the beginning of the next 6 rows = 30(34, 38) sts. On the next RS row, * k 2 tog; rep from * across = 15(17, 19) sts. P 1 row. Bind off all sts.

FINISHING: Join shoulder seams. Join sleeve seams.

For sleeves: Run a basting thread along the sleeve cap and pull to slightly gather. Set in sleeves, easing fullness across shoulder area. With the RS facing using crochet hook, join green to bodice at underarm seam close to sleeve seam. Work 46(50, 54) sl sts around; at end, sl st in beginning sl st and fasten off. For scalloped edging, join green 1(1½, 2) inches from underarm seam and in a green sl st (draw up a lp, ch 1). * In next sl st (3 dc), sl st in next sl st; rep from * for sixteen times more and end about 1(1½, 2) inches from underarm seam = seventeen scallops. At end, fasten off.

Join skirt seam from lower edge up 10½(13, 15½) inches. Turn hem to WS along the eyelet row forming a picot edge and sew in place.

For left back placket: With the RS facing using smaller needle and green, pick up and k 40 sts from top of skirt seam to neck edge. K 6 rows. Bind off all sts.

For right back placket: With the RS facing using smaller needle and green, pick up and k 40 sts from neck edge to top of skirt seam. K 2 rows.

Buttonholes: K 8, * bind off 2 sts, k 5 sts; rep from * across for 5 buttonholes and ending last rep k to end of row. On the next row, k across and cast on 2 sts over each buttonhole. K 2 more rows. Bind off all sts. Sew buttons opposite buttonholes. Join lower placket ends tog and to top of skirt seam.

For collar: With smaller needle and white, cast on 97(113, 129) sts. Work collar pat as follows:

Row 1 (RS): K 1, * yo, (k 1, p 1) 7 times, k 1, yo, k 1; rep from * across.

Row 2: K 1, * p 2, (k 1, p 1) 7 times, p 1, k 1; rep from * across.

Row 3: K 2, * yo, (k 1, p 1) 7 times, k 1, yo, k 3; rep from * across, ending last rep k 2.

Row 4: K 2, * p 2, (k 1, p 1) 7 times, p 1, k 3; rep from * across, ending last rep k 2.

Row 5: K 3, * yo, (k 1, p 1) 7 times, k 1, yo, k 5; rep from * across, ending last rep k 3.

Row 6: K 3, * p 2, (k 1, p 1) 7 times, p 1, k 5; rep from * across, ending last rep k 3.

Row 7: K 4, * yo, (k 1, p 1) 7 times, k 1, yo, k 7; rep from * across, ending last rep k 4.

Row 8: K 4, * p 2, (k 1, p 1) 7 times, p 1, k 7; rep from * across, ending last rep k 4.

Row 9: K 5, * (ssk) 3 times, sl 1, k 2 tog, psso, (k 2 tog) 3 times, k 9; rep from * across, ending last rep k 5.

Row 10: Purl.

Row 11: K 1, * k 2 tog; rep from * across = 49(57, 65) sts.

With the RS facing, using smaller needle and white, leaving green plackets free, pick up and k 49(57, 65) sts along neck edge. P 1 row. Holding the collar next to the WS of the bodice at neck edge, k tog the first st from each needle, * k tog the next st from each needle and bind off; rep from * across to end.

With the RS facing, using crochet hook, attach green to back edge of collar near the neck seam (draw up a lp, ch 1). Sl st in same st, * 3 dc in next st, sl st in next st; rep from * around collar edge. At end, fasten off.

Bear-Paw Quilt

As pictured on page 11, finished size is 70½x84½ inches.

MATERIALS

2¾ yards of 45-inch-wide red cotton fabric
5¾ yards of 45-inch-wide white fabric
5½ yards of 45-inch-wide muslin backing
81x96-inch piece of quilt batting
9 yards of white bias binding
Cardboard or plastic for templates
Graph paper
Sewing and quilting thread

INSTRUCTIONS

The quilt consists of thirty 10-inch pieced blocks and 20 plain blocks set together on the diagonal. Pieced blocks are arranged in five rows of six blocks each. Top is pieced out with 18 side triangles and four corner triangles.

CUTTING PLAIN BLOCKS: Make a template for a 10-inch square. (Templates for plain blocks and setting triangles are finished size.) Add ¼-inch seam allowances to all sides when cutting pieces from fabric. Cut 20 white cotton squares.

For side and corner triangles, cut square template in half diagonally; label one triangle "side." Cut other piece in half again; label one triangle "corner." Cut 18 side triangles and four corner triangles. *Note: Cut side triangles with long side on the straight of grain and corner triangles with short side on the straight of grain.*

CUTTING PIECED BLOCKS: Using full-size pattern diagram, *page 18,* make templates for A-C pieces from cardboard or plastic, adding ¼-inch seam allowances all around; cut out. To use templates, draw around them with pencil on wrong side of fabric. *Note: Cutting instructions are for one block. Amounts in ()s are for cutting 30 pieced blocks.* From white fabric cut 24 (720) A, four (120) B, and four (120) C pieces. From red fabric, cut 24 (720) A and four (120) B pieces.

PIECED BLOCK ASSEMBLY: Sew white B triangle to red B triangle to form square. Join six white A triangles to six red A pieces similarly to form six small squares. Sew squares together into two strips of three squares each. Sew one strip to one red side of large square, red edges together. Add white C piece to red end of second strip and sew to other red side of square. Make three more squares. Sew four squares together to make pieced block. Make 30 pieced blocks.

QUILT ASSEMBLY: Lay out the blocks according to the quilt assembly diagram, *page 18.* Stitch together in diagonal rows; stitch rows together.

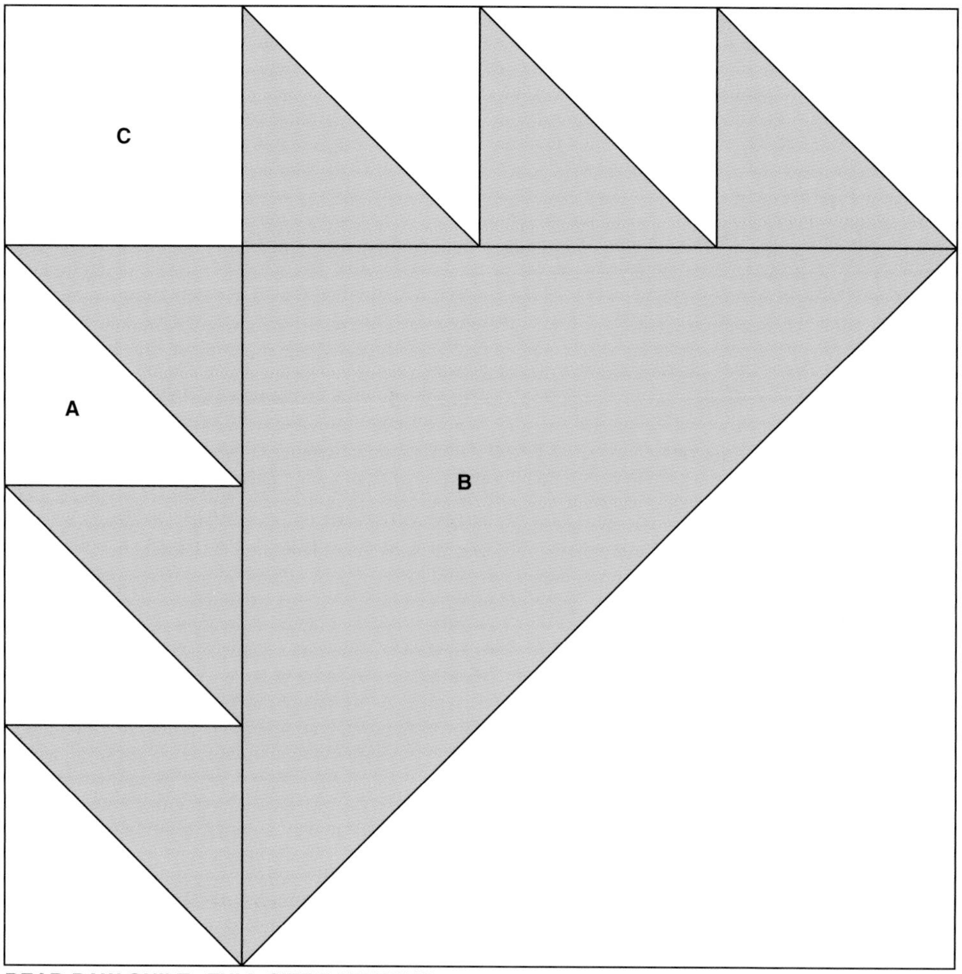

BEAR-PAW QUILT–FULL-SIZE PATTERNS

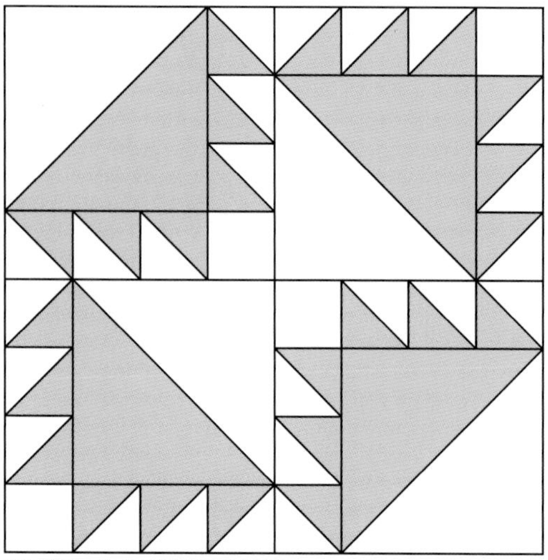

PIECED BLOCK DIAGRAM

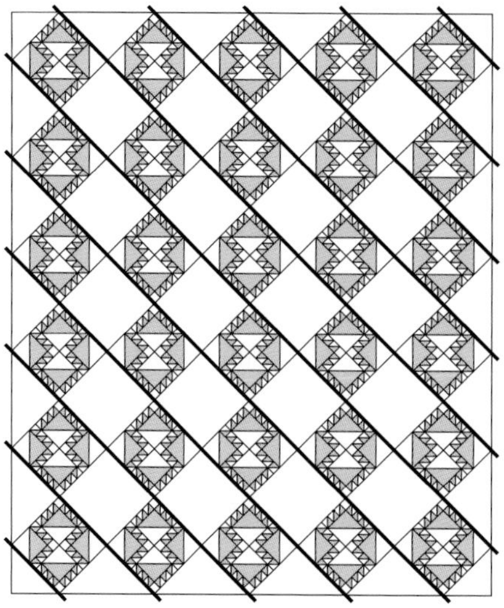

QUILT ASSEMBLY DIAGRAM

FINISHING: Cut muslin yardage in half across width; sew long edges together using ½-inch seam allowances. Piece batting to fit and sandwich between backing and quilt top. Baste layers together in several directions across the quilt to hold; quilt as desired. Bind the raw edges with bias binding.

Festive Holiday Eggnog

Pictured on page 12.

INGREDIENTS

- **6 beaten egg yolks**
- **2 cups milk**
- **⅓ cup sugar**
- **1 to 3 tablespoons light rum**
- **1 to 3 tablespoons bourbon**
- **1 teaspoon vanilla**
- **1 cup whipping cream**
- **2 tablespoons sugar**
- **Whipped cream; ground nutmeg**

METHOD

Stir together the egg yolks, milk, and ⅓ cup sugar in a large heavy saucepan. Cook and stir over medium heat till mixture just coats a metal spoon. Remove from heat. Cool quickly by placing pan in a sink or bowl of ice water and stirring for 2 minutes. Stir in rum, bourbon, and vanilla. Cover and chill 4 to 24 hours.

At serving time, whip 1 cup cream and 2 tablespoons sugar till soft peaks form. Transfer chilled egg mixture to a punch bowl. Fold in whipped cream mixture. Top each serving with whipped cream; sprinkle with nutmeg. Serve at once. Makes about 10 (4-ounce) servings.

Cranberry-Nut Pinwheels

Pictured on page 12.

INGREDIENTS

- **1 cup cranberries**
- **½ cup sugar**
- **1 teaspoon cornstarch**
- **¼ cup water**
- **⅔ cup cashews**
- **2 tablespoons butter, softened**
- **¾ cup butter**
- **3 cups all-purpose flour**
- **1 cup sugar**
- **1 egg**
- **3 tablespoons milk**
- **½ teaspoon baking soda**
- **½ teaspoon vanilla**

METHOD

For filling, in a small saucepan combine the cranberries, ½ cup sugar, and cornstarch. Add water. Bring to a boil, stirring to dissolve the sugar. Boil gently over medium heat for 5 minutes, stirring frequently. Remove from heat. Press the hot mixture through a sieve. Discard the solids. Cover the surface of the hot mixture and cool without stirring.

Place the cashews in a blender container or food processor bowl. Cover and blend or process till finely ground. Add the 2 tablespoons butter. Cover and blend or process about 3 minutes more or till mixture is smooth and spreadable. Stop and scrape down sides of container as necessary.

In a large mixing bowl, beat the ¾ cup butter and cashew mixture with an electric mixer on medium to high speed about 30 seconds or till softened. Add about half of the flour to the butter mixture. Then add the 1 cup sugar, egg, milk, baking soda, and vanilla. Beat till thoroughly combined, scraping the sides of the bowl occasionally. Then beat or stir in the remaining flour. Cover and chill about 1 hour or till dough is easy to handle.

Divide dough in half. Place each half of the dough between 2 sheets of waxed paper. Using a rolling pin, roll each half into a 16×12-inch rectangle.

Spread half of the filling over each half of dough. From a short side, roll up each half jelly-roll style, removing waxed paper as you roll. Moisten and pinch the edges to seal. Wrap each in waxed paper or plastic wrap. Chill for 4 to 48 hours. Cut the dough into ¼-inch-thick slices. Place about 2 inches apart on greased cookie sheets. (If you wish, place some cookies in pairs, with edges touching.)

Bake in a 375° oven for 10 to 12 minutes or till edges are firm and bottoms are lightly browned. Remove cookies and cool on wire racks. Makes 96 pinwheels or about 48 double pinwheels.

Honey Sand Balls

Pictured on page 12.

INGREDIENTS

- **1 cup butter, softened**
- **½ cup sifted powdered sugar**
- **2 tablespoons honey**
- **2 cups all-purpose flour**
- **¾ cup chopped walnuts**
- **1 teaspoon vanilla**
- **¼ teaspoon salt**
- **Sifted powdered sugar**

METHOD

In a large mixing bowl, beat the butter, the ½ cup powdered sugar, and honey with an electric mixer on medium speed till combined. Beat or stir in the flour, walnuts, vanilla, and salt. Mix thoroughly, using your hands, if necessary.

Shape dough into 1-inch balls. Place balls 1½ inches apart on greased cookie sheets. Bake in a 325° oven 14 to 16 minutes or till cookies are lightly browned. While cookies are still warm, roll them in powdered sugar. Cool cookies on wire racks. Roll cookies in powdered sugar again. Makes about 48.

Holiday Pfeffernüesse

Pictured on page 12.

INGREDIENTS

- **⅓ cup molasses**
- **¼ cup margarine or butter**
- **2 cups all-purpose flour**
- **¼ cup packed brown sugar**
- **½ teaspoon baking soda**
- **¾ teaspoon ground cinnamon**
- **¼ teaspoon ground cardamom**
- **¼ teaspoon ground allspice**
- **⅛ teaspoon pepper**
- **1 beaten egg**

METHOD

Combine molasses and margarine in a large saucepan. Heat and stir over low heat till margarine melts. Remove from heat. Cool to room temperature.

Stir together flour, brown sugar, soda, cinnamon, cardamom, allspice, and pepper in a large bowl; set aside.

Stir egg into molasses mixture. Gradually stir in flour mixture till combined. Transfer dough to a bowl. Cover; chill 1 hour or till easy to handle.

Divide dough into 12 portions. On a lightly floured surface roll each portion into a 10-inch rope. Cut ropes into ½-inch pieces. Place pieces ½ inch apart in an ungreased shallow baking pan. Bake in a 350° oven 10 to 12 minutes or till edges are firm and bottoms are lightly browned. Remove cookies; cool on paper towels. Makes about 240.

Candy-Cane Wreaths

Pictured on page 12.

INGREDIENTS

- **¾ cup butter or margarine**
- **¾ cup sugar**
- **¼ teaspoon baking powder**
- **1 egg**
- **½ teaspoon vanilla**
- **¼ teaspoon peppermint or almond extract**
- **2 cups all-purpose flour**
- **Red food coloring**

METHOD

Beat butter or margarine in a mixing bowl with an electric mixer on medium to high speed for 30 seconds. Add sugar and baking powder and beat till combined. Beat in egg, vanilla, and extract till combined. Beat in as much flour as you can with the mixer. Stir in any remaining flour with a wooden spoon. Divide dough in half. Stir desired amount of food coloring into one half. Cover each half and chill 30 minutes or till easy to handle.

Shape about ½ tablespoon of plain dough into a 5-inch rope on a lightly floured surface. Repeat with about ½ tablespoon of red dough. Place ropes side by side and twist together about six times.

Form twisted ropes into a circle, gently pinching where ends meet.

Place on an ungreased cookie sheet. Repeat with remaining dough, leaving 2 inches between cookies. Bake in a 375° oven about 10 minutes or till firm and bottoms are lightly browned. Cool on cookie sheet about 1 minute; remove cookies and cool on wire rack. Makes about 24.

Crazy Patchwork Jacket

Pictured on page 13.

MATERIALS

Folkwear pattern No. 133, or jacket pattern with similar collar
Green wool outer fabric and red lining fabric in amount specified on pattern
¼ yard each of 45-inch-wide dark green, medium green, light green, bright red, medium red, dark red, rose, and cream corduroy fabric
Green batiste in amount sufficient to back collar
Notions and interfacing as specified on pattern envelope
28 various Christmas buttons and charms

INSTRUCTIONS

Sew all seams with right sides of fabric facing unless otherwise indicated. Use ¼-inch seam allowances for patchwork. Construct jacket using seam allowances as specified in pattern instructions.

To make patchwork yardage, cut corduroy fabrics in strips, varying widths between 2 and 3 inches. Sew strips together in random color order to make yardage. Cut pieced yardage at various angles, cutting across seams. Restitch pieces to create yardage once again. Repeat if necessary, making patchwork shapes as small as desired.

Cut out jacket collar from patchwork and batiste; cut out remainder of jacket from fabrics as instructed in pattern. Baste batiste pieces to wrong sides of collar pieces. Continue constructing the jacket according to the pattern instructions.

When jacket is completed, sew charms and buttons to patchwork collar at random.

12-Days Necklace

Pictured on page 14.

MATERIALS

FABRICS

6x6-inch piece of white 22-count needlepoint canvas
6x6-inch piece of lightweight fusible interfacing

THREADS

Thread for basting
Cotton embroidery floss in colors listed in key on page 21
Metallic #8 braid in colors listed in key

SUPPLIES

Needle
Twelve 1⅛x⅞-inch gold jewelry finding charm frames with backs
3⅜x3½-inch piece of fusible transweb paper
3⅜x3½-inch piece of mat board
12 jump rings
24-inch length of desired gold neck chain with clasp

INSTRUCTIONS

Use a basting stitch to divide the needlepoint canvas into 12 equal rectangles, each measuring 2x1½ inches. Find the center of one chart for necklace piece, *page 21*, and of one rectangle; begin stitching there.

Use two plies of floss or one strand of cord to work half cross-stitches over one thread of the needlepoint canvas. Work French knots and backstitches using one ply of embroidery floss.

Fuse interfacing to back side of stitchery. Trace frame back onto transweb paper and mat board; cut out 12 of each. Carefully cut around each stitched design to make twelve 1⅛x⅞-inch rectangles. Fuse cross-stitch to mat board using transweb paper.

Slip the stitched pieces into the jewelry frames. Insert the frame backs behind stitchery. Starting 8 inches from chain clasp, attach framed partridge stitchery to neck chain using jump ring. Continue adding charms in consecutive order every 1¼ inches.

12-Days Sampler

Pictured on page 14.

MATERIALS

FABRIC

20x17-inch piece of 22-count white Hardanger fabric

THREADS

Cotton embroidery floss in colors listed in key on page 21
1 additional skein each of DMC 310 and 986
Metallic #8 braid as listed in key
Metallic cord as listed in key

SUPPLIES

Embroidery hoop
Needle
Mat and frame

INSTRUCTIONS

Tape or zigzag the edges of the Hardanger fabric to prevent fraying. Find the center of the chart, *page 22*, and the center of the fabric; begin stitching there.

Use three plies of floss, four strands of cord, or one strand of braid to work cross-stitches over two threads of Hardanger fabric. Work French knots using two plies of floss. Use two plies of floss to work backstitches.

Press the finished stitchery from the back. Mat and frame stitched piece as desired.

Cross-Stitch Pillows

As shown on page 15, poinsettia pillow, including ruffle, measures 18½ inches in diameter; bow pillow, including ruffle, measures 18×18 inches.

MATERIALS

FABRICS FOR POINSETTIA PILLOW

20x20-inch piece of 7-count ivory Klostern fabric
1¼ yards of red and green Christmas print fabric; ⅛ yard of coordinating Christmas print fabric
15x15-inch piece of ivory cotton fabric

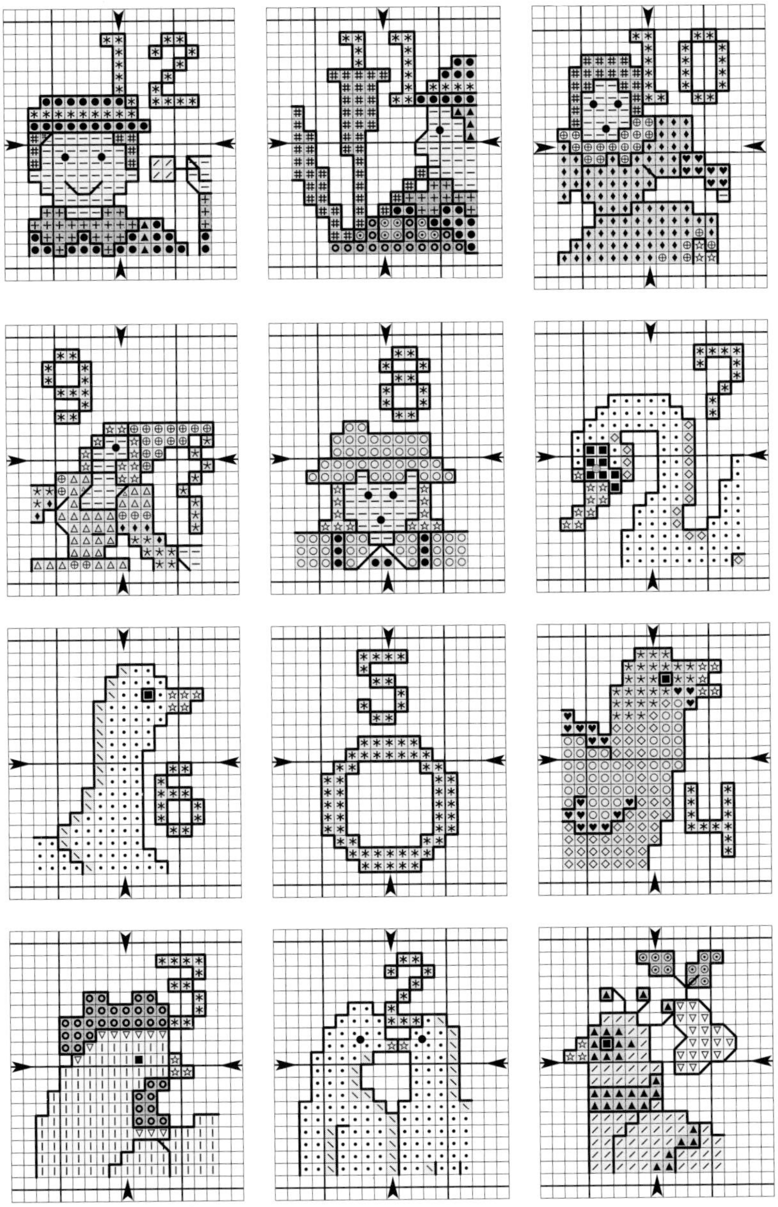

12-DAYS NECKLACE

12-DAYS SAMPLER AND NECKLACE

ANCHOR		DMC	
002	•	000	White
110	♦	208	Dark lavender
109	✴	209	Medium lavender
403	■	310	Black
9046	✚	321	True Christmas red
358	▲	433	Dark chestnut
310	▦	434	Medium chestnut
362	▢	437	Medium tan
1005	◉	498	Dark Christmas red
890	☆	729	Old gold
361	╱	738	Light tan
301	▽	744	Medium yellow
300	▯	745	Light yellow
1012	▬	754	Peach
234	╲	762	Pearl gray
1016	～	778	Antique mauve
132	●	797	Royal blue
144	◇	800	Delft blue
246	✕	986	Dark forest green
244	⊙	987	Medium forest green
888	▨	3045	Yellow beige
264	△	3348	Yellow green
087	♥	3607	Dark fuchsia
086	◯	3608	Medium fuchsia
	⊕	001	Kreinik silver #8 braid
	✳	002	Kreinik gold #8 braid
	◈	205C	Kreinik antique gold Balger cord

BACKSTITCH

403	╱	310 Black—all stitches

FRENCH KNOT

002	●	000 White—swan's eye
403	●	310 Black—eyes and mouths

Sampler stitch count: 149 high x 114 wide
Sampler finished design sizes:
22-count fabric – 13½ x 10⅜ inches
14-count fabric – 10⅝ x 8⅛ inches
18-count fabric – 8¼ x 6⅜ inches

#1, 2, 4, and 8
Necklace stitch count: 18 high x 14 wide
#1, 2, 4, and 8
Necklace finished design sizes:
22-count fabric – ⅞ x ⅝ inch
14-count fabric – 1¼ x 1 inches
18-count fabric – 1 x ¾ inch

#3, 7, 9, 11, and 12
Necklace stitch count: 18 high x 15 wide
#3, 7, 9, 11, and 12
Necklace finished design sizes:
22-count fabric – ⅞ x ⅝ inch
14-count fabric – 1¼ x 1⅛ inches
18-count fabric – 1 x ⅞ inch

#5 Necklace stitch count: 18 high x 11 wide
#5 Necklace finished design sizes:
22-count fabric – ⅞ x ½ inch
14-count fabric – 1¼ x ¾ inches
18-count fabric – 1 x ⅝ inch

#6 Necklace stitch count: 17 high x 14 wide
#6 Necklace finished design sizes:
22-count fabric – ¾ x ⅝ inch
14-count fabric – 1¼ x 1 inches
18-count fabric – ⅞ x ¾ inch

#10 Necklace stitch count: 19 high x 14 wide
#10 Necklace finished design sizes:
22-count fabric – ⅞ x ⅝ inch
14-count fabric – 1⅜ x 1 inches
18-count fabric – 1⅛ x ¾ inches

FABRICS FOR BOW PILLOW

22x22-inch piece of 7-count ivory
 Klostern fabric
1¼ yards of red and green Christmas
 print fabric; ⅛ yard of coordinating
 Christmas print fabric
16-inch-diameter circle of ivory cotton
 fabric

THREADS

Cotton embroidery floss in colors listed in
 keys, *pages 23–24*; red ⅛-inch ribbon

SUPPLIES

Embroidery hoop; needle
27 gold ⅛-inch-diameter beads
21 green ⅛-inch-diameter glass beads
⅛-inch-diameter cording; polyester fiberfill

INSTRUCTIONS

For each pillow design, tape or
zigzag edges of fabric to prevent
fraying. Find center of desired chart,
pages 23–24, and of fabric; begin
stitching there.

Use four plies of floss or one strand
of ribbon to work cross-stitches over
one square of fabric. Work backstitches
using two plies; work green backstitches on bow pillow using four plies.

For poinsettia pillow, attach
beads to center of poinsettia using
yellow floss.

For bow pillow, work weaving
stitch using one strand of ribbon as
shown on the chart, *page 24.* Attach
the green beads using Christmas
green floss.

Trim poinsettia pillow fabric to a
16-inch-diameter circle; trim bow
pillow fabric to 15 inches square.

Continued on page 23

12-DAYS SAMPLER

Key on page 21.

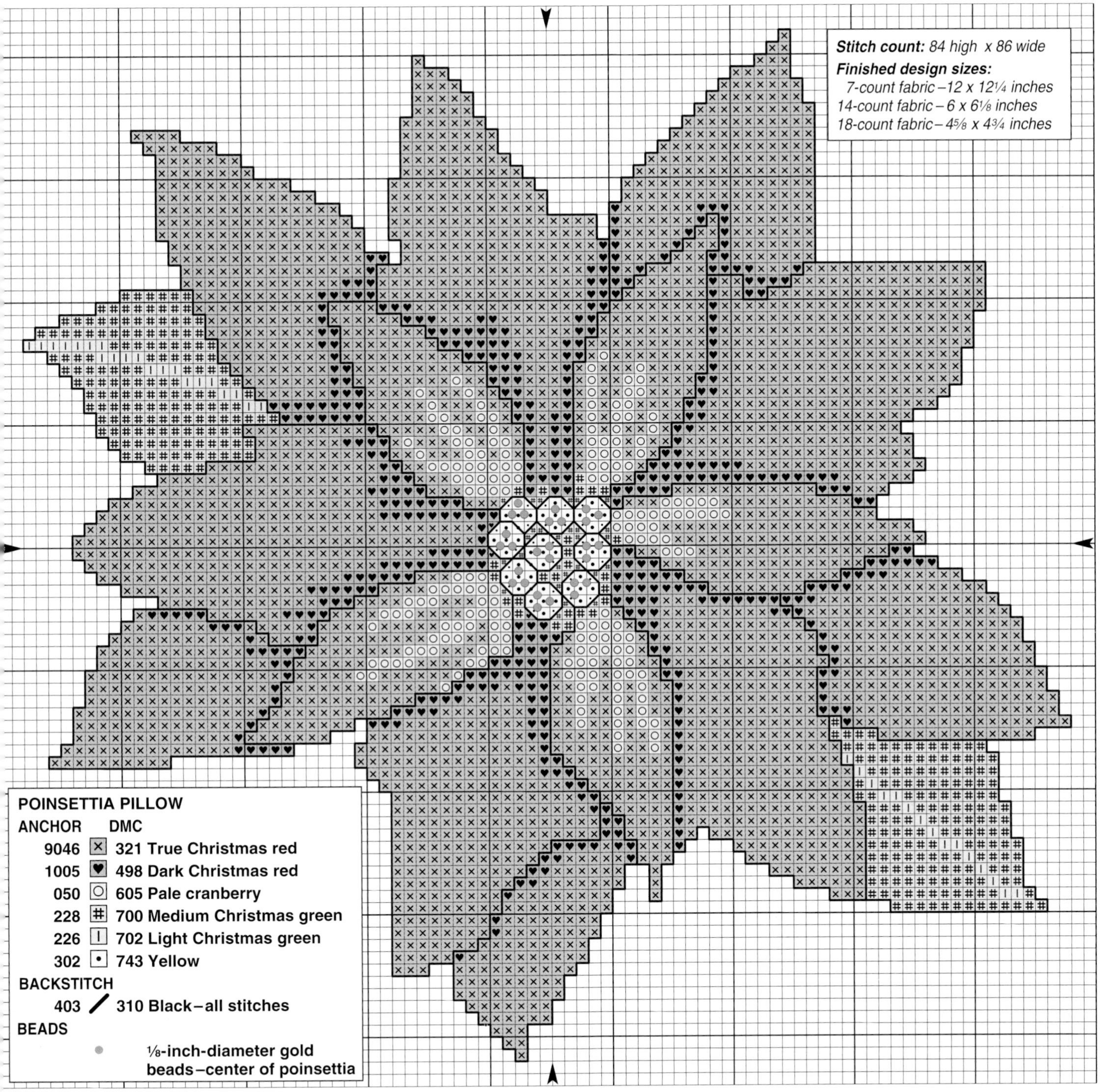
Stitch count: 84 high x 86 wide
Finished design sizes:
7-count fabric – 12 x 12¼ inches
14-count fabric – 6 x 6⅛ inches
18-count fabric – 4⅝ x 4¾ inches
POINSETTIA PILLOW
ANCHOR DMC
9046 321 True Christmas red
1005 498 Dark Christmas red
050 605 Pale cranberry
228 700 Medium Christmas green
226 702 Light Christmas green
302 743 Yellow
BACKSTITCH
403 310 Black – all stitches
BEADS
⅛-inch-diameter gold beads – center of poinsettia

POINSETTIA PILLOW

For poinsettia pillow, cut a 16-inch-diameter round pillow back, three 6×45-inch ruffle strips, and one 6×22-inch ruffle strip from red and green Christmas print. Cut two 1¼×25-inch piping strips from coordinating fabric.

For bow pillow, cut an 18-inch square pillow back and four 6×45-inch ruffle strips from red and green Christmas print. Cut two 1¼×32-inch piping strips from the coordinating fabric. All measurements include ½-inch seam allowances. Sew fabrics with right sides facing unless otherwise indicated in the instructions.

For each pillow, baste ivory cotton fabric to back side of stitched pillow top.

Sew short ends of the piping strips together to make one long strip. Cut cording to match length; center lengthwise on wrong side of piping strip. Fold fabric around the cording, raw edges together. Use zipper foot to sew through both layers close to cording. Baste piping to pillow front, raw edges even.

Sew short ends of ruffle strips together to form a circle. Fold fabric wrong sides facing with raw edges even, making one continuous folded edge; press. Sew gathering thread through both layers of ruffle ½ inch

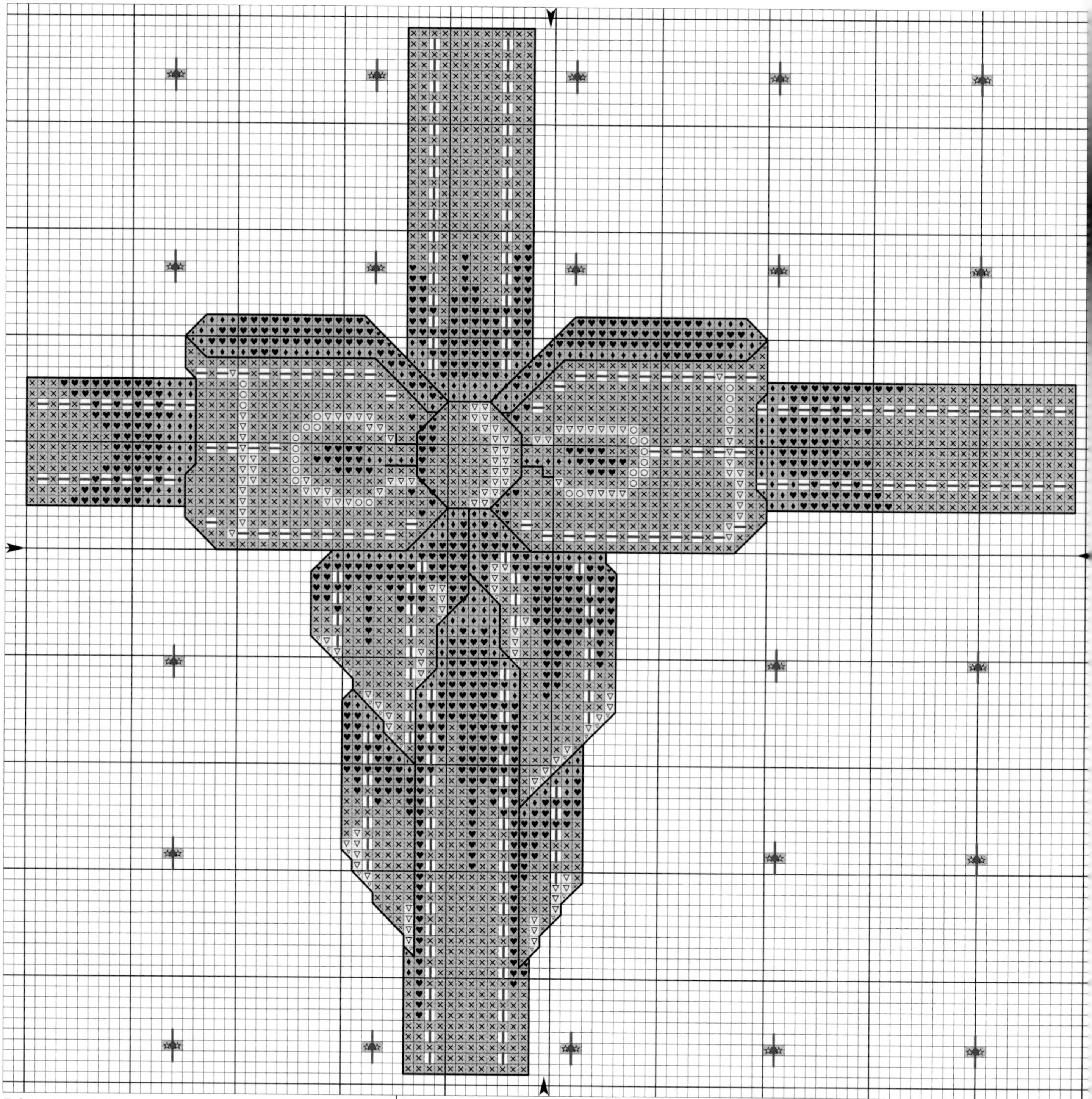

BOW PILLOW

from raw edges. Pull gathers to fit perimeter of pillow front with raw edges even; adjust gathers evenly. Sew ruffle to pillow along piping stitching line.

Sew pillow front to back, leaving an opening for turning. Clip curves and corners, turn right side out, and press. Stuff pillow firmly; slipstitch opening closed.

BOW PILLOW

ANCHOR		DMC
9046	☒	321 True Christmas red
1005	♥	498 Dark Christmas red
062	▽	603 True cranberry
050	○	605 Pale cranberry
043	♦	815 Garnet
	☆	003 Kreinik red 1/16-inch ribbon

BACKSTITCH

205	/	911 Emerald–background
403	/	310 Black–all remaining stitches

WEAVING STITCH

/ 003 Kreinik red 1/8-inch ribbon – bow detail

BEADS

• 1/8-inch-diameter green beads–background

Stitch count: *98 high x 99 wide*

Finished design sizes:
7-count fabric–14 x 14 1/4 inches
14-count fabric–7 x 7 1/8 inches
18-count fabric–5 3/8 x 5 1/2 inches

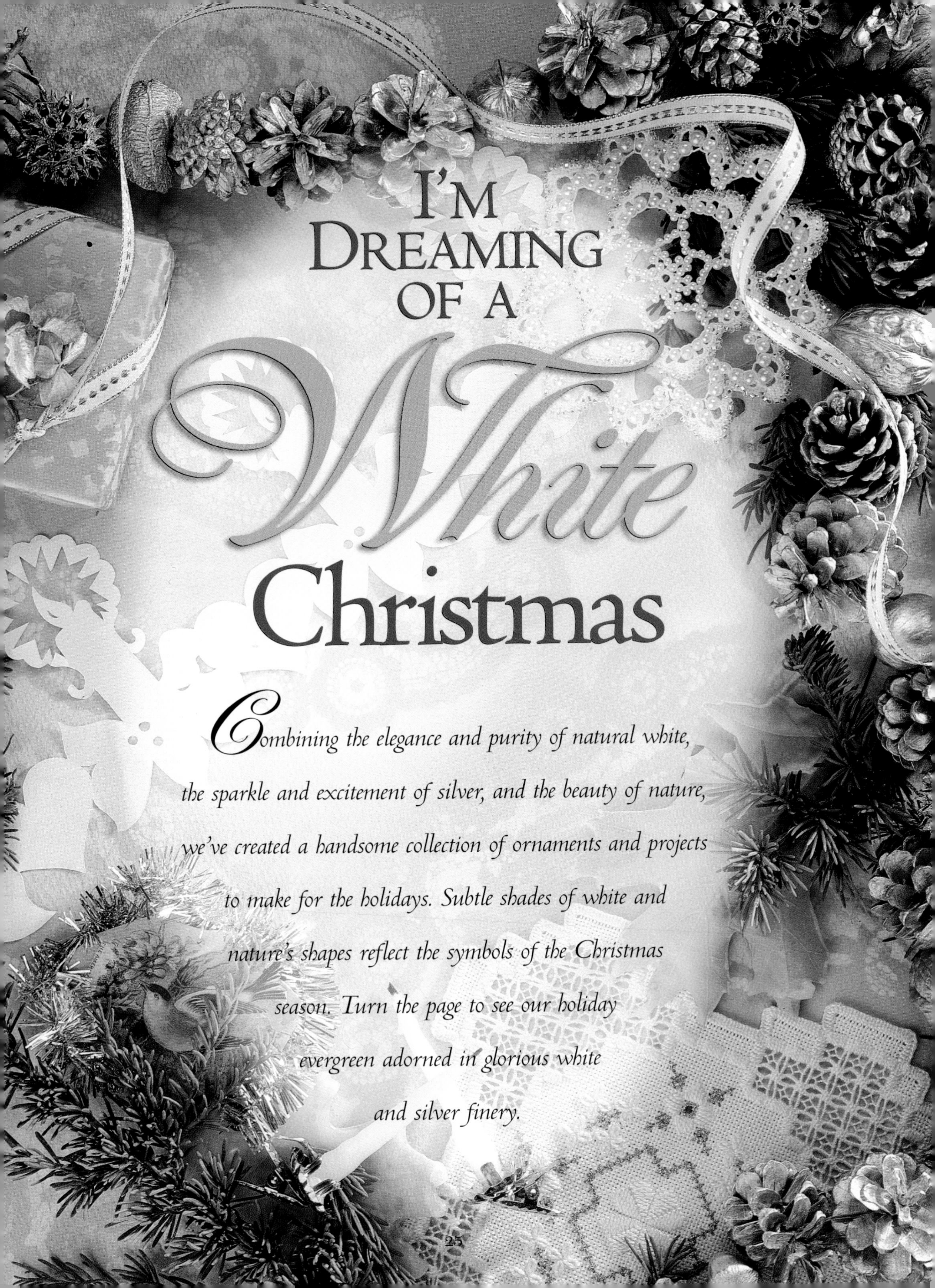

I'M DREAMING OF A *White* Christmas

Combining the elegance and purity of natural white, the sparkle and excitement of silver, and the beauty of nature, we've created a handsome collection of ornaments and projects to make for the holidays. Subtle shades of white and nature's shapes reflect the symbols of the Christmas season. Turn the page to see our holiday evergreen adorned in glorious white and silver finery.

Naturally *White-on-White* Holiday Evergreen

White-as-snow paper candles, sparkling beaded crocheted snowflakes, nature's own leaves dipped in shiny white wax, and creamy-colored sugar cookies are only a few of the elegant yet natural ornaments on our wintry tree. Using only neutral colors to accent an already beautiful tree from the forest, our white and silver masterpiece is sure to be the centerpiece of your holiday decorating. For a closer look at each of the ornaments and garlands, and for instructions for each project, turn to pages 34–38.

Designs: Cut Paper Candle Garland, Linda Arthur; Hand-Dipped Candles and Wax-Dipped Leaves, Carol Dahlstrom; Crocheted Snowflakes, Melody MacDuffee; Silver Pinecone Garland, Donna Chesnut

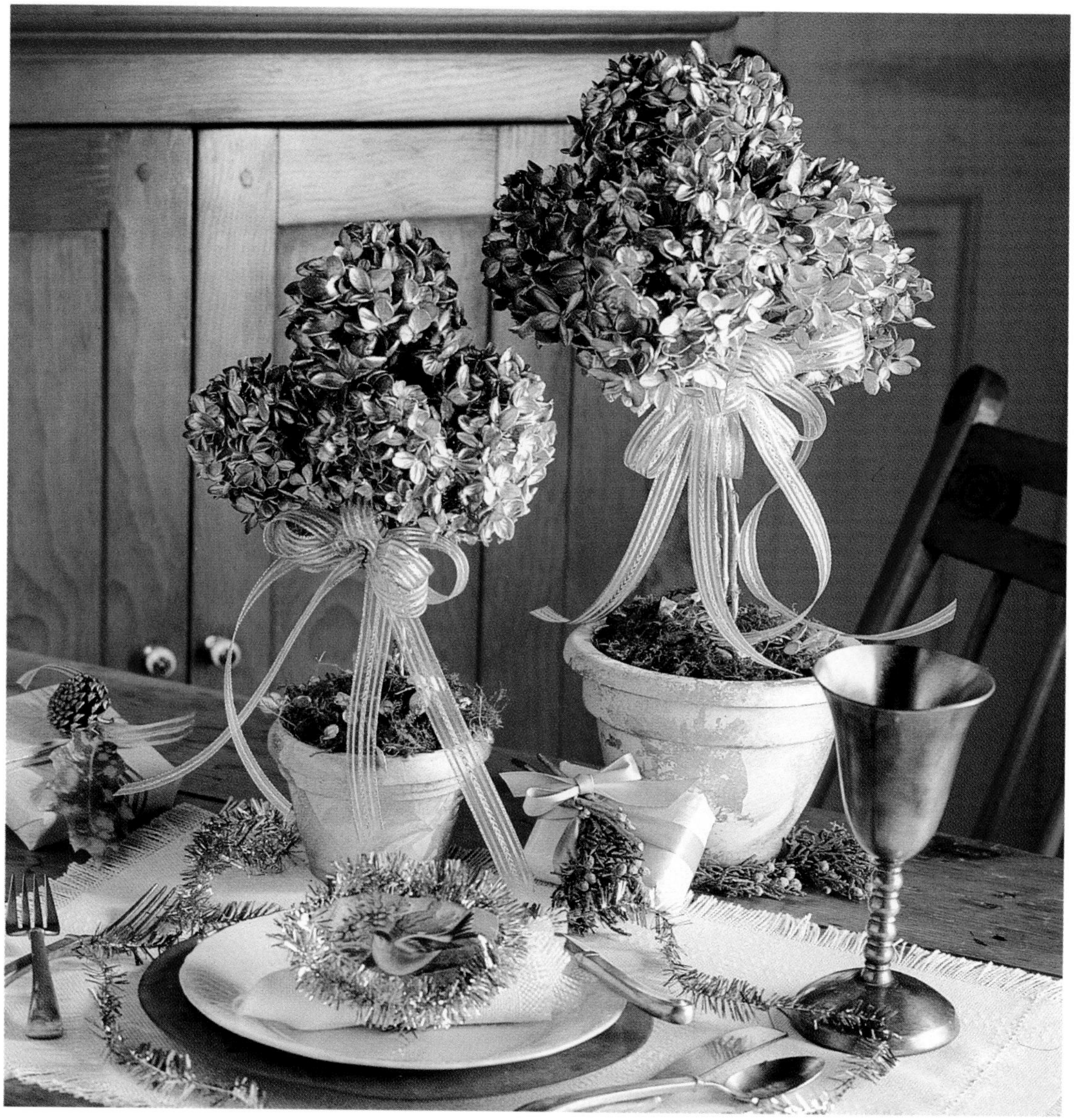

Tinsel and Hydrangea *Tabletop*

Glittering silver garland and painted hydrangeas combine to create a festive table setting. The centerpiece features a sparkling hydrangea topiary arranged in a silver-and-white marbleized pot. The quick-to-make antique paper napkin ring is trimmed in tinsel. A pewter charger and tableware complement the festive tinsel accents. Complete instructions for these projects are on pages 38–39.

Designs: Donna Chesnut and Carol Dahlstrom

Chenille Snowflake *Afghan*

Cuddle up with the luxurious feel of chenille in our ivory-and-white snowflake afghan. Crocheted with lush acrylic worsted-weight yarn, this piece works up quickly and is sure to keep out the winter chills. *Instructions for the afghan are on page 39.*

Design: Ann Smith for Monsanto-Designers for America

Nature Lover's *Candles and Leaves*

Positioned in natural wood holders, our hand-dipped candles and charming waxed leaves create a feeling of Christmas past. Each candle, carefully hand-dipped in pairs, has its own personality. The holders are made simply by drilling a hole in a small piece of natural wood. The step-by-step instructions for hand-dipping the candles and leaves are on page 40.

Designs: Holders, Jil Severson; Candles and Leaves, Carol Dahlstrom

Creamy White *Gardenia Wreath*

Dried gardenias, silver pinecones, and sparkling Christmas balls mirror the beauty of the season as they adorn our holiday wreath. The embellishments are added to a purchased wreath and topped with an ivory wire-edged ribbon. Instructions are on page 41.

Design: Gerry Bauman

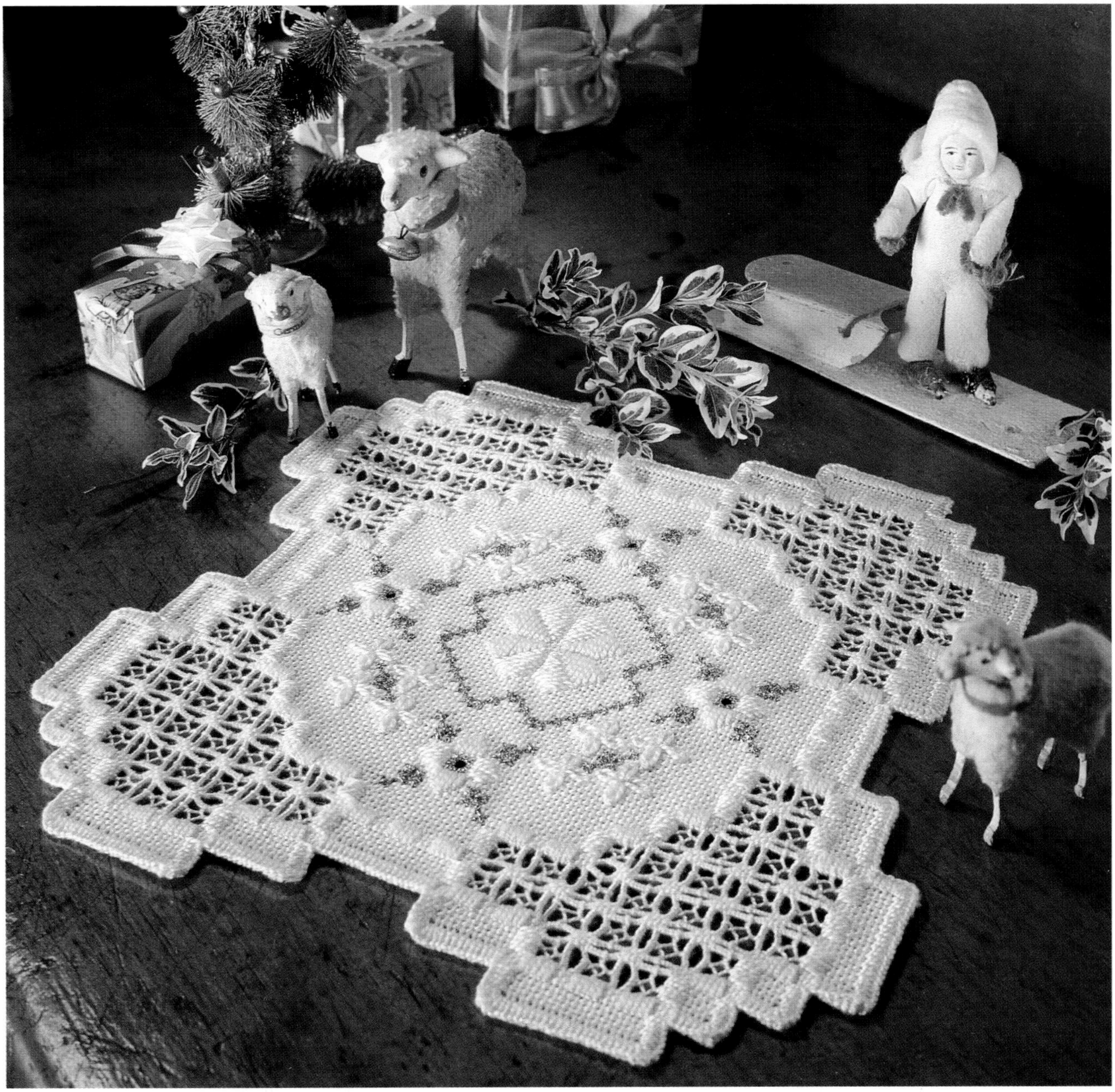

Elegant *Hardanger Doily*

Stitches of cream and metallic threads combine to create our heirloom-quality Hardanger doily. This lovely 12-inch-square piece is worked on 20-count ivory Jobelan fabric. *Instructions, chart, and stitching diagrams begin on page 41.*

Design: Lynne Hermanson

Candle and Heart Garland

As shown on pages 26–27, each motif measures 4⅝×4⅜ inches.

MATERIALS

Tracing paper
#2 pencil
5-inch-wide strip of white butcher paper, cut to desired length
Teaspoon
Scherenschnitte scissors or crafts knife and cutting mat or old magazine
Cellophane tape

INSTRUCTIONS

Trace pattern, *right*, onto tracing paper, using pencil. Place pencil-sketched side of tracing paper facing white paper strip, centering design between top and bottom edges and aligning one side edge. Using rim of teaspoon, stroke firmly along pencil lines until complete image is transferred.

Accordion fold butcher paper strip at each end of design, using dotted lines on pattern as a guide and keeping top and bottom edges even.

To cut design, use scherenschnitte scissors to cut around outside lines of design. (Be sure not to cut along fold lines.) *Or,* tape edges of paper to cutting mat and use crafts knife.

Unfold garland and retrace inside cut lines on every repeat. Cut out carefully with scherenschnitte scissors or crafts knife.

To finish, press on the pencil-traced (wrong) side with a warm iron.

PAPER CANDLE GARLAND

Crocheted Snowflakes

Shown on pages 26–27, round ornament has a 5-inch diameter, the six-pointed star measures 5 inches across widest points, and the 12-pointed star measures 6 inches across widest points.

MATERIALS

Coats Big Ball cotton crochet thread, size 30: one ball of white will make several ornaments
Size 14 steel crochet hook
Beading needle
Stiffy Fabric Stiffener
Waxed paper
Cardboard
Straight pins
Paintbrush
One 12-inch length of white satin ribbon for each ornament

For Round Ornament

114 size 3mm pearls
54 size 4mm pearls
54 size 5mm pearls
12 size 6mm pearls
402 silver-lined rochailles beads

For Six-Pointed Star Ornament
90 size 3 mm pearls
6 size 4 mm pearls
18 size 5 mm pearls
582 silver-lined rochailles beads
For 12-Pointed Star Ornament
384 size 3 mm pearls
512 silver-lined rochailles beads

TECHNIQUES

Beaded Chain Stitch (bch): Bring up a bead, yo behind the bead and draw through lp on hook.

Pearled Chain Stitch (pch): Bring up a pearl, yo behind the pearl and draw through lp on hook.

Beaded Single Crochet (bsc): Insert hook into stitch, bring up a bead, yo behind the bead, yo and draw through both lps on hook.

Pearled Single Crochet (psc): Work as for bsc using a pearl.

Right Thread (RT): The thread running through the pearl or bead on the right-hand side.

Left Thread (LT): The thread running through the pearl or bead on the left-hand side.

FOR ALL TECHNIQUES

To string the beads or pearls, cut about a 1-yard length of cotton, and thread into the needle. Follow the directions for the numbers and sequence of beads or pearls to string.

FOR FINISHING

To block an ornament, pin it face down onto cardboard which has been covered with waxed paper. Following the manufacturer's instructions, paint the fabric stiffener onto the thread portions of the ornaments and leave to dry. Repeat the paint process once more. After completely dry, remove the pins and peel the ornament away from the waxed paper.

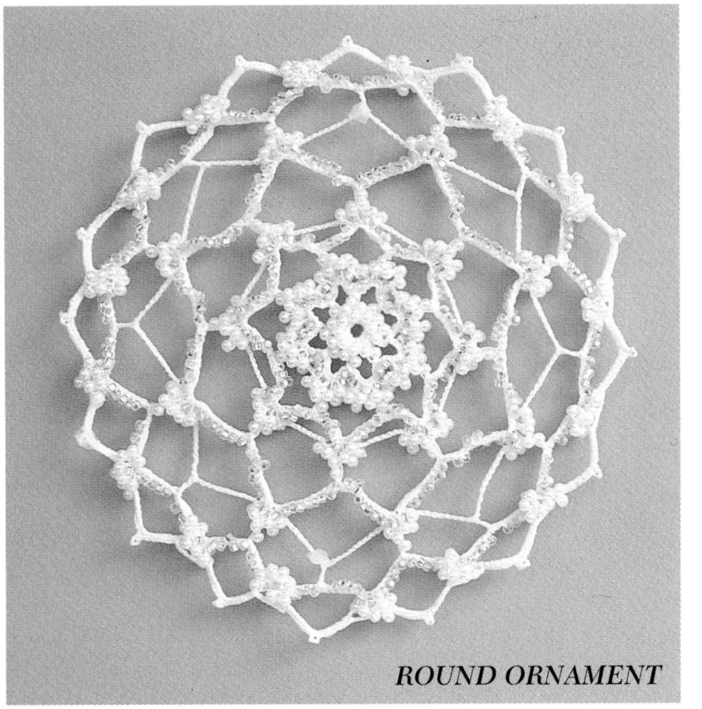
ROUND ORNAMENT

INSTRUCTIONS

ROUND ORNAMENT

String 30 (3 mm) pearls. Ch 6; join with sl st to form ring.

Rnd 1 (RS): Ch 1, 12 sc in ring; join with sl st in first sc; turn.

Rnd 2: (5 pch, sk 1 sc, sl st in next sc) 6 times. Fasten off.

Rnd 3: String [3 (3 mm) pearls, 1 (4 mm) pearl, 3 (3 mm) pearls] 6 times. With the WS facing, join thread with a sl st in RT of the third pearl in any 5-pch group, ch 1, (7 pch, sl st in RT of third pearl of next 5-pch group) 6 times. Fasten off.

Rnd 4: String [3 (3 mm) pearls, 2 (4 mm) pearls, 1 (5 mm) pearl, 2 (4 mm) pearls, and 1 (3 mm) pearl] 6 times. With the WS facing, join thread in RT of any 4-mm-pearl with sl st. Ch 1, (9 pch, sl st RT in next 4-mm-pearl) 6 times. Fasten off.

Rnd 5: String 126 beads. With the RS facing, join thread with sl st in RT of second 3-mm-pearl of any 9-pch-group. * Ch 2, sc RT next pearl, (ch 3, sc RT next pearl) twice, ch 5, sc RT next pearl, (ch 3, sc RT next pearl) twice, ch 4, sk last 3-mm-pearl of this group and first 3-mm-pearl of next group, sc RT next pearl; rep from * around for 5 times more.

Rnd 6: * 3 sc in ch-2 sp, 4 sc in each of next 2 ch-3 sps, in ch-5 sp (sc, hdc, 2 dc, trc, 2 dc, hdc, sc), 4 sc in each of next 2 ch-3 sps, sk ch-4 sp; rep from * for 5 times more; turn.

Rnd 7: * (bsc in each of next 3 sc, sk 1 sc) twice, sk 1 sc, bsc in each of next 7 sts, (sk 1 sc, bsc in each of next 3 sc) twice, sk next sc, bsc in each of next 2 sc; rep from * around for 5 times more, ending with sl st in skipped sc at beginning of rnd. Fasten off.

Rnd 8: String [1 (3 mm) pearl, 1 (4 mm) pearl, 2 (5 mm) pearls, 1 (6 mm) pearl, 2 (5 mm) pearls, 1 (4 mm) pearl, and 1 (3 mm) pearl] 12 times. With the WS facing, join thread in RT of seventh bead from Rnd 7 join. * 9 pch, sk 9 beads, sl st RT next bead, 9 pch, sk 10 beads, sl st RT next bead; rep from * for 5 times more. Fasten off.

Rnd 9: String 276 beads. With the RS facing, join thread with sl st in RT of first 4-mm-pearl of any 9-pch-group. * Ch 3, sc RT next pearl, (ch 4, sc RT next pearl) twice, ch 6, sc RT next pearl, (ch 4, sc RT next pearl) twice, ch 3, sk 2 (3 mm) pearls, sc RT next 4-mm-pearl; rep from * around for 11 times more.

Rnd 10: Ch 2, sl st in next ch-3 lp, * 5 sc in each of next 2 ch-4 lps, in ch-6 lp (sc, hdc, 2 dc, trc, 2 dc, hdc, sc), 5 sc in each of next 2 ch-4 lps, sk next 2 ch-3 lps; rep from * for 11 times more, ending with sl st in first sc; turn.

Rnd 11: * (Sk 1 sc, bsc in each of next 4 sc) twice, sk 1 st, bsc in each of next 7 sts, sk 1 st, (bsc in each of next 4 sc, sk 1 sc) twice; rep from * for 11 times more, ending with sl st in first sc. Fasten off.

Block ornament. Slip a 12-inch length of ribbon through one scallop for hanging loop.

SIX-POINTED STAR ORNAMENT

12-POINTED STAR ORNAMENT

SIX-POINTED STAR ORNAMENT

String 42 beads. Ch 6; join with sl st to form ring.

Rnd 1: Ch 1, 12 sc in ring; join with sl st in first sc; turn.

Rnd 2: (7 bch, sk 1 sc, sl st in next sc) 6 times. Fasten off.

Rnd 3: String [4 beads, 1 (4 mm) pearl, and 4 beads] 6 times. With the WS facing, join thread with sl st in RT of second bead of any 7-bead group. * (Ch 2, sc RT next bead) twice, ch 4, sc RT next bead, ch 2, sc RT next bead, ch 2, sk 2 beads, sc RT next bead; rep from * for 5 times more, ending with sl st in join; turn.

Rnd 4: * 2 sc in each of next 2 ch-2 sps, in ch-4 lp (sc, ch 3, sc), 2 sc in each of next 2 ch-2 sps; rep from * for 5 times more; turn.

Rnd 5: * Bsc in each of next 4 sc, ch 2, sk next sc, psc in ch-3 lp, ch 2, sk next sc, bsc in each of next 4 sc; rep from * for 5 times more, ending with sl st in beg bsc. Fasten off.

Rnd 6: String [5 (3mm) pearls, 7 beads, 1 (5 mm) pearl, and 7 beads] 6 times. With the WS facing, join thread with sl st in ch-2 sp before any pearl; * sc RT next pearl, 5 pch, sc LT in same pearl, sc next ch-2 sp, 7 bch, pch, 7 bch, sc next ch-2 sp; rep from * for 5 times more, ending with sl st in first sc. Fasten off.

Rnd 7: String [5 (3 mm) pearls, 10 beads, 1 (5 mm) pearl, 10 beads] 6 times. With the WS facing, join thread with sl st in RT of bead just before any 5-mm-pearl. Ch 1, sc in join; * ch 2, sc RT next pearl, 5 pch, sc LT same pearl, ch 2, sc LT next bead, 10 bch, 1 pch, 10 bch, sk (6 beads, 5 pearls, and 6 beads), sc RT next bead; rep from * for 5 times more, ending with sl st in first sc. Fasten off.

Rnd 8: String [12 beads, 1 (5 mm) pearl, 12 beads] 6 times. With the RS facing, join thread with sl st in RT of center pearl of any 5-pearl group. * (Ch 2, sc RT next pearl) twice, (ch 2, sc RT next bead) 10 times, ch 2, sc RT next pearl, ch 5, sc RT of third pearl of next 5-pearl group; rep from * for 5 times more.

Rnd 9: * 3 sc in each of next 13 ch-2 sps, ch 1, sk ch-5 lp; rep from * for 5 times more, ending with sl st in first sc; turn.

Rnd 10: (Sc in next ch, 12 bch, pch, 12 bch, sk 39 sc) 6 times, ending with sl st in first sc; turn.

Rnd 11: Ch 1, sl st RT next bead, ch 3 (counts as first dc); * (ch 1, dc RT next bead) 11 times, ch 1, dc RT pearl, ch 3, dc LT same pearl, (ch 1, dc LT next bead) 12 times, dc RT next bead; rep from * for 5 times more, omitting final dc in last rep and ending with sl st in third ch of beg ch-3; turn.

Rnd 12: String [12 beads, 5 (3 mm) pearls, 12 beads] 6 times. (Bsc in each of next 12 ch-1 sps, 5 psc in ch-3 sp, bsc in each of next 12 ch-1 sps) 6 times; at end, sl st in first sc and fasten off.

Block ornament. Slip a 12-inch length of ribbon through one point for a hanging loop.

12-POINTED STAR ORNAMENT

String 24 (3 mm) pearls. Ch 8; join with sl st to form ring.

Rnd 1: Ch 1, 16 sc in ring; join with sl st in first sc; turn.

Rnd 2: (3 pch, sk 1 sc, sl st in next sc) 8 times; turn.

Rnd 3: Ch 3, sk 1 pearl, sl st RT of next pearl, (ch 8, sk 2 pearls, sl st RT of next pearl) 8 times; turn.

Rnd 4: String 48 beads. (Sc in next ch, bsc in each of next 6 ch, sc in next ch, sc into same thread of Rnd 2 pearl as before) 8 times, ending with sl st in first sc. Fasten off.

Rnd 5: String 72 (3 mm) pearls. With the WS facing, join thread with sl st in LT of second bead of any 6-bead group; * 3 pch, sl st LT next bead, (3 pch, sl st RT next bead) twice, ch 3, sl st LT second bead of next 6-bead group; rep from * for 7 times more. Fasten off.

Rnd 6: String 96 beads. With the WS facing, join thread with sl st in RT of fifth pearl of any 9-pearl group. (Ch 14, sl st RT corresponding pearl of next 9-pearl group) 8 times.

Rnd 7: (Sc next ch, bsc in each of next 12 ch, sc in next ch, sc around Rnd 6 and into RT of same Rnd 5 pearl as before) 8 times, ending with sl st in first sc. Fasten off.

SILVER PINECONE GARLAND

Rnd 8: String 72 (3 mm) pearls. With the WS facing, join thread with sl st in LT of fifth bead of any 12-bead group. * 3 pch, sl st LT of next bead, (3 pch, sl st RT of next bead) twice, ch 8, sl st LT of fifth bead of next 12-bead group; rep from * 7 times more. Fasten off.

Rnd 9: String 160 beads. With the WS facing, join thread in RT of fifth pearl of any 9-pearl group. (Ch 22, sl st RT fifth pearl of next 9-pearl group) 8 times.

Rnd 10: * Sc next ch, bsc in each of next 20 ch, sc in next ch, sc around Rnd 9 into RT of same Rnd 8 pearl as before; rep from * for 7 times more, ending with sl st in first sc. Fasten off.

Rnd 11: String 72 (3 mm) pearls. With the WS facing, join thread with sl st in LT of ninth bead of any 20-bead group. * (3 pch, sl st LT next bead, (3 pch, sl st RT next bead) twice, ch 20, sl st LT of ninth bead in next 20-bead group; rep from * for 7 times more. Fasten off.

Rnd 12: String 208 beads. With the RS facing, join thread in RT of fifth pearl of any 9-pearl group, (ch 15, trc in next ch-20 lp, ch 15, sl st RT of fifth pearl of next 9-pearl group) 8 times; turn.

Rnd 13: * (Sc in next ch, bsc in each of next 13 ch, sc in next ch), sc in trc, rep bet ( ) again, sc around Rnd 12 into RT of same Rnd 11 pearl as before; rep from * for 7 times more. Fasten off.

Rnd 14: String 144 (3 mm) pearls. With the WS facing join thread with sl st in LT of sixth bead of any 13-bead group. * 3 pch, sl st RT of next bead, 3 pch, sl st LT of same bead, 3 pch, sl st RT of next bead, ch 12, sl st LT of sixth bead of next 13-bead group; rep from * for 7 times more; turn.

Rnd 15: * In ch-12 lp [8 sc, (ch 3, sl st in st prior to ch-3 just made = picot made), 8 sc], ch 6, pass the ch-6 lp behind the pearl cluster; rep from * for 15 times more; at end, join with sl st in first sc. Fasten off.

Block ornament. Cut a 12-inch length of ribbon and slip through one point for a hanging loop.

Silver Pinecone Garland

As shown on pages 26–27, garland measures approximately 5 feet long.

MATERIALS

25 pinecones; 10 to 15 nuts
6 large seed pods or similar dried natural material
Drill; ⅛-inch-diameter drill bit
6-foot-long piece of strong fishing line
Large-eyed needle
Silver spray paint

INSTRUCTIONS

Drill ⅛-inch-diameter hole through each nut, pinecone, and seed pod. Thread needle with one end of fishing line. Thread first pinecone onto line, push to end leaving 6-inch tail. Knot tail around pinecone to secure end of garland. Randomly thread materials onto line. Secure end of line around last piece.

Spray paint entire garland silver; allow to dry.

Eucalyptus Tree Topper

As shown on page 26, star measures 10×11 inches.

MATERIALS

Tracing paper
Carbon paper
Ballpoint pen
12x12-inch piece of ¼-inch plywood
Scroll saw
Drill with ⅛-inch bit
12 inches of medium gauge wire
Fine grit sandpaper
White acrylic paint
Silver glitter brush-on paint
5 to 7 stems of eucalyptus
Hot-glue gun
Hot-glue stick
Silver spray paint
Crocheted Ornament (Instructions, pages 34–37)
1⅓ yards of 3-inch-wide silver mesh ribbon

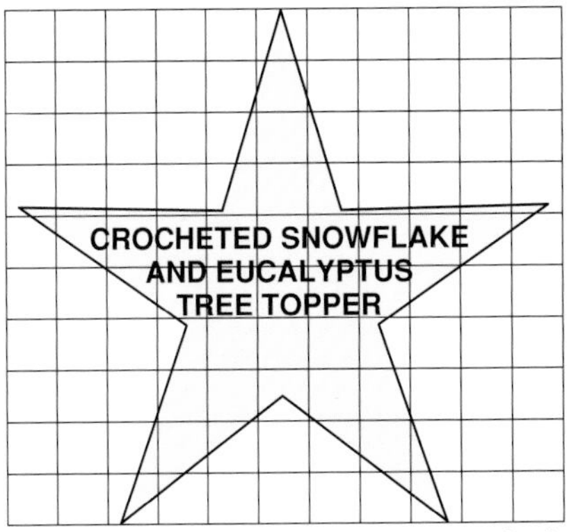

1 Square = 1 Inch

INSTRUCTIONS

Enlarge star pattern, *page 37*, and trace onto tracing paper. Place carbon paper between pattern and wood; transfer outline, tracing over lines with ballpoint pen.

Cut out star with scroll saw. Drill two holes through the center, approximately 1¼ inches apart. Sand edges smooth.

Paint entire star white; allow to dry thoroughly. Brush silver glitter paint over front.

Thread ends of wire through holes from front to back; twist wires together at back to secure.

Spray paint eucalyptus silver; allow to dry. Bend stems of eucalyptus as necessary to form star shape and hot-glue to star, covering wood. Carefully secure crocheted snowflake to front of star atop eucalyptus, using dabs of hot glue.

Wire ribbon to back of star, leaving long tails. Use wire ends to secure star to treetop.

White-as-Snow Cookies

Shown on pages 26–27.

INGREDIENTS

- **1 recipe Rolled Sugar Cookie Dough**
- **8 ounces vanilla-flavored candy coating, cut up**
- **3 tablespoons shortening**
- **Edible glitter, optional**

METHOD

On a lightly floured surface, roll a portion of chilled cookie dough ⅛ inch thick. With a 3- or 3½-inch star or snowflake cookie cutter or a 5-inch tree cookie cutter, cut out cookies. Reroll the scraps. With a smaller star or flower cutter (about ¾ inch in diameter), cut out a shape in the center of each cookie, if desired. Use ¼-inch assorted-shaped cutters or a sharp knife to cut smaller designs. Use a straw to cut a hole in top for hanging, if desired. Place on ungreased cookie sheets.

Bake in a 375° oven for 7 to 8 minutes or till edges are firm and bottoms are very lightly browned. Transfer cookies to wire racks; cool.

Heat and stir 8 ounces candy coating and shortening over very low heat till mixture begins to melt. Remove from heat; stir till smooth. Dip cooled cookies, face down, into melted mixture, shaking cookies gently to smooth any ripples in the coating. Transfer cookies to wire racks. Sprinkle with edible glitter, if desired. Makes 24 cookies.

Rolled Sugar Cookie Dough: In a large mixing bowl beat ⅓ cup *butter* and ⅓ cup *shortening* with an electric mixer on medium speed for 30 seconds. Add 1 cup *all-purpose flour,* ¾ cup *sugar,* 1 *egg,* 1 tablespoon *milk,* 1 teaspoon *baking powder,* 1 teaspoon *vanilla,* and dash *salt.* Beat till combined. Beat in 1 cup *all-purpose flour.* Divide in half. Cover and chill 3 hours or till easy to handle.

Hydrangea Topiary

As shown on page 28, topiary stands 14 inches tall.

MATERIALS

Terra-cotta pot in desired size; old pail
Water; oil-based silver spray paint
4 large hydrangea flower blossoms on long stems, dried
Florist's foam block to fit inside pot
1 yard of ¾-inch-wide silver ribbon
Florist's wire; Spanish and sphagnum moss

INSTRUCTIONS

For marbleized pot, fill pail half full with cold water. Spray silver paint on top of water. Submerge clay pot in the water and pull back up through paint. Allow to dry thoroughly. Repeat if necessary to achieve the desired effect.

For hydrangea arrangement, spray paint hydrangea blossoms silver; allow to dry. Set aside.

Fit the foam block into the silver-painted pot. Group the blossoms together with one slightly higher than the others; wire stems together below the blossoms. Push stems into foam block until bottom of blossoms are approximately 4 inches above top edge of pot.

Make a bow from ribbon and wire to the stems at the base of the blossoms. Fill the pot with Spanish moss. Arrange sphagnum moss on the top.

Bird Napkin Ring

As shown on page 28, napkin ring measures approximately 3×4½ inches, excluding ring to hold napkin.

MATERIALS

Small reproduction bird print, cut to approximately 3x4 inches
3x4-inch piece of heavyweight art paper, in color to blend with background of bird print
Crafts glue
24 inches of silver tinsel garland
Hot-glue gun
Hot-glue stick

INSTRUCTIONS

Trim bird print carefully around bird and leaf detail as desired, making sure print still measures at least 2×3 inches.

Glue print to art paper using crafts glue. Trim art paper around print, leaving borders as desired around edges of print.

Trim fringe on garland to ½ inch. Glue the garland around back of

print, allowing fringe to show from the front.

Using remainder of garland, form a 1½-inch-diameter loop on the back of print to hold the napkin; hot-glue ends securely in place.

Snowflake Afghan

As shown on page 29, afghan measures 46×55 inches. Skill Level: For the intermediate crocheter.

MATERIALS

Lion Chenille Sensations "100% Monsanto acrylic" worsted-weight yarn (1.4-oz./87-yd. skein): 19 skeins of antique white (80761.01) for MC Berella "4" "Monsanto Acrylic with Bounce-Back Fibers" worsted-weight yarn (3.5-oz./100-gm. skein): 6 skeins of winter white (8941) for CC

Size 5/F (3.75 mm) and 6/G (4.25 mm) aluminum crochet hooks or size to obtain gauge

GAUGE: With CC and larger hook, Rnd 1 = 2-inch-diameter; one finished block = 9-inches-square.

INSTRUCTIONS

FIRST BLOCK

Beginning at the center using larger hook and CC, ch 8; join with sl st to form ring.

Rnd 1: Ch 3 (counts as dc), work 23 more dc in ring; join with sl st in 3rd ch of beginning ch-3.

Rnd 2: (Ch 3 (counts as dc), dc in same dc as join = beginning cl made), ch 3, *(dc 2 tog in same dc as join = cl made)*; * ch 3, sk 2 dc, in next dc (cl, ch 3, cl); rep from * around, ending ch 3, join with sl st in top of first cl = 8 double cl.

Rnd 3: Sl st in first ch-3 sp, in same sp (beginning cl, ch 3, cl); * ch 3, sk next ch-3 sp, (cl, ch 3, cl) in next ch-3 sp; rep from * around, ending ch 3, sl st in top of first cl.

Rnd 4: Sl st in first ch-3 sp, in same sp (beginning cl, ch 3, cl); * ch 2, sc over ch-3 lps from rnds 2 and 3, ch 2 **, (cl, ch 3, cl) in next ch-3 sp; rep from * around, ending last rep at **; join with sl st in top of first cl. Fasten off CC.

Rnd 5: With the RS facing and smaller hook, join MC with sl st in any ch-3 sp. In same sp as join (beginning cl, ch 3, cl); * 5 trc in next sc, in next ch-3 sp (cl, ch 3, cl), 3 trc in next sc **, in next ch-3 sp (cl, ch 3, cl); rep from * around, ending last rep at **; join with sl st in top of beginning cl.

Rnd 6: Ch 3 (counts as dc); * 3 dc in ch-3 sp, dc in top of next cl, dc in each of next 2 trc, 5 dc in next trc, dc in each of next 2 trc, dc in top of next cl, 3 dc in ch-3 sp, dc in top of next cl, dc in each of next 3 trc **, dc in top of next cl; rep from * around, ending last rep at **; join with sl st in third ch of beg ch-3 = 17 dc along each side, excluding the corner 5-dc groups. Fasten off MC.

Rnd 7: With the RS facing and larger hook, join CC with sl st in third dc of any 5-dc corner. Ch 1, 3 sc in same dc as join; * sc in each of next 21 dc **, 3 sc in next dc; rep from * around, ending last rep at **; join with sl st in first sc.

Rnd 8: Ch 1, sc in same sc as join; * 3 sc in next sc **, sc in each of next 23 sc; rep from * around, ending last rep at **, sc in each of last 22 sc; join and fasten off.

Rnd 9: With the RS facing and smaller hook, join MC with sl st in second sc of any corner 3-sc group. Ch 1, 3 sc in same sc as join, sc in next sc, [(working over the center dc post from Rnd 6, make a dc = fpdc made)], * sk the sc behind the fpdc, sc in next sc, sk next dc, fpdc over post of next dc from Rnd 6 **; rep from * for 10 times more, 3 sc in next sc, sc in next sc, fpdc over same post as last fpdc; rep from * around, ending last rep at **, rep from * for 9 times, fpdc over same post as first fpdc, sc in next sc; join = 12 fpdc along each side.

Rnd 10: Ch 3 (counts as dc); * 3 dc in next sc, dc in each of next 2 sc, (fpdc over fpdc, dc in next sc) 12 times, dc in next dc; rep from * around; join with sl st in third ch of beginning ch-3.

Rnd 11: Ch 1, sc in join; * sc in next dc, 3 sc in next dc, sc in each of next 3 dc, (fpsc over fpdc, sc in next dc) 12 times, sc in next sc; rep from * around; join and fasten off. Make 29 more blocks as for First Block. Sc blocks tog on WS using CC and in six rows, each with 5 blocks.

BORDER: With the RS facing and larger hook, join CC with sl st in second sc of any 3-sc-corner group; ch 1, 3 sc in same sc, * sc in each sc to joining, [(yo and draw up a lp in corner of each of next 2 blocks, yo and draw through all 5 lps on hook = puff st made)]; rep from * around, working 3 sc in each corner; at end, join with sl st in first sc.

Rnd 2: Ch 1, sc in first sc, in next sc *(sc, ch 3, sl st in sc just made = picot made)* for first corner, sc in each sc to fourth sc before puff st, (picot in sc, sc in next sc) twice, picot in puff st, (sc in next sc, picot in next sc) twice; cont as est around, working next corners as for first corner.

Rnd 3: Sl st in each sc around, sl stitching beneath each picot; at end, sl st in first sl st and fasten off.

Hand-Dipped Candles and Leaves

As shown on pages 30–31.

MATERIALS

Candle wax
Hammer, chisel, or screwdriver
Small pail; old tin can
Hot plate or stove
Old saucepan
For Candles:
Candle wicking
1-inch dowel or broomstick for hanging
For Leaves:
Natural leaves
Waxed paper

INSTRUCTIONS

Break wax into small pieces using hammer and chisel. Place wax into old tin can and place can in water in saucepan. Water should be at least ⅓ the depth of the pan. Place pan over low to medium heat. Water will bubble and melt wax in can. NEVER put wax directly on the burner.

After the wax is melted, remove the can and saucepan from stove and place on a covered surface.

Fill pail at least ¾ full with very cold water.

Cut a piece of candle wicking twice the length of desired candle plus 6 inches. Holding wicking in the middle, dip wick into hot wax then into the cold water. (At first, little wax seems to stay on wicking, but after dipping a few times, candles will start to form.) By holding wick in middle, you create two candles. Be sure to keep candles separated while dipping. Repeat, dipping candles back and forth from wax to water until the desired thickness is obtained. Hang candles over a suspended dowel or broomstick until dry.

To make Hand-Dipped Leaves, choose leaves that are complete and in good shape. They need not be dry. Holding the leaf by the stem, dip the leaf into the hot wax. Suspend in the air for about 30 seconds. Lay on waxed paper to dry.

Step-by-Step Hand-Dipped Candles

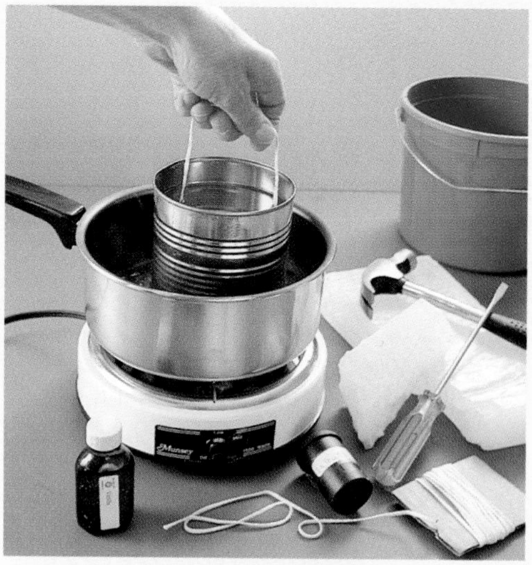

1

Dip candle wicking into melted wax by holding the wicking in the center.

2

Repeat, dipping back and forth between candle wax and cold water until desired thickness of candle is obtained.

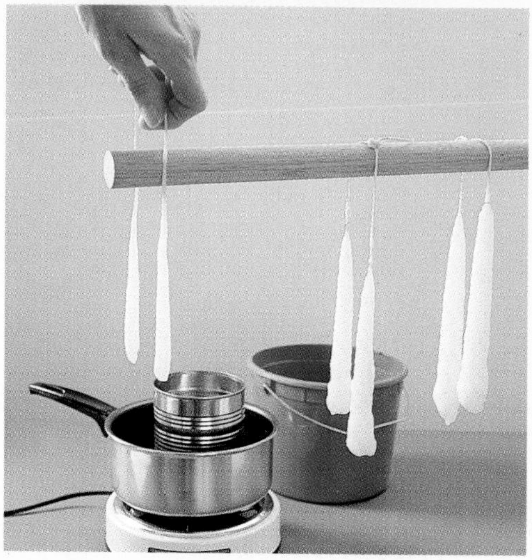

3

Hang candles over a suspended dowel or broomstick until completely dry.

White Gardenia Wreath

As shown on page 32.

MATERIALS

24-inch-diameter silk evergreen wreath
White spray paint
2 yards of 2-inch-wide ivory wire-edged ribbon
Hot-glue gun; hot-glue sticks
3 freeze-dried gardenia blossoms
9 freeze-dried white peony blossoms
12 freeze-dried bridal white roses
6 white pinecones
White 1-inch-diameter glass ball ornaments
Queen-Anne's-lace; globe thistle
White yarrow; silver king artemisia
1-yard strand of small white pearls

INSTRUCTIONS

Spray wreath lightly with white paint; allow to dry. Make a multiloop bow from ribbon, leaving streamers; hot-glue to top.

Glue pinecones and sprigs of globe thistle, yarrow, and artemisia to wreath, alternating materials for desired effect. Next, glue three gardenias evenly spaced around wreath, and add 11 roses, peonies, and sprigs of Queen-Anne's-lace.

To finish, glue remaining rose to center of bow; add tiny sprigs of desired materials. Loop pearls and glue to back of bow, allowing loops to hang 6 or 8 inches.

Hardanger Doily

As shown on page 33.

MATERIALS

FABRIC

12x12-inch piece of 20-count ivory Jobelan fabric

THREADS

#8 and #5 cream pearl cotton
1 spool of #8 braid in color listed in key, *page 42*

SUPPLIES

Needle
Embroidery hoop

INSTRUCTIONS

Tape or zigzag the edges of Jobelan fabric. Find the top row of satin stitches on the chart, *page 42*, and the vertical center of fabric. Measure 3¼ inches from top of fabric and two threads to left of vertical center; begin first satin stitch there. For all stitches, refer to diagrams, *right*.

Work the satin-stitch Kloster blocks and flowers first, using one strand of #5 pearl cotton. Next, use one strand of #5 pearl cotton to work lazy daisy stitches and buttonhole stitch edging.

Use one strand of gold metallic braid to work the cross-stitches and eyelets; give each eyelet stitch a gentle tug to open up hole.

Cut and remove threads, referring to the chart. Thread needle with 30-inch length of #8 pearl cotton. Wrap remaining threads, making divided wrapped bars with dove's eyes.

Trim fabric around outside edge of doily, close to stitching. Rinse doily in warm water; roll in towel. While still damp, press doily face down on terry towel.

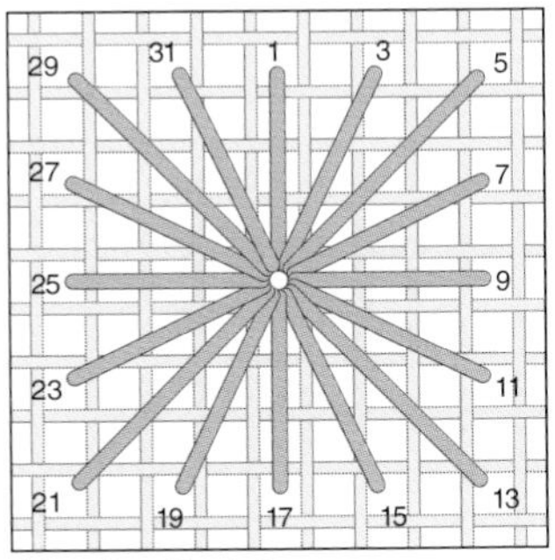

Algerian Eyelet

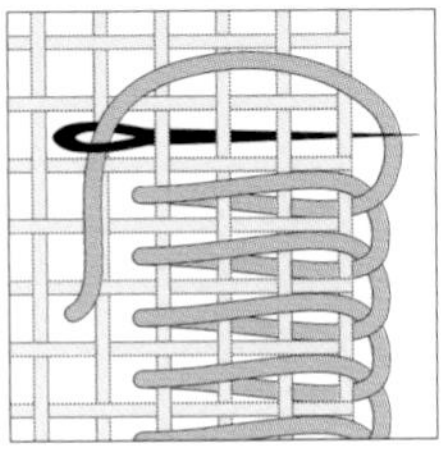

Buttonhole Stitch

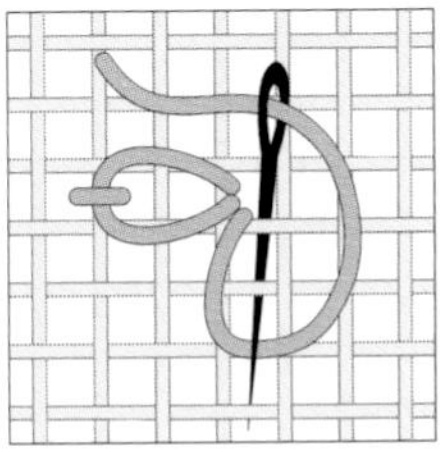

Lazy Daisy

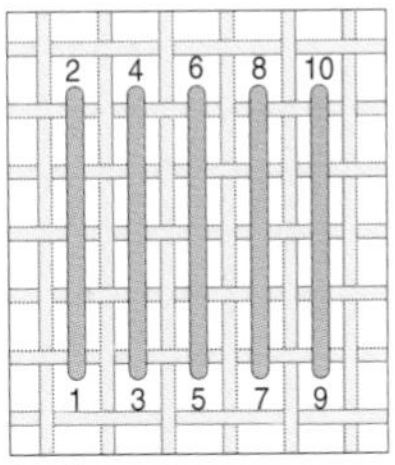

Satin Stitch

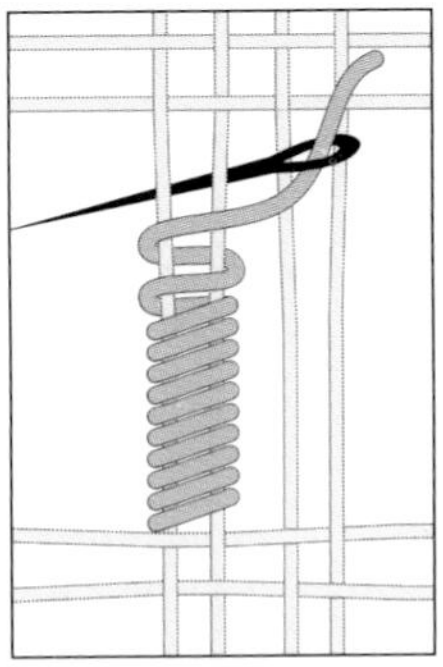

Wrapped Bars

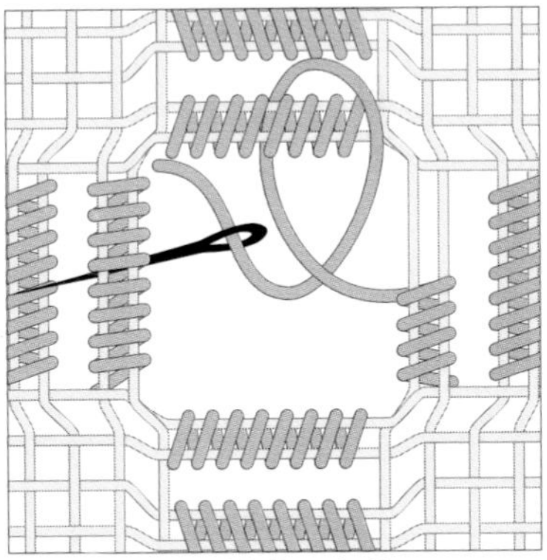

Wrapped Bars with Dove's Eye

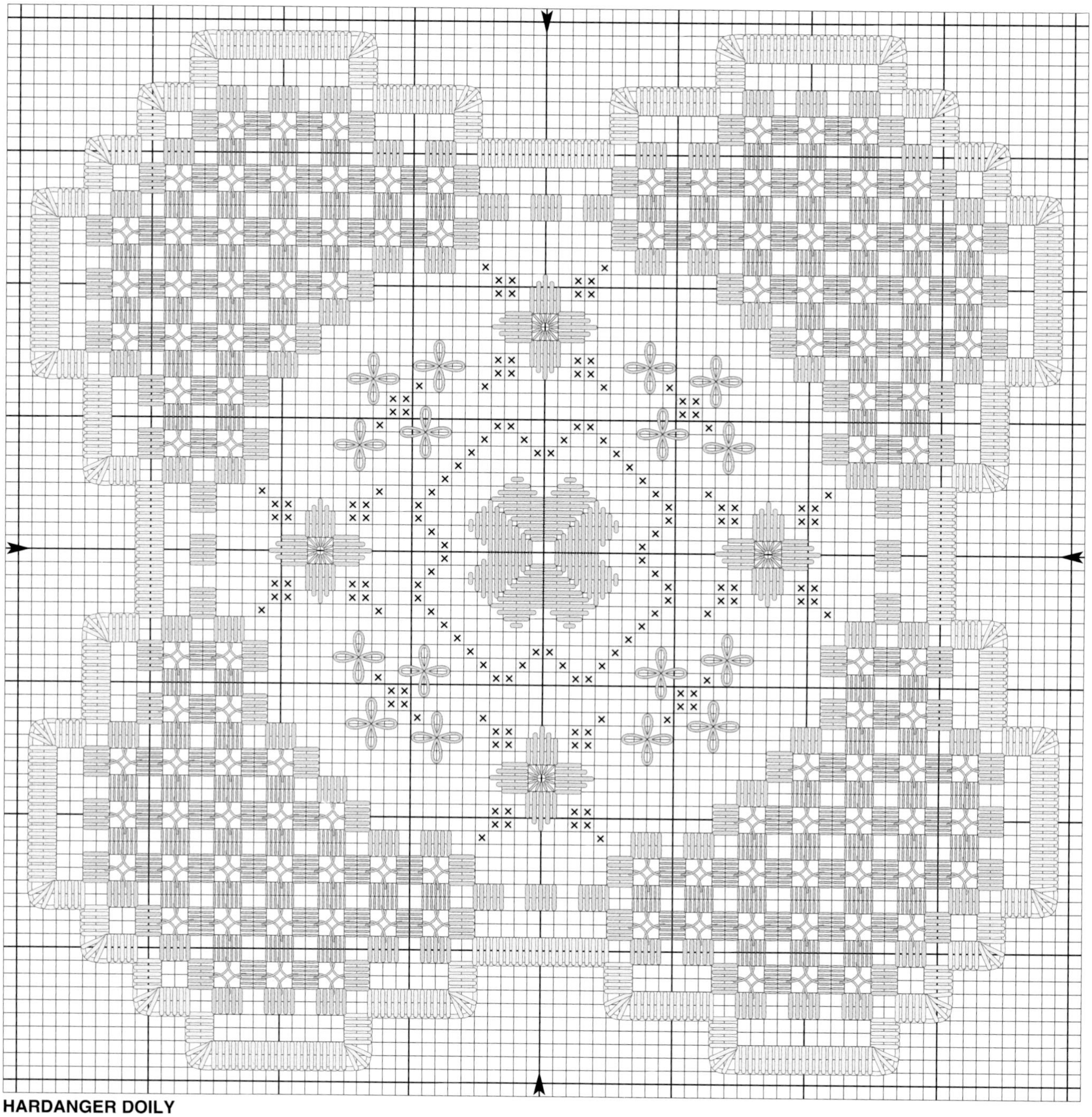

HARDANGER DOILY

HARDANGER DOILY

ANCHOR		DMC
	☒	102HL Kreinik gold #8 braid

SATIN STITCH

| 926 | ▯ | 712 Cream #5 pearl cotton |

LAZY DAISY

| 926 | ◊ | 712 Cream #5 pearl cotton |

BUTTONHOLE STITCH

| 926 | ▥ | 712 Cream #5 pearl cotton |

ALGERIAN EYELET

| | ✳ | 102HL Kreinik gold #8 braid |

ANCHOR	DMC
WRAPPED BARS WITH DOVE'S EYE	
926	712 Cream #5 pearl cotton

Stitch count: 78 high x 78 wide

Finished design sizes:
20-count fabric–7⅞ x 7⅞ inches
28-count fabric–5⅝ x 5⅝ inches
36-count fabric–4⅜ x 4⅜ inches

Jolly Fellows

Santas and Snowmen

Celebrate the Christmas season with two of the most beloved holiday characters—merry ol' Santa and the heartwarming snowman. Whether on tiny lapel pins, an eye-catching banner, or a clever holiday quilt, their jolly smiles remind us of the joy surrounding this special time of year. These magical fellows will brighten any room of your holiday home, perk up your Christmas gatherings, and add a festive touch to wintry wearables.

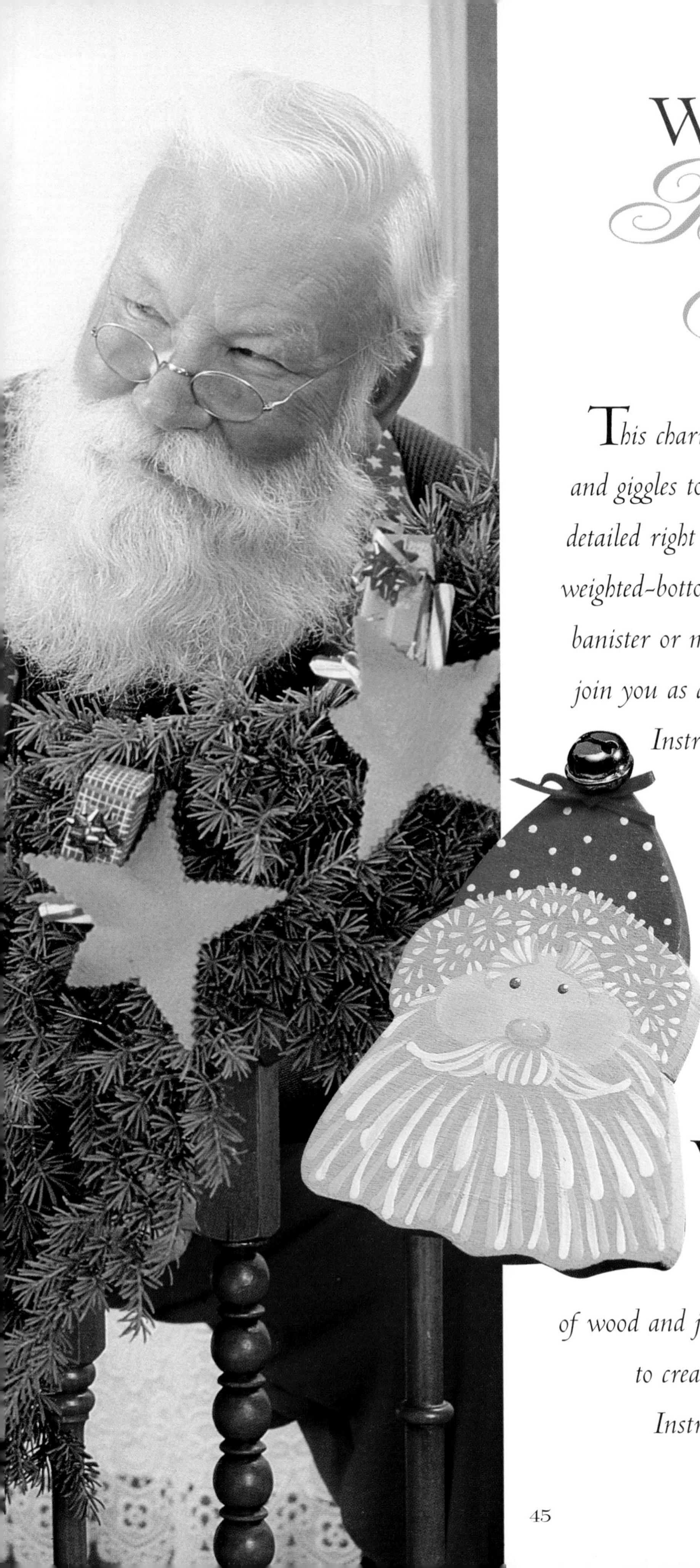

Welcoming *Banister Santa*

This charming St. Nick will bring smiles and giggles to children of all ages. Delightfully detailed right down to his cheesecloth beard, this weighted-bottom Santa would love to perch on a banister or mantel or sit in a small chair and join you as a guest during Christmas dinner.

Instructions begin on page 51.

Design: Phyllis Dunstan

Dear St. Nick Pin

With a jingle-bell tassel, this wood pin makes a much appreciated gift for friends and family. Scraps of wood and just a touch of paint are all it takes to create this jolly piece of jewelry.

Instructions begin on page 55.

Design: Susan Cage-Knoch

Friendly Frosty Hot Pad

As a fun gift or for your own kitchen, this whimsical pot holder isn't one that will be tucked away in a drawer. Primitive stitches on flannel and cotton fabrics make this snowman hot pad precious enough to frame. Instructions begin on page 55.

Design: Susan Cage-Knoch

Snow Family Pin

This adorable trio adds a happy note to even the coldest winter days. This clay pin is made of easy-to-find supplies and can be worn on a holiday jacket or favorite sweater and enjoyed long after the Christmas decorations are packed away. Instructions begin on page 57.

Design: Rachel Sindelar

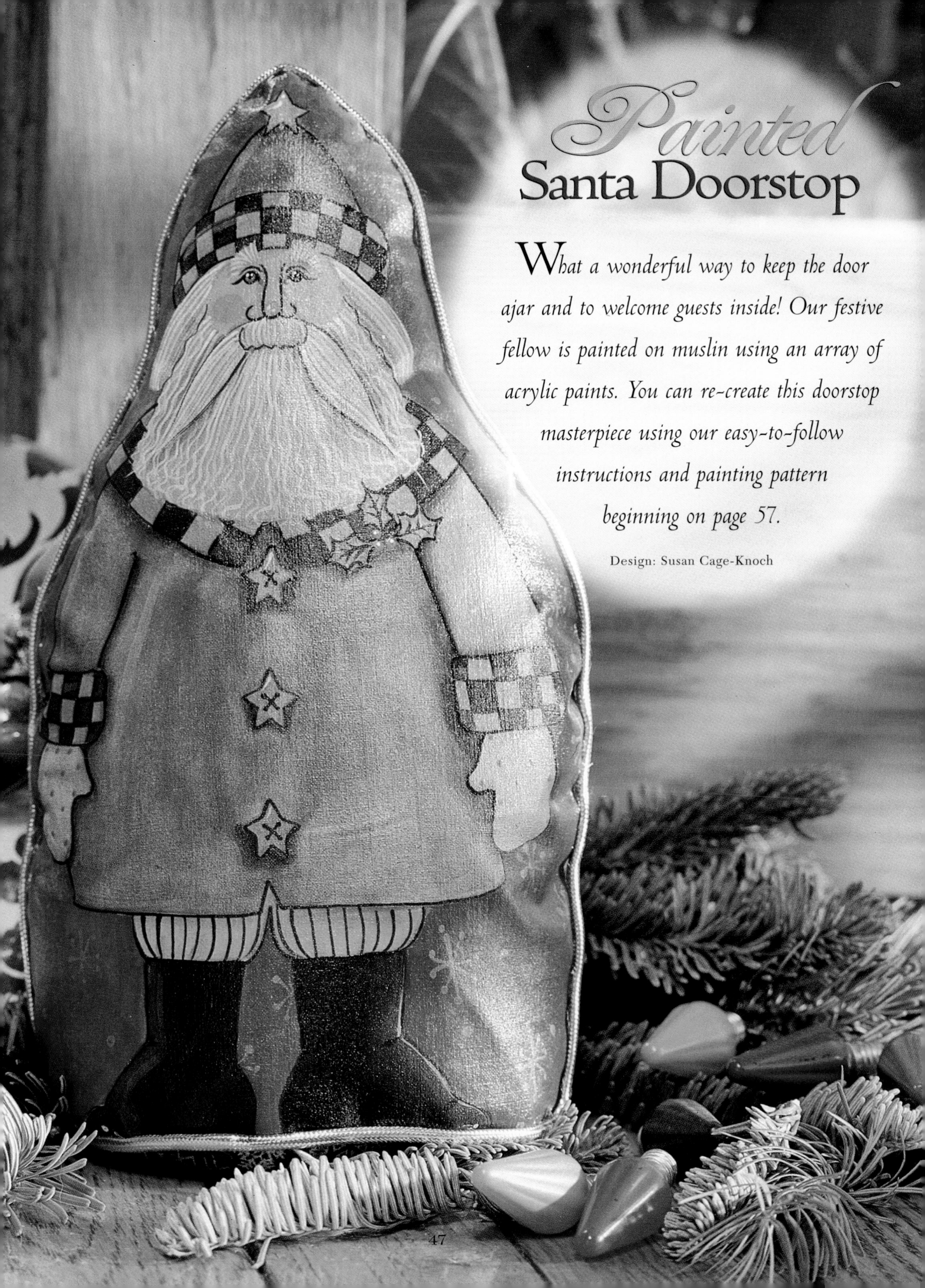

Painted Santa Doorstop

What a wonderful way to keep the door ajar and to welcome guests inside! Our festive fellow is painted on muslin using an array of acrylic paints. You can re-create this doorstop masterpiece using our easy-to-follow instructions and painting pattern beginning on page 57.

Design: Susan Cage-Knoch

Happy Snowmen Banner and Doll

This collection of frolicking snowmen will add the magic of Christmas to any room in the house. The banner stitches up quickly using colorful felts and flosses, and the cute-as-a-button fleece doll is trimmed with buttons, sticks, felt, and fabric pen paint. Instructions for both these lighthearted projects begin on page 59.

Designs: Banner, Sue Banker; Doll, Jeff Julseth

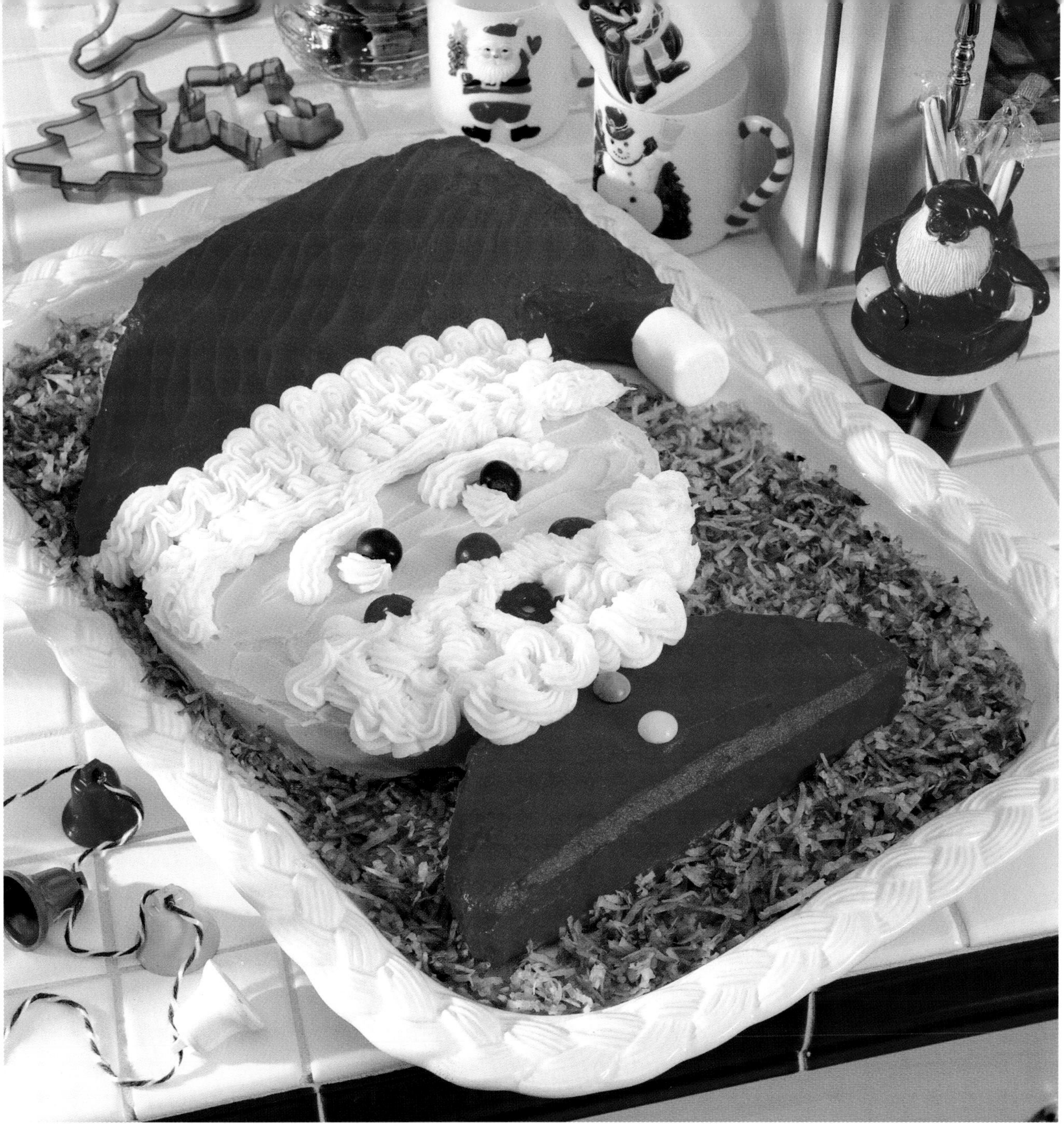

Clever Cut-Up *Santa Cake*

Here's a fun-to-make dessert that the kids will want to help create. This "ho-ho-holiday" delight starts with a simple cake mix. With a few clever cuts—like magic—Santa takes shape. Trim with assorted candies and treat dinner guests to an extra-special finale. *The recipe is on page 64.*

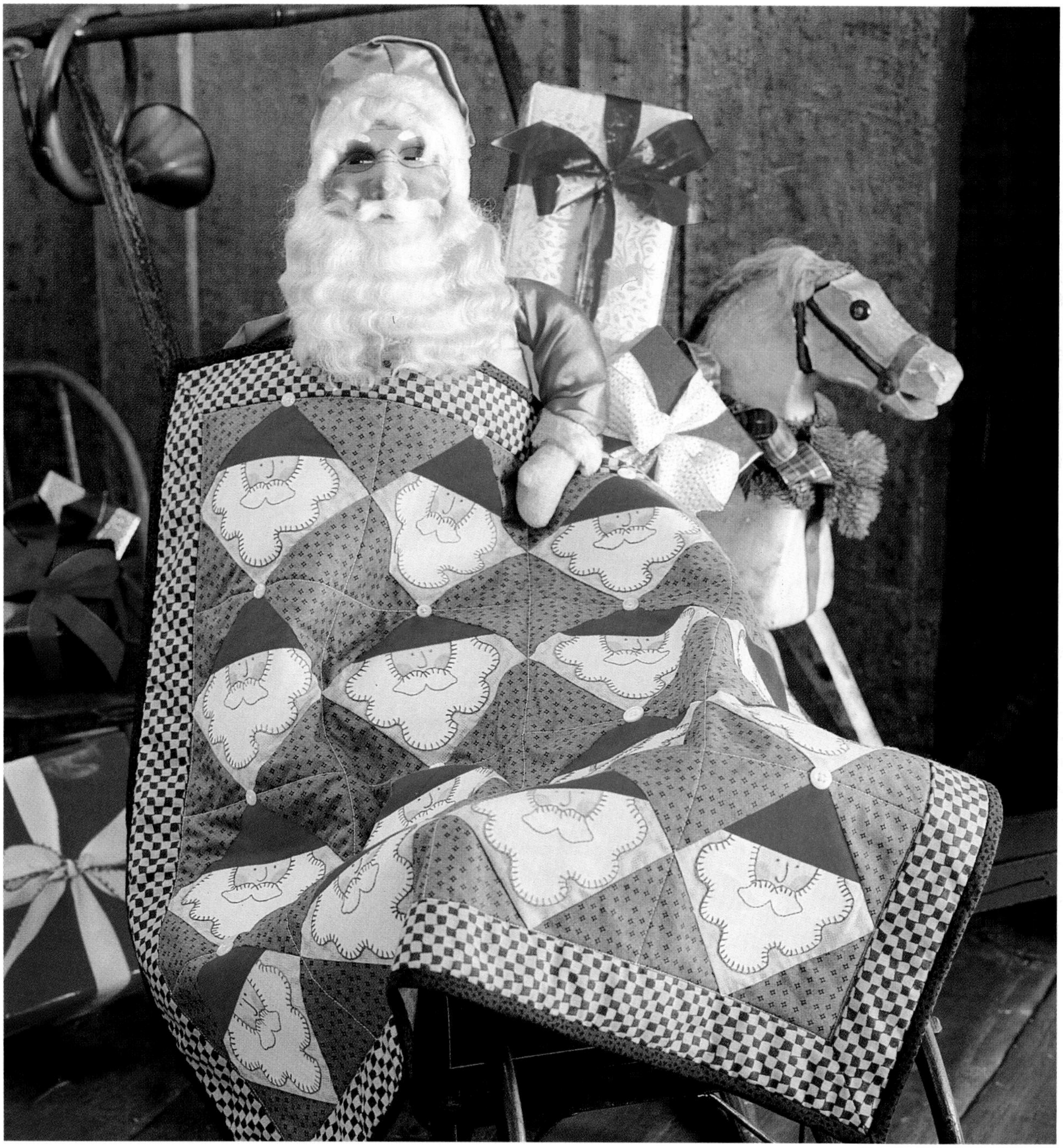

Santa *Wall Quilt*

This small quilt will be cherished for many Christmases. For the beginner or experienced quilter, this fun-to-quilt piece comes alive with soft hues, blanket stitches, and the cheerful face of the jolly old fellow himself. *Complete instructions begin on page 65.*

Design: Terrece Beesley

Welcoming Banister Santa

As shown on pages 44–45, the Santa doll measures 29½ inches tall and sits 14 inches tall.

MATERIALS

Note: Fabric yardages are for 45-inch-wide fabrics

4 tea bags
¼ yard of unbleached muslin
Tracing paper
½ yard of rose and tan large check fabric
⅓ yard of rose and maroon small check fabric
⅓ yard of forest green felt
¼ yard of forest green with gold star print fabric
¼ yard of maroon with black stripe fabric
¼ yard of maroon print flannel
Two 9x12-inch tan felt rectangles
6x6-inch piece of gold felt
6x6-inch piece of black felt
6x6-inch piece of heavy cardboard
Tailors' chalk pencil
Dark brown sewing thread
Threads to match fabrics
Dressmakers' carbon
.01 black permanent artists' pen
Colored pencils: red and blue-gray
Unscented hairspray
Polyester fiberfill
Black carpet thread
Two 1¼-inch-diameter tan buttons
Twelve ½-inch-diameter gold jingle bells
1¼ yard of ⅜-inch-diameter navy blue cord
7 inches of 18-gauge wire
Needle-nosed pliers
Large gold star charm
Package of cheesecloth
Waxed paper
Fabric stiffener
Hot-glue gun
Hot-glue stick
Fabric glue

INSTRUCTIONS

Prepare a strong tea solution by steeping the tea bags in one quart of hot water; remove tea bags. Soak muslin in solution until fabric is slightly darker than desired. Squeeze out excess tea. Allow fabric to dry thoroughly; press. Reserve excess tea and set aside.

Enlarge and trace the beard, hair, and mustache from patterns, *page 52*, onto tracing paper; do not cut out. Trace remaining patterns there and on *pages 53 and 54*, and cut out. Patterns and all measurements include ¼-inch seam allowances. Sew all seams with the right sides of the fabric facing, unless otherwise specified. Clip the curves as necessary.

Cut the head pieces from the tea-dyed muslin, bodies and sleeves from rose and maroon check, trousers from rose and tan check, hat from green felt, and stars from gold felt. In addition, cut two 4½×5-inch sleeve cuffs from the maroon flannel and two 5×8½-inch trouser cuffs from the maroon with black stripe. Cut the shoe soles from cardboard.

Draw around nose onto doubled thickness of muslin, around lower arm twice onto doubled thickness of tan felt, around lower leg twice onto doubled thickness of star print, around vest front and back onto doubled thickness of green felt, and around sleeve cap twice onto doubled thickness of maroon felt. Set pieces aside uncut, to be stitched then cut out during assembly.

For face, stitch through both layers of muslin along nose outline, using shortened stitch length and dark brown thread. Cut out close to stitching. Brush front and back with fabric stiffener. Crease along dotted lines shown on pattern to add dimension. Set nose aside and allow to dry.

Using dressmakers' carbon, transfer the face detail to one head piece. Outline eyes and mouth with black pen. Color irises blue-gray and lip red using colored pencils. Blush cheeks using red pencil. Spray doll face with unscented hairspray to set color.

For head and body, sew bottom edge of head to top of each body piece. Sew fronts to backs, leaving an opening for turning. Turn right side out and stuff with fiberfill. Sew the opening closed.

For arms, stitch along lower arm outlines drawn on doubled thickness of tan felt, leaving top edges unstitched. Cut out, leaving a ⅛-inch seam allowance and turn right side out; stuff. Using carpet thread, gather top openings. Pull gathers tight to close openings; knot.

Sew each sleeve side seam, leaving small opening for stuffing. Stitch across top and turn right side out. Gather bottom edge; slide lower arm into sleeve bottom. Pull gathers tight around top of lower arm, adjust gathers, and whipstitch to secure.

Stuff arms lightly through side openings; sew openings closed. Fold each cuff in half lengthwise, right sides facing. Stitch across one end and down long edge; turn right side out. Wrap around bottom edge of sleeve, lapping edges so finished edge is on top; stitch lapped edges to secure. Wrap finished arm around each shoulder on body; whipstitch in place.

For legs, glue one side of each cardboard sole to black felt. Cut around sole, leaving ¼-inch border of felt. Glue felt edge to back. Stitch along lower leg outlines drawn on doubled thickness of fabric, leaving marked openings. Cut out, leaving a ⅛-inch seam allowance and turn right side out. Turn under ¼ inch along bottom raw edge; finger press.

Align sole center front and back with foot front and back seams; whipstitch together. Stuff firmly. Gather and close top as for the lower arms.

Sew inside seam on each trouser leg. Turn one leg right side out and slip inside other. Sew together curved edges; turn right side out. Gather bottom of each leg. Insert top ½ inch of lower leg into each trouser leg and pull gathers tight. Adjust gathers and whipstitch to lower legs. Lightly stuff trouser legs, stopping halfway to knee. Slide

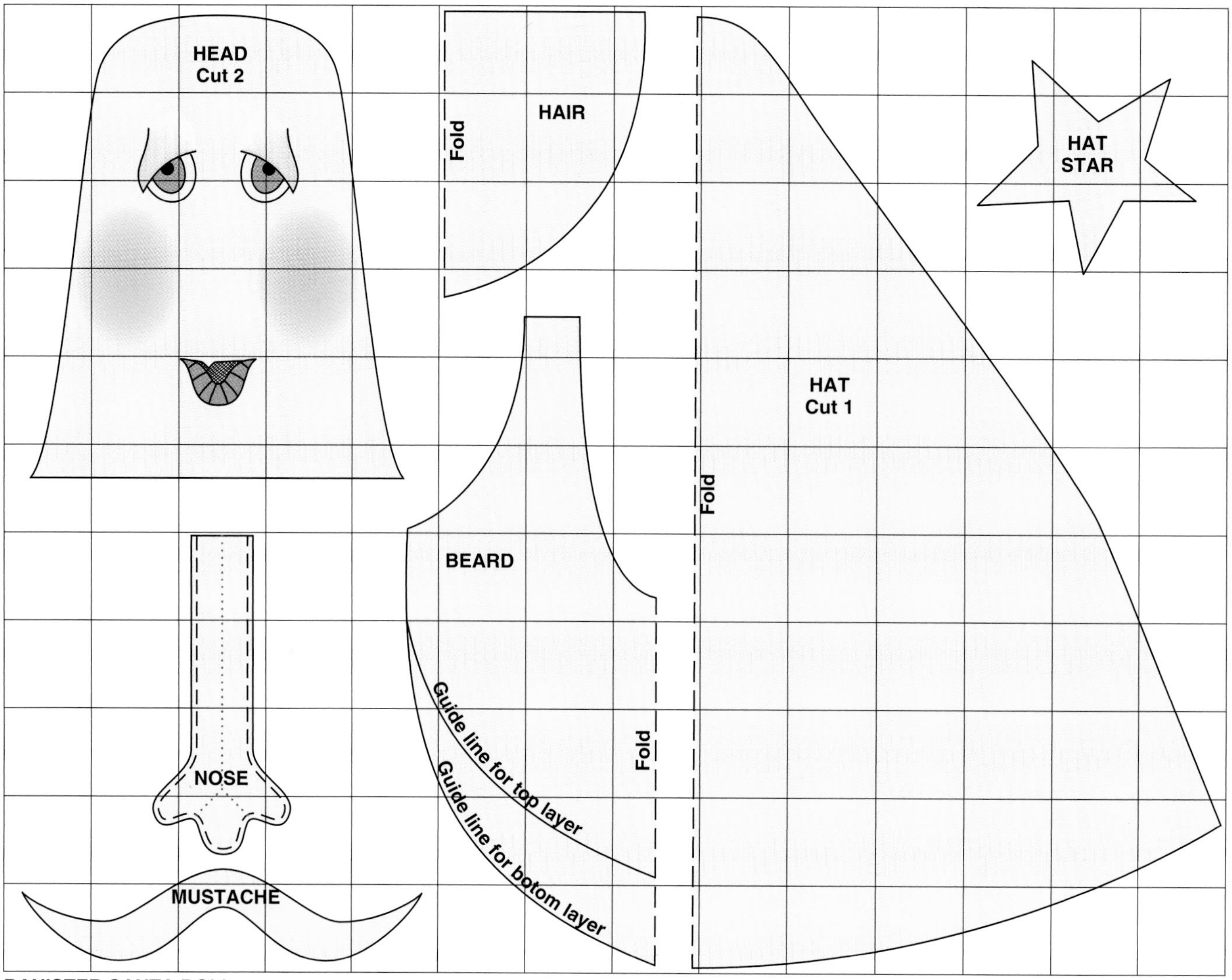

BANISTER SANTA DOLL

1 Square = 1 Inch

trousers onto body up to dotted line, gather trouser top to fit, and whipstitch to secure.

Fold and stitch trouser cuffs as for sleeve cuffs. Turn right side out and lightly stuff; stitch across raw edges. Wrap cuff around bottom of each trouser leg, lapping finished edge over raw edge at outside of leg. Tack cuff to secure. Sew large tan button to each.

For vest, stitch along front and back outlines drawn on doubled thickness of green felt. Cut out close to stitching. Overlap back pieces ¼ inch and zigzag center seam from top to dot.

Stitch along sleeve cap outlines drawn on doubled thickness of flannel, leaving marked openings. Cut out, leaving a ⅛-inch seam allowance and turn right side out. Blindstitch opening closed.

Lap vest armhole ¼ inch over straight edge of each cap, matching top shoulder fold to dot on sleeve cap. Whipstitch sleeve caps to vest on inside. Butt vest side edges to back side edges at Xs; tack. Sew bells, evenly spaced, around vest bottom edge, using three for each front piece and six across back. Glue the smaller stars to vest front, one on upper left, and one on lower right.

Put vest on Santa, lap front edges, and hot-glue closed. Wrap cord around waist several times and knot in front.

For hat, sew side seam. Using pliers, twist tight loop in each end of wire. Sew one loop to tip of hat. Position wire along seamline; tack remaining looped end to seam. Turn hat right side out. Turn up bottom edge 1 inch; tack to secure. Turn up once again to make doubled cuff.

Bend wire inside hat to shape as desired. Tack star charm to tip. Glue remaining gold star to front of hat.

For beard and hair, slide patterns under pieces of waxed paper. Cut 8-inch length of cheesecloth for beard. Unfold and cut into two equal sized pieces. Mix equal parts fabric stiffener and strong tea until thickness of whipping cream. Coat cheese cloth with mixture. Lay each piece atop one beard pattern and shape to conform to the outline.

Continued on page 54

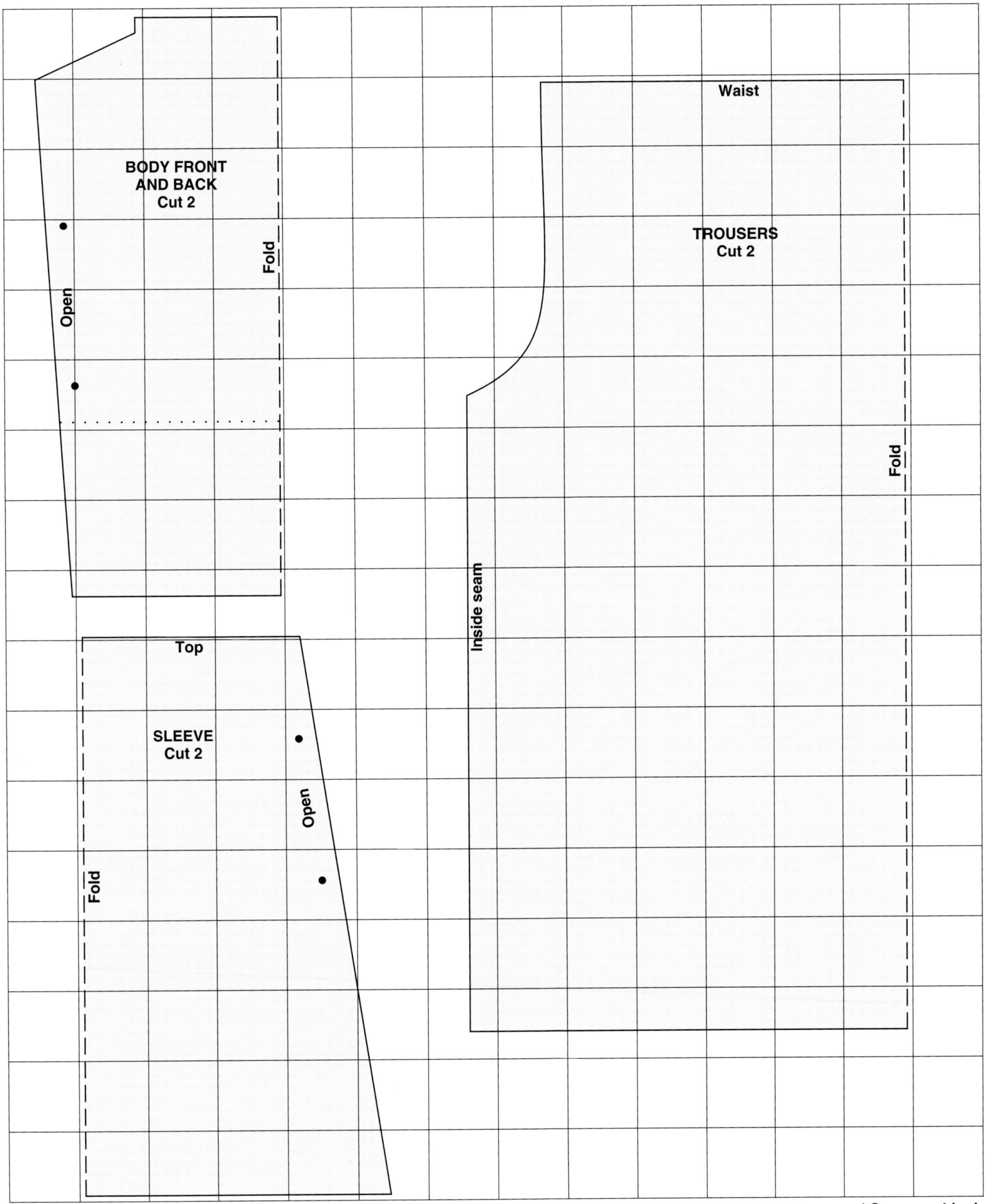

BANISTER SANTA DOLL

1 Square = 1 Inch

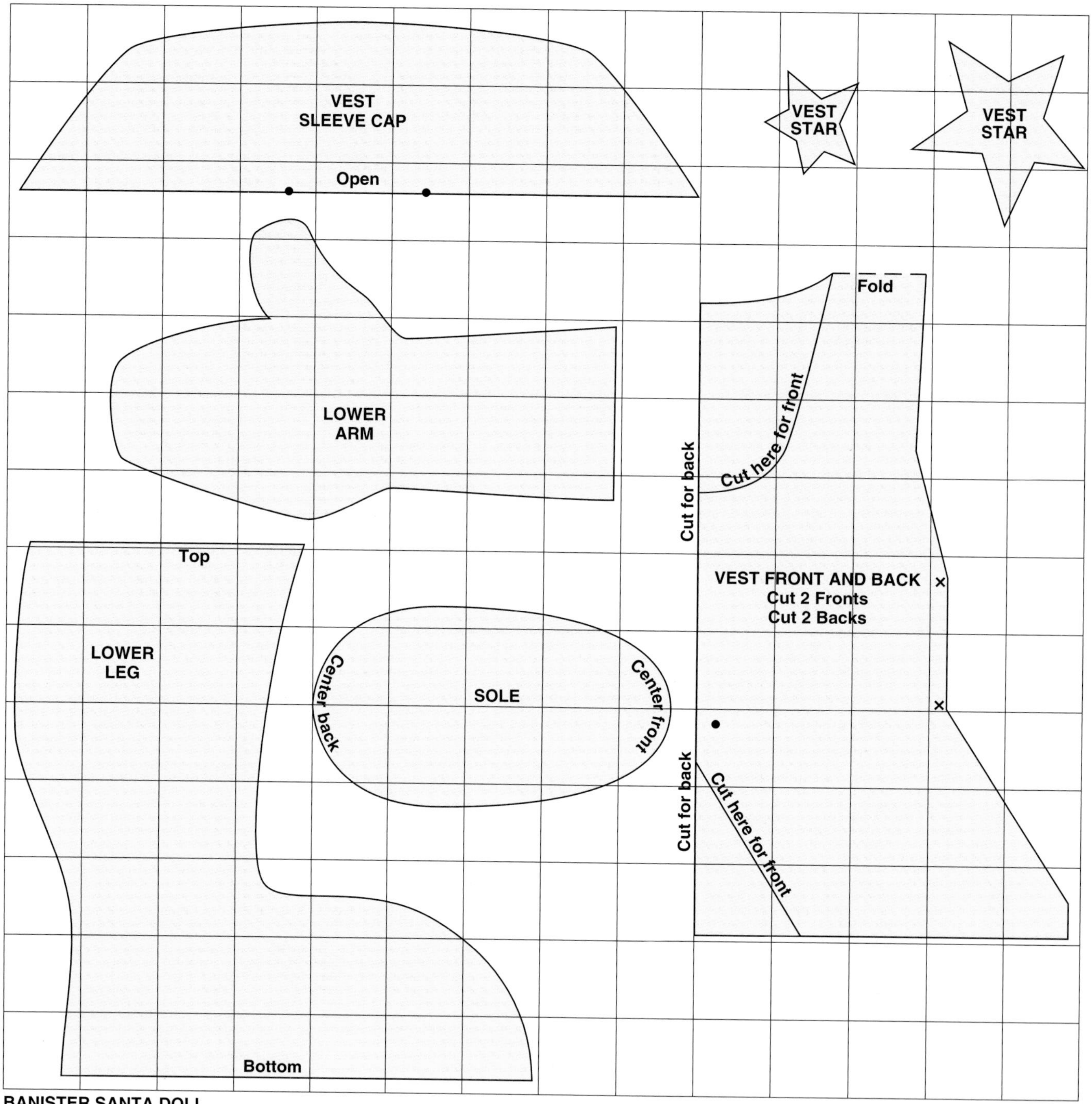

BANISTER SANTA DOLL

1 Square = 1 Inch

Make irregular edges to resemble curls. Repeat process, using 4×9-inch piece of cheesecloth for hair and narrow strip for mustache. When pieces are partially dry, peel waxed paper from back and allow to dry thoroughly.

Bend the hair to fit around the back of the head. Hot-glue top edge to the back of the head, 2½ inches from the top seam. Bend bottom layer of beard to fit around front of face, shaping it so the sides run along the side seams and the center curves under the mouth. Hot-glue the sides to the head.

Repeat for the top layer of the beard, gluing sides atop those of lower beard. Glue the nose down the center of the face, positioning tip at dotted line on pattern and gluing along straight side edges only. Glue the mustache under the tip of the nose; glue the edges of the nostrils to the mustache.

Push a handful of fiberfill into the hat. Slide the hat onto head, pulling it down over the top edge of the hair and the sides of beard. Hot-glue the hat in place.

Dear St. Nick Pin

As shown on page 45, pin measures 3½x2¾ inches.

MATERIALS

Tracing paper
Carbon paper
Ballpoint pen
4x3½-inch piece of ¼-inch poplar or pine
Scroll saw
Fine grit sandpaper
Delta Ceramcoat acrylic paints: Santa's flesh, bouquet pink, liberty blue, Quaker gray, sandstone, white, berry red, barn red, lichen gray, and black
Artists' brushes
Polyurethane spray
6 inches of 1/16-inch-wide red satin ribbon
⅜-inch-diameter green jingle bell
1-inch-long pin back
Hot-glue gun
Hot-glue stick

INSTRUCTIONS

Trace pattern, below, onto tracing paper. Place carbon paper between pattern and wood; transfer pattern, tracing over all but fine detail lines using ballpoint pen. Cut out ornament with scroll saw. Sand edges smooth.

DEAR ST. NICK PIN

Paint Santa's face Santa's flesh; blend bouquet pink into nose and cheeks. Paint hat and back of pin berry red. Shade hat with barn red. Dot eyes liberty blue. Paint hat fur lichen gray and beard, mustache, and eyebrows Quaker gray. Shade Santa's nose with Quaker gray.

Referring to pattern for detail, add tiny slashes of white to hat fur, grouping slashes as shown. Use longer slashes of sandstone to detail hair on beard and eyebrows; top with white slashes. Detail mustache with strokes of white. Add tiny white highlights to eyes and nose.

Spray entire pin with polyurethane. Tie ribbon into bow; glue to tip of hat. Glue jingle bell atop bow and pin back to center back of face.

Friendly Frosty Hot Pad

As shown on page 46, hot pad measures 9x9 inches.

MATERIALS

FABRICS

¼ yard of 45-inch-wide dove gray flannel
¼ yard of 45-inch-wide cream and burgundy print cotton fabric
8x9½-inch piece of white cotton fabric
2x4-inch piece of burgundy chintz
9x9-inch piece of fleece

FLOSS

Cotton embroidery floss: white, dark charcoal (DMC 3799), medium watermelon (DMC 3706), and dark khaki (DMC 3011)

SUPPLIES

Tracing paper
Rub-on transfer pen and paper
Embroidery needle
Embroidery hoop
Sewing threads to match fabrics

INSTRUCTIONS

Trace snowman, hat, and snow from pattern, *page 56*, onto tracing paper. Add ⅛-inch seam allowances all around snowman and hat, and to curved top edge of snow. Cut out patterns. Fold white and burgundy fabrics in half for double layer, cut two of each snow and snowman from white fabric, and two hats from burgundy chintz. In addition, cut two 9x9-inch squares from gray flannel, and 38 linear inches of 1¼-inch-wide bias strips from cream and burgundy print.

Trace tree and bird from pattern, *page 56*, onto tracing paper. Draw over lines using regular black pen. Using back of tracing so pattern is reversed, transfer pattern to transfer paper using transfer pen according to manufacturer's instructions. Next, transfer markings to right side of one flannel square, following the pattern placement.

Sew snowman pieces together, right sides facing, using ⅛-inch seam allowance. Use small hand stitches or machine stitches as desired. Leave an opening for turning. Turn snowman right side out, press, and slipstitch opening closed. Repeat for hat. Sew snow pieces together along curved edge. Turn to right side and press. Baste sides and bottom together close to edge. Stitch each piece in place on front flannel square, using appliqué stitch and following pattern for placement.

Trace snowman's arms, features, and hat detail onto tracing paper. Transfer these to transfer paper and then to flannel square as for tree and bird.

Use two plies of floss for all embroidery. Stitch tree trunk using a long and short stitch and dark khaki floss. Outline stitch branches and straight stitch needles using same color.

Work bird body using satin stitch and dark charcoal floss; straight stitch tail feathers in same color. Use medium watermelon to straight stitch beak and feet.

Work straight stitches for hat detail and satin stitch snowman's nose using medium watermelon.

Use dark charcoal floss to work French knot eyes, mouth, and buttons on snowman.

FRIENDLY FROSTY HOT PAD

Stitch base of each arm branch using long and short stitches, and outline stitch remainder of each branch in dark charcoal.

Work varied sizes of white straight-stitch snowflakes over design square at random, using snowflake next to hat on pattern as a guide.

For hat tassel, work five ¾-inch-long medium watermelon floss loops, each beginning in same place at tip of hat. Cut loops and trim ends even. Satin stitch several times over base of stitches at tip of hat.

To assemble hot pad, layer fleece between wrong sides of hot pad front and back flannel pieces; baste. Trim all edges to match. Sew short ends of bias strips together for one long strip. Using a ¼-inch seam allowance, sew binding around hot pad front. Turn raw edges to back, turn under ¼ inch, and hand-sew in place along seam line.

Snow Family Pin

As shown on page 46, finished pin measures 1¾×2¼ inches. Large snowman is 1 inch tall, medium is ¾ inch tall, and small is ½ inch tall.

MATERIALS

White Fimo or Sculpey oven-bakable clay
Three 1¼-inch-long jewelry finding head pins
Jewelry wire cutters
Acrylic artists' paints: orange and black
Artists' brushes: ¼-inch flat and fine detail
Black ultra fine point permanent marker
5 black seed beads
Clear gloss suitable for bakable clay
Wool needlepoint yarn: 3 inches each of green, red, and blue
2 black sequins
1 gold sequin
2¼-inch-long curved jewelry pin with three attached rings for charms, or similar jewelry suitable for three charms

INSTRUCTIONS

Knead clay until it is pliable. For large snowman, roll clay into ⅝-inch-diameter ball for body and ⅜-inch-diameter ball for head. For medium snowman, roll a ½-inch-diameter ball for body and a ¼-inch-diameter ball for head. For small snowman, roll a ⅜-inch-diameter ball for body and a scant ¼-inch-diameter ball for the head.

For each snowman, push head pin up through body and then head. Bake the clay according to the manufacturer's directions.

Using photograph, page 46, as a guide, paint eyes and carrot nose with liner brush. Draw stick arms on sides of body using marker. Glue two beads onto large and medium snowman bodies and one bead onto small snowman body for buttons. Brush snowmen with gloss; allow to dry. Knot desired color yarn around neck for scarf; trim ends. Turn scarf so knot is off center and glue ends to the body.

Thread black sequin onto head pins of large and small snowmen and gold sequin onto head pin of medium snowman. Attach each snowman by threading head pin through loop on jewelry pin; twist end of head pin into loop and end.

Santa Doorstop

As shown on page 47, doorstop stands 10¼ inches tall.

MATERIALS

Tracing paper
8x12-inch piece of muslin
¼ yard of navy blue fabric with gold snowflake print, or similar blue holiday print
8x12-inch piece of freezer paper
Gesso
1-inch paint brush
Fine grit sandpaper
Tack cloth
Carbon paper
Ballpoint pen
Delta Ceramcoat acrylic paints: grape, metallic gold, navy blue, leaf green, wild rose, desert sun, medium flesh, black, denim blue, lichen gray, hammered iron, sandstone, magnolia white, yellow, blue jay, and mocha
Artists' brushes
Exterior varnish
Navy blue sewing thread
Polyester fiberfill
Polyfill pellet beads
Small funnel
32 inches of ⅛-inch-diameter metallic gold cord
Hot-glue gun; hot-glue stick

INSTRUCTIONS

Trace base pattern and doorstop outline, page 58, onto tracing paper and cut out. Cut base and back piece from blue and gold print. Lay muslin rectangle atop shiny side of freezer paper. Using medium heat, iron fabric to paper. After paper has cooled, apply thin coat of gesso to fabric. Allow gesso to dry. Sand over gesso lightly in one direction; wipe with tack cloth. Apply second thin coat of gesso, sand, and wipe with tack cloth. Place carbon paper between pattern and doorstop front; transfer front piece outline and Santa, excluding face detail, by tracing over lines with ballpoint pen. Do not cut out doorstop front until all painting is completed.

Paint background grape. Add snowflakes and dots at random using metallic gold. Next, paint Santa's face medium flesh; allow to dry. Using pattern and carbon paper, transfer face detail. Shade nose and eyelids with desert sun. Blend wild rose into cheeks and tip of nose. Paint irises denim blue with black pupils. Dot inner corner of each eye with wild rose. Outline eyes and nose in black.

Paint coat and hat denim blue with navy blue shading. Paint mittens blue jay; shade with denim blue. When mittens are dry, dot with gold.

Paint pants, coat buttons, hat cuff, sleeve cuffs, collar, star buttons, and star on hat yellow. Add navy blue checks to cuffs and collar, following pattern. Shade pants with mocha and add thin navy blue stripes when dry. Paint star button thread lines using black.

Paint boots black; highlight with lichen gray.

Paint beard, mustache, and eyebrows lichen gray; shade with hammered iron. First using sandstone and then magnolia white, paint thin lines to detail all hair.

Paint holly leaves green and berries wild rose.

Using liner brush, outline clothing detail and holly leaves in black. Highlight eyes, tip of nose, all stars, boots, and holly berries with magnolia white. Allow all paint to dry thoroughly.

Apply coat of varnish to painted doorstop front; allow to dry. Cut out front along cutting line.

Sew doorstop front to back, using ⅛-inch seam allowance. Leave an

Continued on page 59

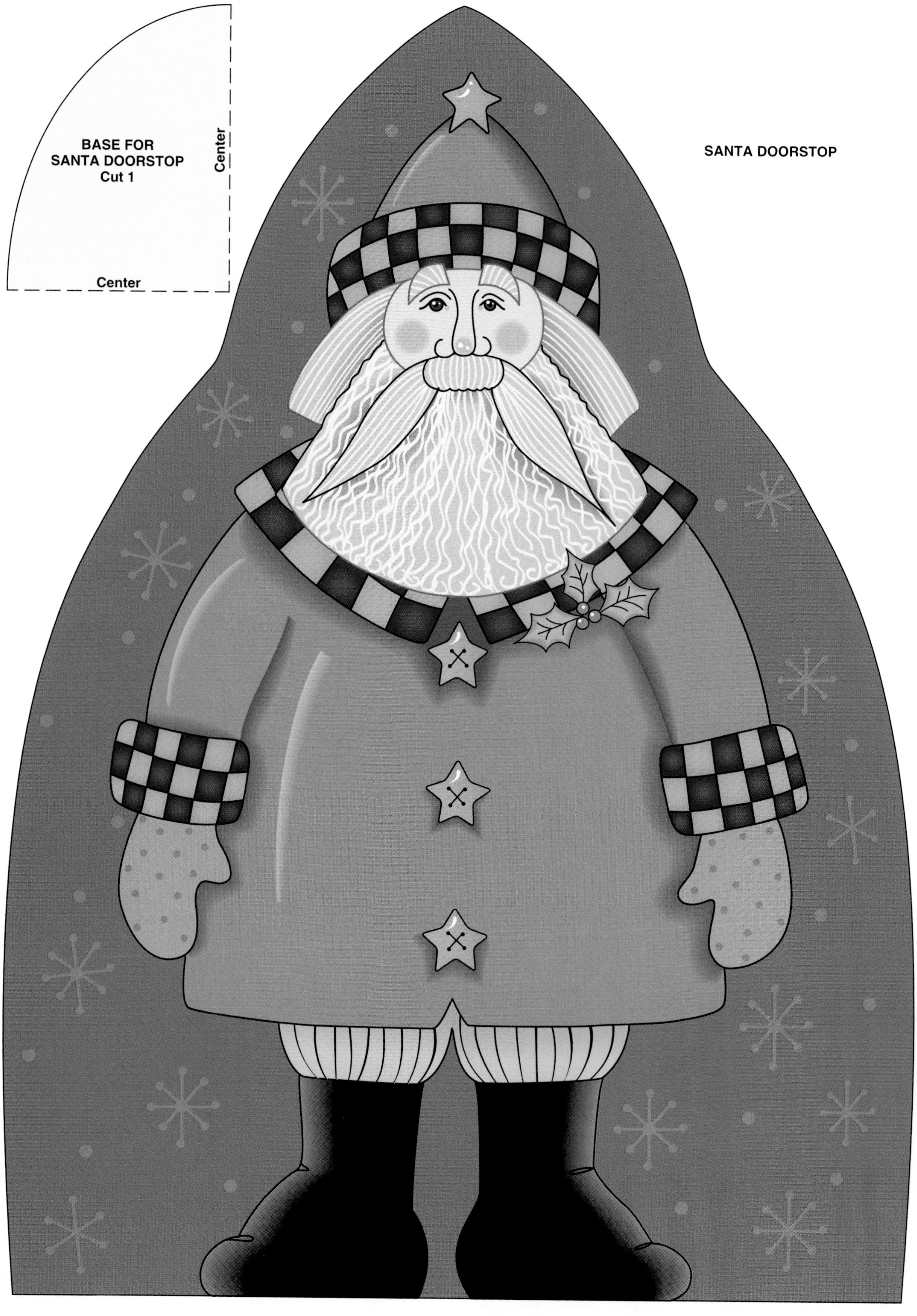
BASE FOR
SANTA DOORSTOP
Cut 1
Center
Center
SANTA DOORSTOP

opening for turning. Sew base to bottom; clip curves. Turn doorstop right side out and stuff top ¾ of figure firmly with polyester fiberfill.

Pour polyfill pellet beads into the bottom, using a funnel if necessary. Whipstitch the opening closed. Hot-glue the gold cord over the seamed edges.

Snowmen Banner

As shown on page 48, banner measures 28½×22½ inches.

MATERIALS

Tracing paper
Four 9x12-inch sky blue felt rectangles
Four 9x12-inch white felt rectangles
Two 9x12-inch lavender felt rectangles
One 9x12-inch fuchsia felt rectangle
One 9x12-inch teal felt rectangle
4x4-inch piece of orange felt
Cotton embroidery floss: pink, lavender, black, fuchsia, teal, orange, mint green, and white
Embroidery needle
55 assorted white buttons
14 colored buttons, in assorted sizes and shades of rose, blue, and teal
White quilting thread
Large-eyed hand sewing needle

INSTRUCTIONS

Enlarge and trace outlined shapes from each snowman pattern, *page 60,* onto tracing paper. Do not trace shapes indicated only by gray dotted lines. Trace hat, scarf, and bow tie patterns, *page 61.* Cut out all pattern pieces.

For snowman A, cut body pieces and snow from white, nose from orange, and hat pieces from fuchsia felt. In addition, cut a 2×10½-inch scarf from lavender felt.

For snowman B, cut body and snow pieces from white, and nose from orange felt. In addition, cut snowman B bow tie from fuchsia and snowman B hat from teal felt.

For snowman C, cut body piece and snow from white, hat pieces from lavender, and nose from orange felt. In addition, cut a 1½×8-inch scarf from teal felt.

For snowman D, cut body and snow pieces from white, vest and hat pieces from fuchsia, and nose from orange felt. In addition, cut snowman D bow tie from teal felt.

For borders, sashing and tabs, cut four 12×1½-inch strips from teal, four 9×1½-inch and two 12×1½-inch strips from lavender and two 9×1½-inch and two 4½×1½-inch strips from fuchsia felt. Cut nine 1½×1½-inch square blocks from white felt.

Use two plies of floss for all stitching except decorative stitching on hats and scarves, and where otherwise specified. For decorative stitching, use six plies of floss.

For snowman A, sew body pieces to blue background rectangle using white running stitches around perimeters, about ¼ inch in from edge. Sew snow to background along curved top edge using light blue running stitches. Sew hat pieces in place using fuchsia running stitches. Use small orange straight stitches to affix nose. Make straight stitch eyes and work arms using black floss. Work French knot mouth using six plies of black floss. Decorate hat with pink straight stitches around hat brim, lavender French knots scattered across brim, and lavender zigzags and pink French knots on top portion of hat. Make pom-pom as for Snowman Doll instructions, *page 64*; tack pom-pom to tip of hat. Knot the scarf in middle; position on the snowman according to the dotted lines. Secure scarf with pink French knots at dots. Use fuchsia straight stitches in a 'V' pattern for fringe, tacked with pink near base of V, as shown on pattern. Sew button at X on snowman. Scatter and stitch on approximately 11 buttons across blue background for snowflakes.

For snowman B, sew body, snow, and nose pieces in place as for snowman A. Work straight stitch eyes, mouth, and arms using black floss. Fold hat piece from bottom toward top along fold line and position as shown on pattern. Sew in place using fuchsia running stitches. Work a fuchsia straight stitch star at top. Decorate using lazy daisies and French knots in desired colors. Knot bow tie strip in middle; position on snowman according to dotted lines. Secure bow tie with straight stitch 'V's in teal and mint green. Sew buttons at Xs on snowman. Scatter and stitch on approximately 12 buttons across blue background for snowflakes.

For snowman C, sew body pieces, snow, and nose pieces in place as for snowman A. Sew hat pieces in place using tiny lavender straight stitches. Make French knot eyes, running stitch mouth, and straight stitch arms using black floss. Decorate hat top with long teal straight stitches and brim with teal lazy daisies and French knots. Knot scarf in middle; position on snowman according to dotted lines. Secure scarf with lavender lazy daisy flowers with fuchsia French knot centers and scattered teal French knots. Sew buttons to hat and body at Xs. Scatter and stitch on approximately 16 buttons across blue background for the snowflakes.

For snowman D, sew body, snow, and nose pieces in place as for snowman A. Sew hat in place using lavender running stitches, tucking in ends of 1½×¼-inch strip at top as shown on pattern. Straight stitch black eyebrows and arms. Work French knot eyes and mouth using six plies of black floss. Sew vest pieces in place using fuchsia running stitches. Decorate vest with straight stitch stars using two plies of pink floss. Knot the bow tie in middle. Position the tie at base of neck and secure with fuchsia French knots at dots. Sew buttons at Xs. Scatter and stitch on approximately 14 buttons across blue background for the snowflakes.

Arrange snowman blocks with A and B in top row and C and D in bottom row. Sew all assembly seams

Continued on page 61

SNOWMAN BANNER–SNOWMAN A

SNOWMAN BANNER–SNOWMAN B

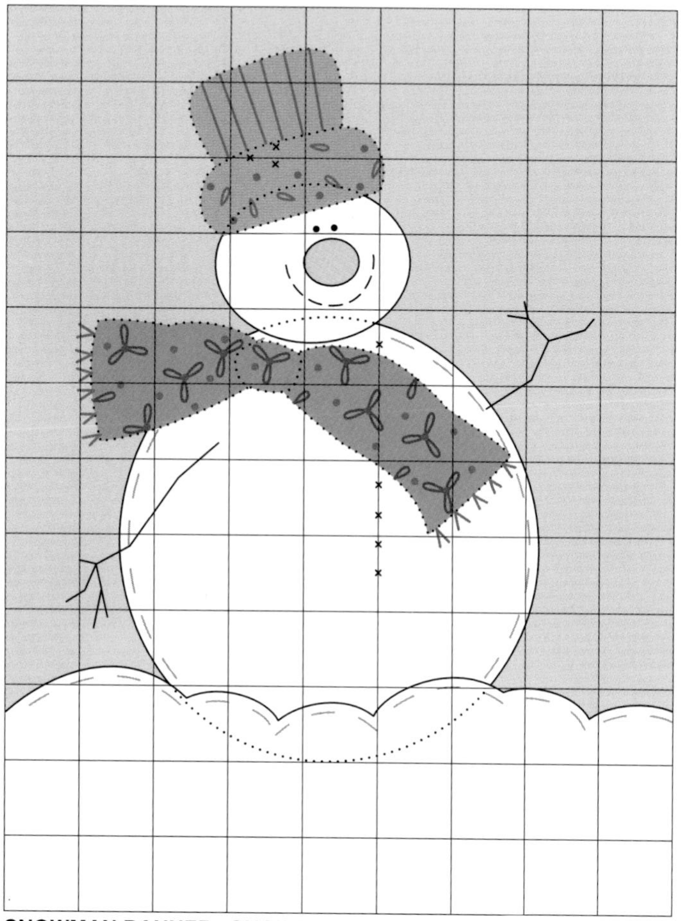

SNOWMAN BANNER–SNOWMAN C

SNOWMAN BANNER–SNOWMAN D

1 Square = 1 Inch

using white quilting thread. Whipstitch seams, piercing felt approximately ⅛ inch from edges. When seams are sewn and opened out, stitches will show.

Sew long side of teal sashing strip to left side of snowman A. In same manner, working left to right, sew 12-inch-long lavender strip to right side of A, Snowman B to right side of lavender strip, and teal strip to right side of snowman B. Repeat for bottom row, using snowmen C and D.

For top horizontal sashing, sew short end of 9-inch-long lavender strip to white block. In same manner, working left to right, sew white block to remaining short end of lavender strip, another strip to white block, ending with another white block at far end. Repeat to make bottom horizontal sashing. Make middle sashing in same manner using white blocks and 9-inch-long fuchsia strips.

Sew middle sashing between rows of snowman blocks, matching seam lines. Sew top and bottom sashing to blocks in same manner.

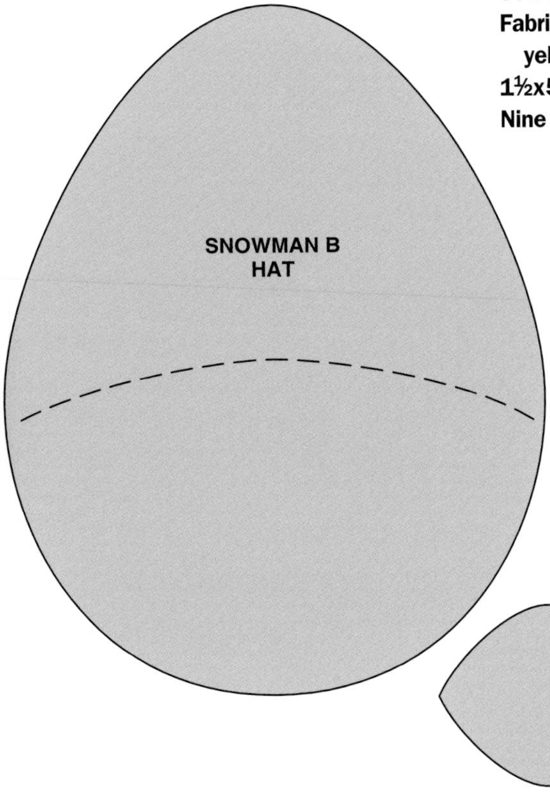

Trim one short end of each tab strip to a point. For each tab, whipstitch straight end of tab to each white top corner block. Fold pointed end to front as shown in photograph, *page 48*, and secure with a white button.

Snowman Doll

As shown on page 48, snowman is 12½ inches tall.

MATERIALS

Tracing paper
28x8-inch piece of white polar fleece
8x8-inch piece of purple polar fleece
3x5-inch piece of light blue polar fleece
2½x20-inch piece of teal polar fleece
½-inch-diameter circle of orange felt
White sewing thread
White button thread
Plastic polyfill pellet beads
Polyester fiberfill
Crafts glue
Cotton embroidery floss: black, yellow, white, light pink, dark pink, and dark lavender
7 size 4-mm round black beads
Two 5-inch-long twigs
Purple sewing thread
Soft sculpture needle
Fabric paint pens: bright pink, bright yellow, and green
1½x5-inch strip of cardboard
Nine white buttons in assorted sizes

Continued on page 64

SNOWMAN DOLL

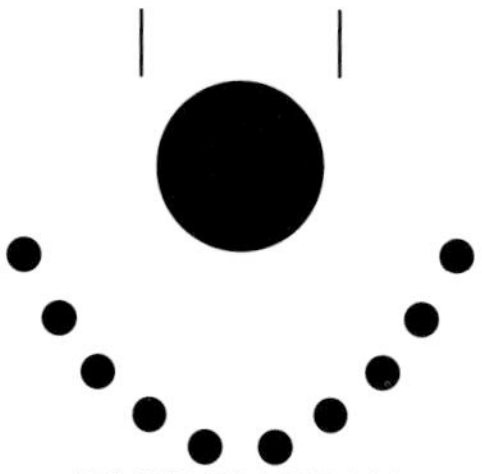

FACE DIAGRAM

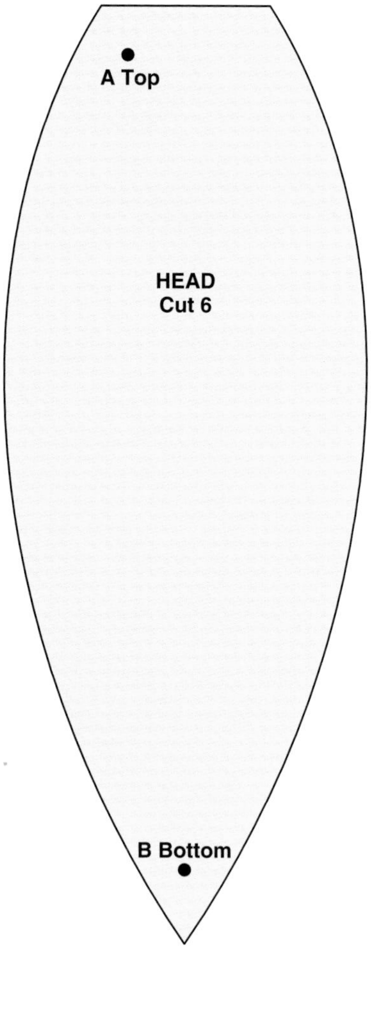

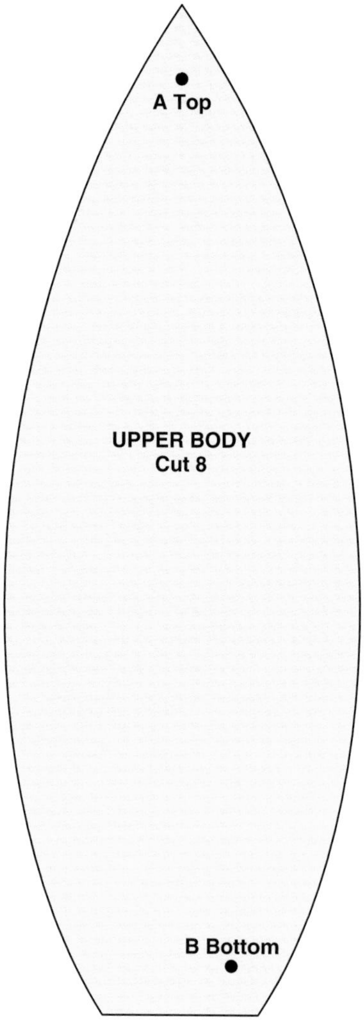

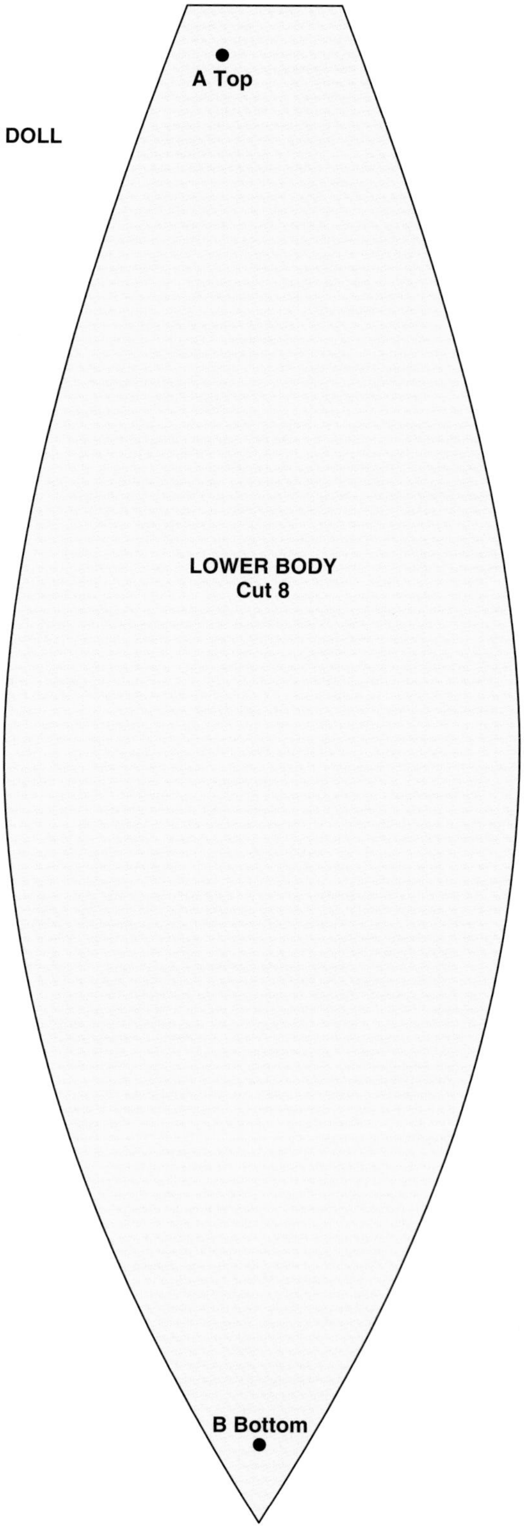

SNOWMAN DOLL

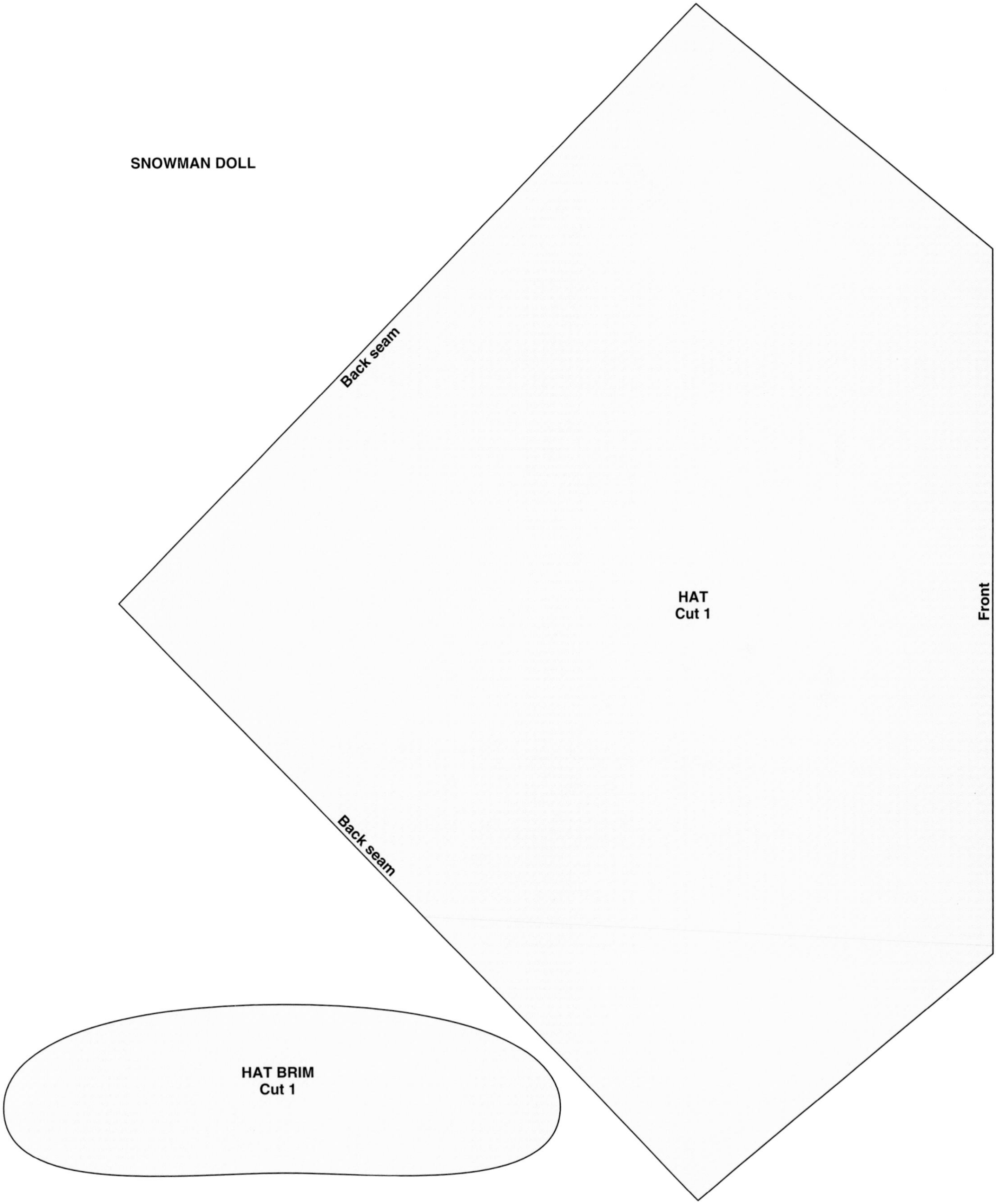

INSTRUCTIONS

Trace patterns, *pages 62–63*, onto tracing paper; cut out. From white polar fleece, cut eight lower body pieces using large body piece pattern, eight upper body pieces using small body piece pattern, and six head pieces. Cut hat brim from blue fleece and hat from purple fleece. Patterns include ¼-inch seam allowances.

Sew four lower body pieces together, sewing from A to B as shown on the pattern. Repeat, making two sets of four pieces. Sew sets together; turn right side out. Fill lower body half full with pellet beads; stuff remainder with fiberfill. Sew opening closed using button thread.

Sew upper body and head in same manner; stuff each with fiberfill, and sew closed. Hand stitch upper body to lower body and then head to upper body to complete the snowman figure.

Glue orange felt circle to center of front of head. Thread needle with 12 plies of black embroidery floss; knot end. Push needle down through top of head and out at top of one eye as shown on face diagram, *page 62*. Stitch down ¼ inch to complete eye; bring needle out at top of other eye and repeat to complete eye. Push needle out through head top. Glue black beads to head to make mouth as shown on the face diagram.

Cut a small hole on each side of the upper body to hold the twig arms. Glue the base of twig to each hole.

Tie teal scarf piece around neck. Using six plies of yellow floss, stitch one bottom edge of scarf to lower body, making floss stitches look like 1-inch-long fringe. On remaining end of scarf, knot floss in four separate places along edge, leaving 1-inch-long tails for fringe. Flip free end over one twig arm; glue to secure.

Sew hat back seam; turn right side out and stuff top. Glue hat to head. Work blanket stitch around hat brim using six plies of yellow floss. Glue brim to bottom of front of hat.

Using paint pens, dot scarf and hat with pink. Dot hat brim and tops of fringe stitches with green. Make two rows of yellow zigzags across front of hat as shown in photograph, *page 48*.

To make pom-pom, use one strand each of light pink, dark pink, and purple floss. Holding three colors together, wrap floss strand 50 times around 1½-inch-wide strip of cardboard. Slide the wraps carefully off the cardboard and tie tightly around the middle. Cut the loops and fluff the strands into a pom-pom, trimming if necessary. Tack pom-pom to hat top.

Glue one button to each side of head to resemble earmuffs. Glue one button to right front side of lower body.

Cut two 8-inch-long strands of white floss. Thread and then knot three buttons on each strand. Tie one strand to each twig arm, allowing buttons to dangle.

Clever Cut-Up Santa Cake

As shown on page 49.

INGREDIENTS

- **1 package 2-layer-size white cake mix**
- **Creamy White Frosting**
- **Red food coloring**
- **1 large marshmallow**
- **2 blue candy-coated, chocolate-covered peanuts (M&M's)**
- **1 red jaw breaker**
- **3 red fruit-flavored circle candies (Lifesavers)**
- **Flaked coconut**
- **3-4 candy-coated, fruit-flavored pieces (Skittles)**

Prepare cake mix according to the package directions, using 1 greased and floured 8-inch round baking pan and 1 greased and floured 8×8×2-inch baking pan. Let cool in pans on wire rack for 10 minutes. Remove from pans and cool completely. If necessary, trim tops of cakes so that both cakes are the same height.

To shape Santa, cut off about one-third of the round cake. Place the larger piece on serving platter or a large piece of cardboard covered with foil, with the flat side facing up. (This will be Santa's head.) Place the smaller piece under the larger piece with the curved edge touching the larger piece. (This will be Santa's shoulders.) Cut a 1-inch strip of cake off of one side of the square cake. (This will be the bottom of Santa's hat.) Place at the top of Santa's head.

Cut the remaining piece of cake into two triangles. For the hat, place one of the triangles with the longer side touching the 1-inch piece at the top of the head. Place the remaining triangle at an angle, fitting it against the other triangle.

Tint ½ cup of the Creamy White Frosting to desired color pink for face, using the red food coloring. Tint 1¼ cups of the frosting to desired red color for hat and shoulders. Leave remaining frosting white.

Frost face, hat, and shoulders with appropriate colors of frosting. Using a small star tip, pipe white frosting onto the brim of Santa's hat. Place marshmallow at the tip of the hat. Add eyes using blue candy-coated, chocolate-covered peanuts (peanut M&M's). Use a red jaw breaker for a nose and red fruit-flavored circle candy for mouth and cheeks (Lifesavers). Secure to face with some of the white frosting. Pipe on a beard, mustache, and eyebrows. Sprinkle beard with coconut. Add candy-coated, fruit-flavored pieces to front of Santa's shirt for buttons. Makes 1 Santa.

Creamy White Frosting: Beat 1 cup *shortening,* 1½ teaspoons *vanilla,* and ½ teaspoon *almond extract* with an electric mixer till combined. Slowly add 2¼ cups *sifted powdered sugar,* beating well. Add 2 tablespoons *milk*. Gradually beat in 2¼ cups more sifted powdered sugar and enough milk to make of spreading consistency. Makes 3 cups.

Santa Wall Quilt

As shown on page 50, wall quilt measures 29½×29½ inches.

MATERIALS

Note: Fabric yardages are for 45-inch-wide fabrics

Tracing paper
Cardboard or template plastic
1¼ yard light blue print fabric
1 yard of medium green print fabric
1 yard of blue and tan check fabric
¾ yard of blue with black print fabric
¼ yard of red fabric
¼ yard of white fabric
⅛ yard of tan fabric
1 yard of fleece
Water-erasable fabric marker
Paper-backed iron-on adhesive
Sewing thread: medium gray and white
Red colored pencil
Gray cotton embroidery floss
16 assorted ½-inch-diameter white buttons

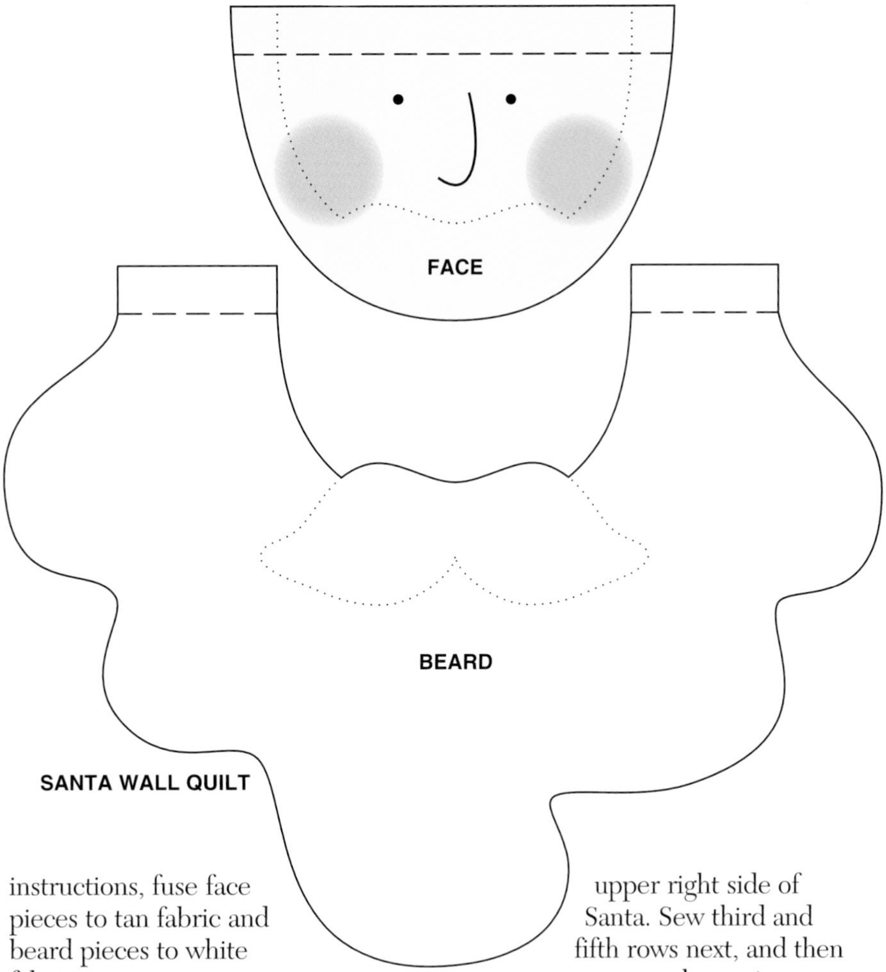

INSTRUCTIONS

The wall quilt consists of 16 Santa blocks in seven diagonal rows, joined by green blocks and surrounded by a border and binding. All pattern pieces and measurements include ¼-inch seam allowances. Sew seams with right sides of fabric facing; press seams toward darker fabric.

Trace face and beard patterns, *right,* and lettered block pieces, *page 66,* onto tracing paper; cut out block piece patterns. Draw around patterns onto template material; cut out. Draw around templates onto right sides of fabrics. From green fabric, cut nine 5×5-inch squares, 12 As, and four Bs. From red fabric, cut 16 Bs. From light blue print, first cut a 30-inch-square backing piece and then cut 16 Cs. From blue and tan check fabric, cut four 2½×32-inch border strips. From blue with black print, cut enough 1-inch-wide bias strips to measure a total of 135 inches.

Trace 16 faces and 16 beards onto paper side of iron-on adhesive. Following the manufacturer's instructions, fuse face pieces to tan fabric and beard pieces to white fabric; cut out.

For Santa block, remove paper backing from face and beard. Match top edge of face to top edge of light blue C piece and fuse, following manufacturer's instructions. Fuse beard over face. Sew long side of red B to top edge of Santa face on C.

Make Santa's cheeks rosy using red pencil. Using three strands of gray floss, work buttonhole stitch around each Santa's beard, spacing stitches approximately $^3/_{16}$ inches apart. Also using gray floss, outline stitch nose, make French knot eyes, and backstitch mustache outline.

To piece quilt top, follow quilt assembly diagram, *page 66,* closely. For first and last diagonal rows, begin with green A triangle; stitch to lower left side of Santa block. Sew green A to upper right side of Santa block to complete row. For second and sixth rows, begin with green A in same manner, sew to lower left of Santa block, sew green 5-inch-square block to upper right side of Santa, sew lower left side of Santa to opposite side, and add green A to upper right side of Santa. Sew third and fifth rows next, and then center row, alternating Santas and green 5-inch-square blocks, and beginning and ending with green A triangles. Sew diagonal rows together; add green A triangle to upper left and lower right corners of square to finish. Sew border strip to each side; miter corners.

Using water-erasable fabric marker, mark stitching lines in square grid pattern. Draw line above and below each Santa block, and along each side of Santa block, so lines intersect in center of each green block. Layer backing, fleece, and pieced quilt top. Trim fleece and backing to match quilt top. Baste layers together, working from center outward. Using white thread, machine quilt along grid lines.

Sew binding strips, end to end, to make one long strip. Sew binding to top, using ½-inch seam allowance; work mitered corners. Press to the back and turn under ½ inch. Pin mitered corners in place; slipstitch binding to back.

Sew button to tip of each Santa hat, stitching through all layers.

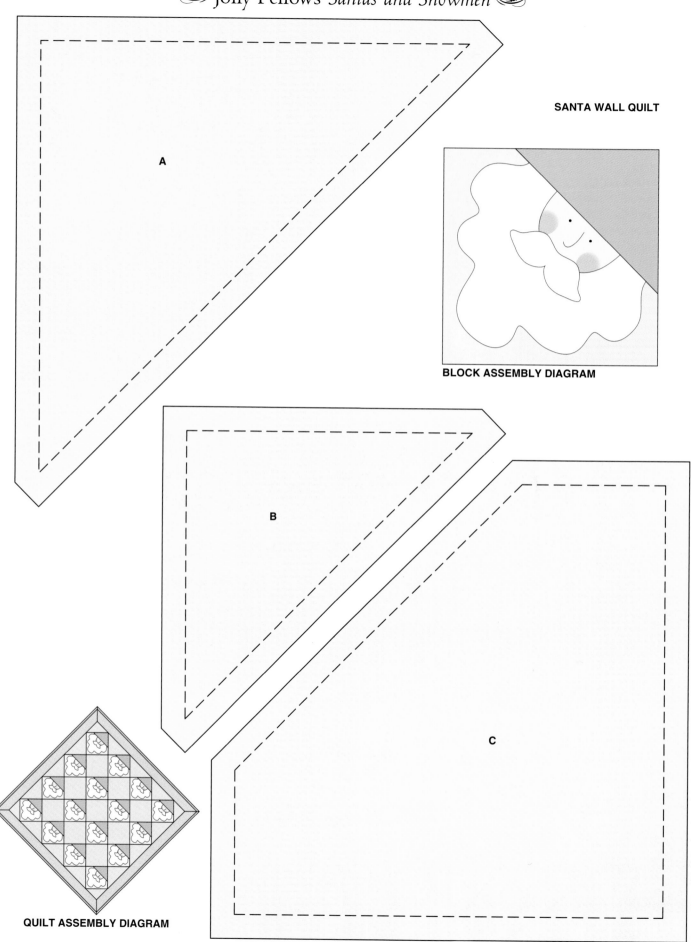

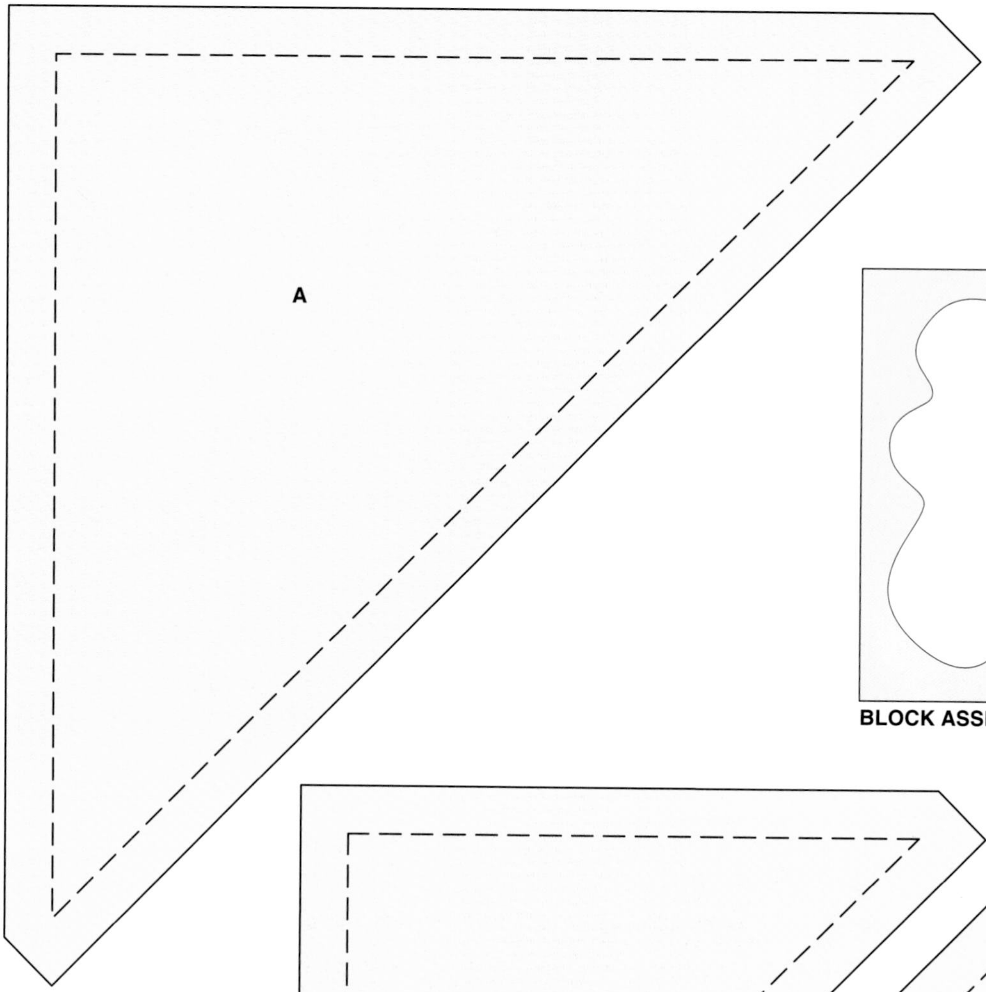

SANTA WALL QUILT

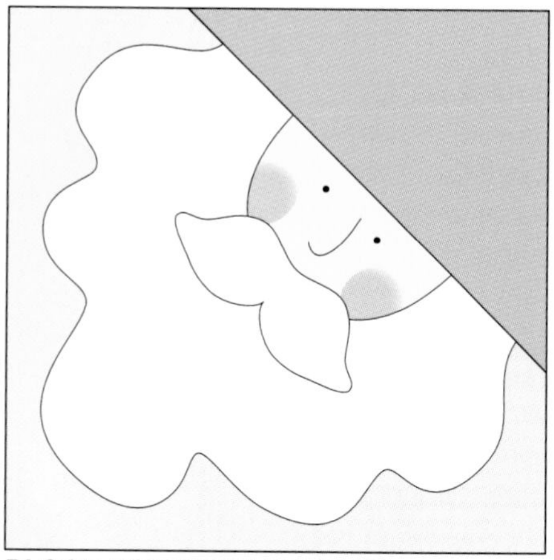

BLOCK ASSEMBLY DIAGRAM

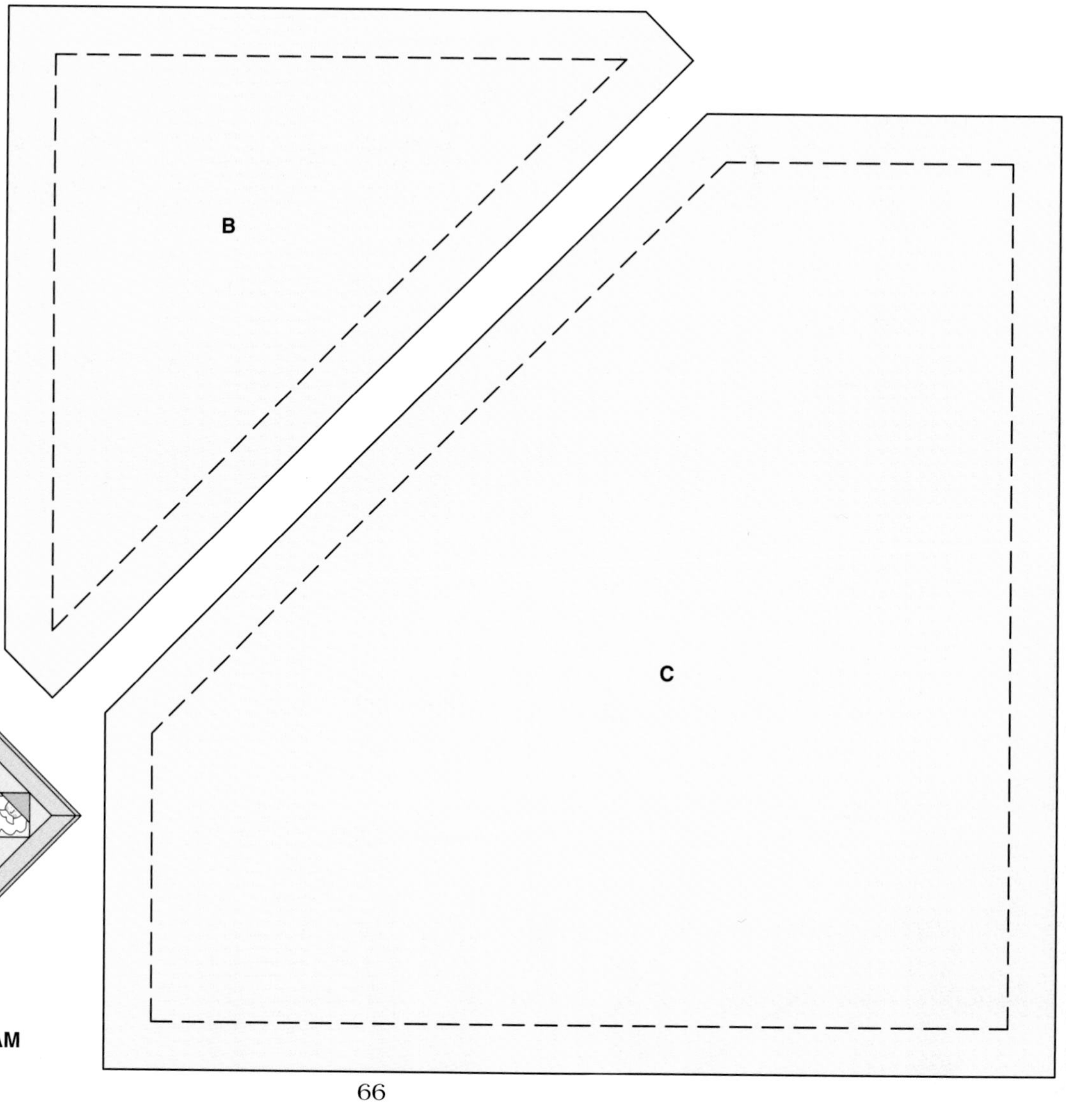

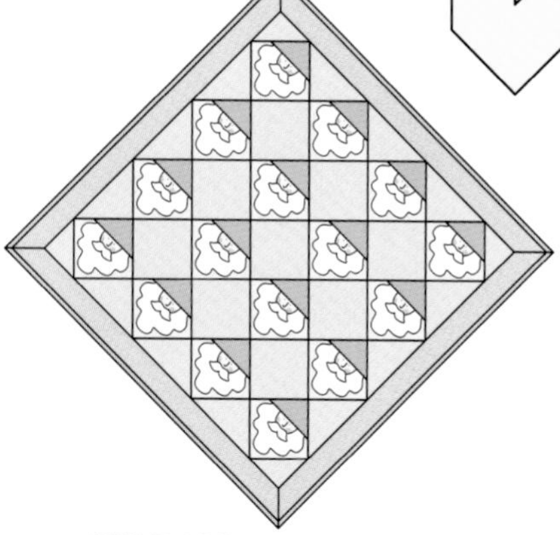

QUILT ASSEMBLY DIAGRAM

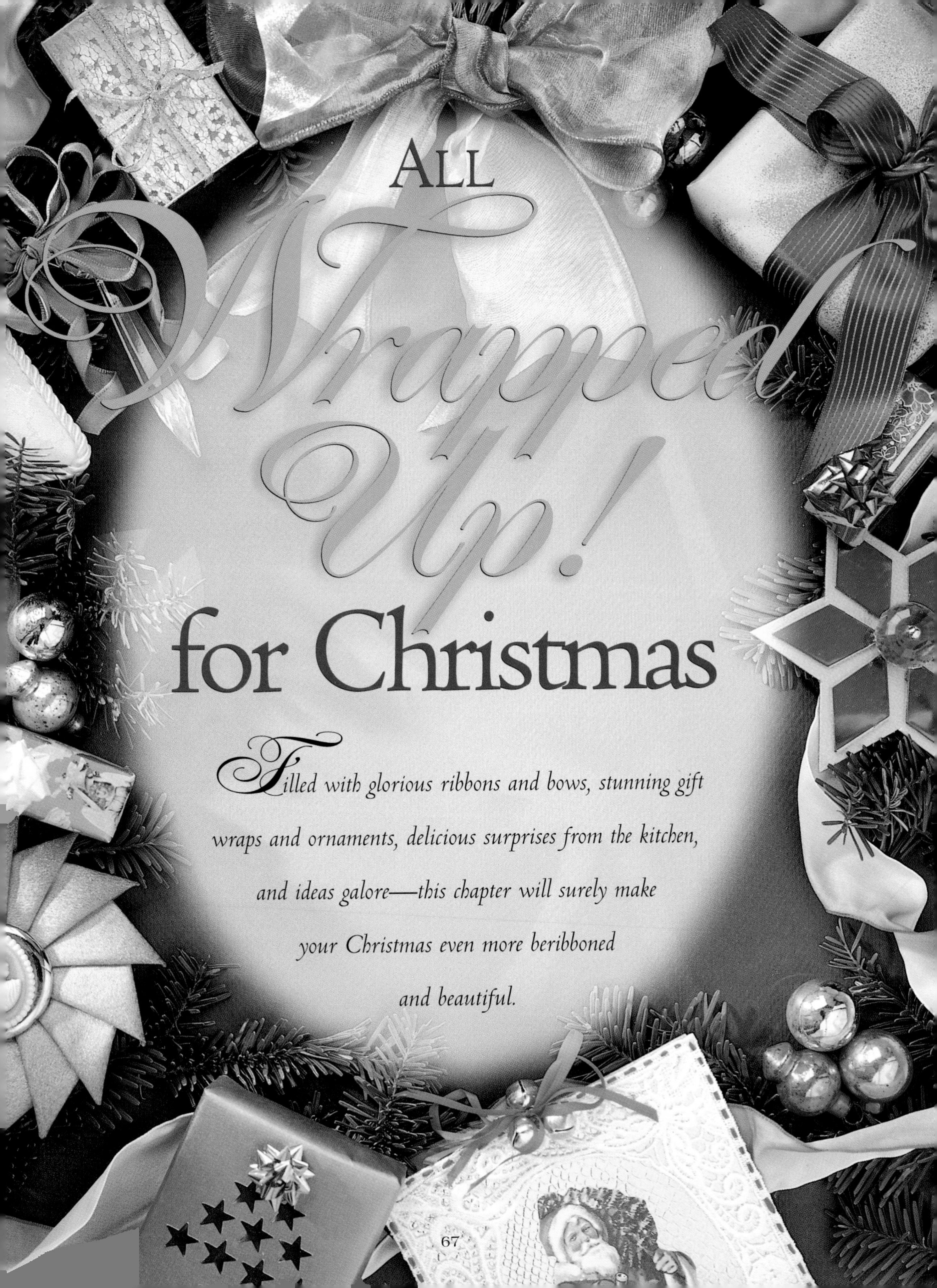

All Wrapped Up! for Christmas

Filled with glorious ribbons and bows, stunning gift wraps and ornaments, delicious surprises from the kitchen, and ideas galore—this chapter will surely make your Christmas even more beribboned and beautiful.

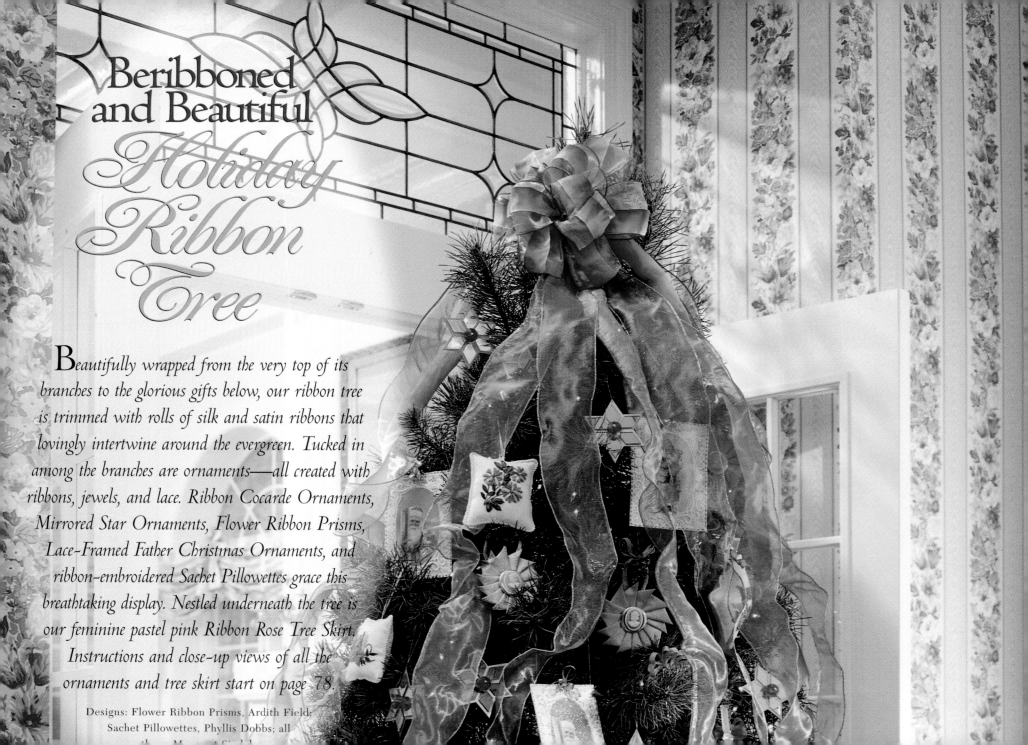

Beribboned and Beautiful

Holiday Ribbon Tree

Beautifully wrapped from the very top of its branches to the glorious gifts below, our ribbon tree is trimmed with rolls of silk and satin ribbons that lovingly intertwine around the evergreen. Tucked in among the branches are ornaments—all created with ribbons, jewels, and lace. Ribbon Cocarde Ornaments, Mirrored Star Ornaments, Flower Ribbon Prisms, Lace-Framed Father Christmas Ornaments, and ribbon-embroidered Sachet Pillowettes grace this breathtaking display. Nestled underneath the tree is our feminine pastel pink Ribbon Rose Tree Skirt.

Instructions and close-up views of all the ornaments and tree skirt start on page 78.

Designs: Flower Ribbon Prisms, Ardith Field; Sachet Pillowettes, Phyllis Dobbs; all

Simply Wrapped Gifts

Dress up your gifts this year with these simple but eye-catching trimmings. Below, from left, are four quick wraps: Just a tiny jar of jelly and golden tinsel will impress that sweet tooth on your list. A beautiful peacock feather tucked in among iridescent teal ribbon is a touch that just takes a minute. A rhinestone-covered circle (available from the bridal section of your fabric store) is the secret to the sparkle of this sparkling gift. There will be kisses all around after you've glued our wrapped-candy variety to a favorite gift.

Designs: Rhinestone trim, Margaret Sindelar; all others, Carol Dahlstrom

Tiny *Clever Packages*

Big *things come in small packages, but sometimes they are a challenge to wrap! We've made these tiny treasures fun from the inside out with clever wraps, from top left: Santa's belt is the inspiration for this tiny wrap made with a small belt buckle and black satin ribbon. Everyone loves to get money for Christmas—even when it is on the outside of the package (we've used white glue so the money comes off easily). Green-checkered ribbon and black-and-white dice make this package a high roller. For the tiniest of presents, just add a holiday button on ⅛-inch ribbon for a festive touch. Simple self-stick stars form a tree shape with a 3-D tiny bow on top.*

Designs: Carol Dahlstrom

Personalized *Festive Bows*

Handsome bows—created all by yourself—are easy to do and add that special touch to your packages. We've shown you how to make that perfect bow, step-by-step, using a dowel and floral oasis to help secure the ribbon as it's made into a bow. To make each bow one-of-a-kind, add a jingle bell, button, silver bell, or other tie-on after the bow is completed.

Designs: Margaret Sindelar

Step-by-Step Bow Making

1

Push dowels into floral oasis about 5 inches apart. Holding ribbon end on top of oasis, wrap dowels at least 3 times. For larger bows, wrap 4-6 times.

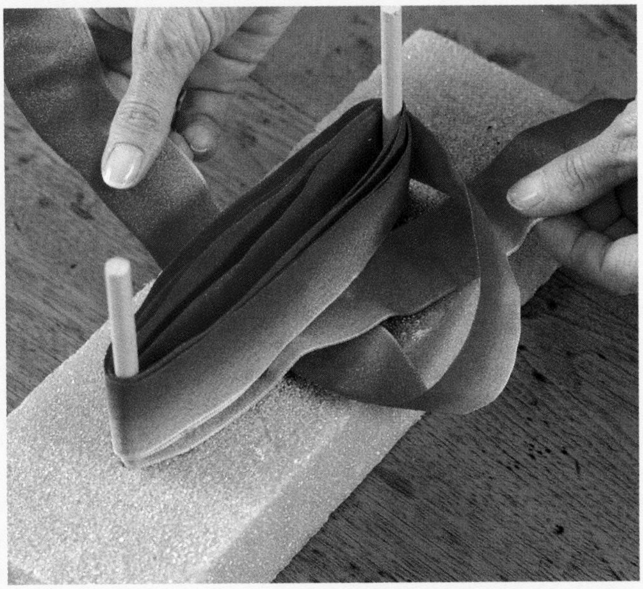

2

After wrapping dowels, cut the ribbon, leaving about an 8-inch tail. Slip tail of ribbon underneath loops, continuing to hold the starting end of ribbon.

3

Before removing the bow loops from dowels, secure by tying the ribbon ends firmly into a knot. Carefully slide the bow loops off dowels.

4

Tie the bow atop intersecting ribbons that wrap around the package. Separate and fluff bow loops. Fold ribbon ends in half and trim on the diagonal.

Clever *Candy-Cane Containers*

In the wink of an eye, you can turn plain carry-out containers into clever wraps by decorating the sides with a candy-cane motif using a foam brush and red and white paint. To make the gift truly one-of-a-kind, fill the boxes with delicious spiced nuts. Instructions for the containers and the recipe for the nuts begin on page 82.

Design: Carol Dahlstrom

Sweet *Holiday Gift Bags*

As sweet as candy, our cross-stitch Santa and reindeer gift bags are sure to be treasured even after the candy is gone. The motifs are stitched on 18-count white Aida then sewn to velveteen to create these holiday treat holders. We've lined our bags with plastic wrap and filled them to the brim with Marbled Bark and Grandma's Fudge.

Instructions for the bags and recipes begin on page 83.

Designs: Cross-stitch, Barbara Sestok; Bags, Margaret Sindelar

Old West *Cactus Breads*

Any old-timer or young cowpoke will love our Cactus Bread served up in resist-painted Western clay pots. The pots are lined with green cellophane and filled with brown sugar before the baked bread is placed in the pot. Designed to be a conversational centerpiece or an individual gift, this present is a real crowd pleaser. *Instructions and recipes begin on page 86.*

Design: Carol Dahlstrom

Roy Rogers
and the
Sure 'Nough
Cowpoke
To Dale

Sachet Pillowettes

As shown on pages 68–69, ornaments measure 4½×4½ inches.

MATERIALS

12x18-inch piece of Zweigart eggshell Puzzle Damask
Tracing paper
Three 6x6-inch squares of netting
Fine-point black permanent marker
Water-soluble fabric marking pen
Medium pistachio (DMC 367) cotton embroidery floss
7-mm-wide embroidery ribbon: wine and teal
4-mm-wide embroidery ribbon: hunter green and light mauve
Embroidery needle
Size 18 chenille needle
Hand-sewing needle
Seven 3x4-mm translucent green pebble beads
24 inches of ⅛-inch-wide ivory satin ribbon
Ivory sewing thread; polyester fiberfill
1½ yards of ¼-inch-diameter ivory satin cord
Potpourri

INSTRUCTIONS

Cut fabric into three 6×6-inch squares and three 4½×4½-inch squares.

Trace designs, *page 79*, onto tracing paper. For each design, position netting over tracing paper and trace design using fine-point marker. Next, position the netting square atop the larger fabric square and trace over the design using fabric marker.

Work stem stitches on each ornament using three plies of green embroidery floss. Complete the design using ribbon. For straight stitches and lazy daisies, keep ribbon as smooth and flat as possible while working.

For Ornament 1, work straight stitches and light green shaded French knots using teal, lazy daisy flowers using wine, and lazy daisy leaves using hunter green. Work pink shaded French knots using light mauve.

For Ornament 2, work straight stitch flowers using wine. Add five straight stitch spokes, evenly spaced, atop wine stitches using light mauve. Stitch three large light green shaded lazy daisy flower petals using teal, and dark green shaded lazy daisy leaves using hunter green.

For Ornament 3, work lazy daisy flowers using wine ribbon and light green shaded flower petals using teal. Work pink shaded lazy daisy petals and colonial knots using light mauve, and dark green shaded lazy daisy leaves using hunter green.

Sew beads to ornaments as on pattern.

For each ornament, trim stitched square to 4½×4½ inches. Cut an 8-inch length of ivory ribbon. Fold the ribbon in half, stack ends, and pin to the center top of stitched square with edges even.

Sew ornament front to back using ¼-inch seam allowance and leaving opening for turning. Turn, press, and stuff. Hand stitch ivory cord around perimeter, tucking ends into opening. Sew opening closed.

SACHET PILLOWETTES

STEM STITCH
- **Seafoam green – stems**

STRAIGHT STITCH
- **Wine 7mm silk ribbon – flowers on Ornament 2**
- **Mauve 4mm silk ribbon – flowers on Ornament 2**
- **Teal 7mm silk ribbon – leaves on Ornament 1**

LAZY DAISY
- **Mauve 4mm silk ribbon – flowers on Ornament 3**
- **Teal 7mm silk ribbon – leaves on Ornaments 2 and 3**
- **Wine 7mm silk ribbon – flowers on Ornaments 1 and 3**
- **Hunter green 4mm silk ribbon – leaves on all Ornaments**

FRENCH KNOT
- **Mauve 7mm silk ribbon – flowers on Ornaments 1 and 3**
- **Teal 4mm silk ribbon – flowers on Ornament 1**

BEADS
- **Green pebble beads – flower centers on all ornaments**

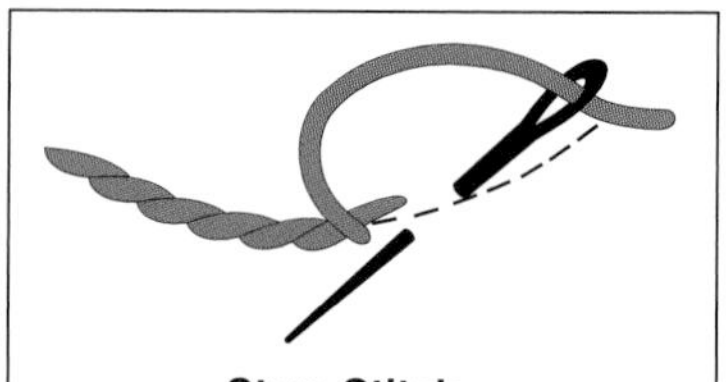

Stem Stitch

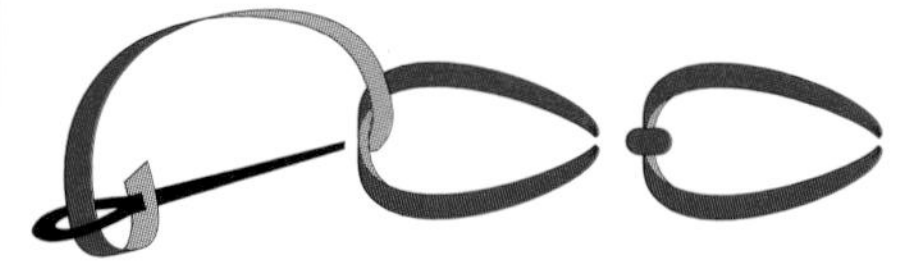

Lazy Daisy

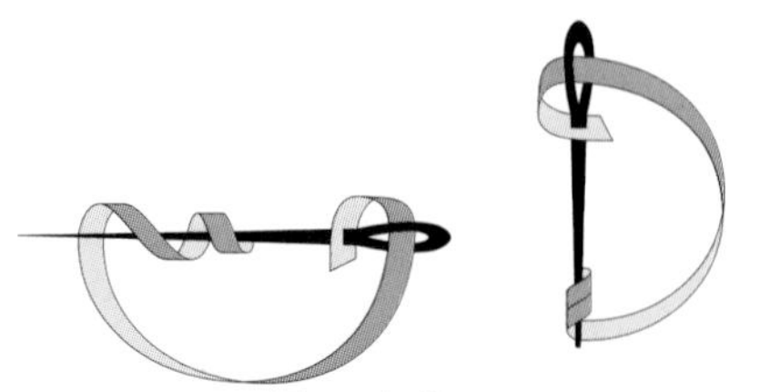

French Knot

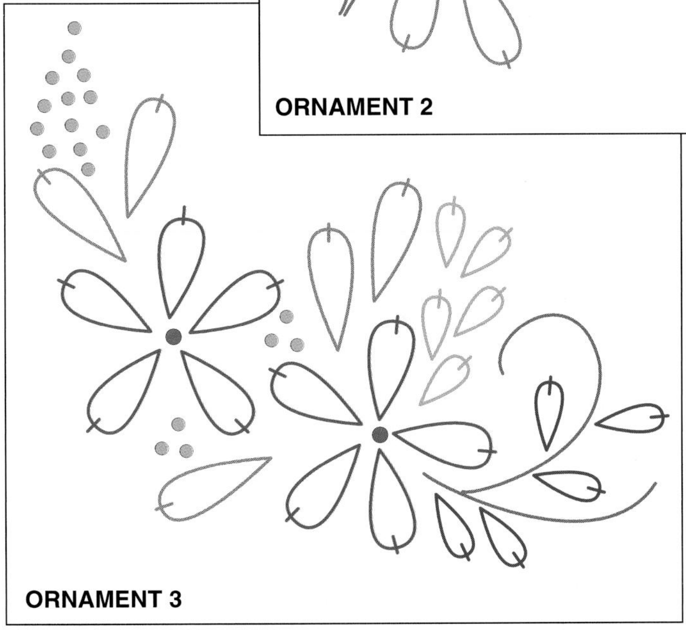

SACHET PILLOWETTES

Flower Ribbon Prisms

As shown on pages 68–69, ornaments measure approximately 4 inches across.

MATERIALS

42 inches of ¼-inch-wide wire-edged ribbon in desired color
10 inches of 24-gauge copper wire
Crystal drop ornament

INSTRUCTIONS

Working from center, loop ribbon back and forth for bow, leaving 8-inch-long streamers. Twist wire around center to secure. Use remaining wire to secure top of prism to bow center and make a hanging loop. Separate and shape ribbon loops as shown in photograph, *above*. Wrap streamers around a pencil to form spirals.

Mirrored Star Ornaments

As shown on pages 68–69, ornaments measure 4×4 inches.

MATERIALS

Tracing paper
5x5-inch piece of matboard
Tapestry needle
Gold metallic spray paint
Clear acrylic spray sealer
Six 40x22.5-mm diamond-shaped mirrors in desired color
6-mm gold bead
18 inches of gold metallic thread
23x15-mm pink acrylic cushion bead
½-inch-diameter clear 2-hole button

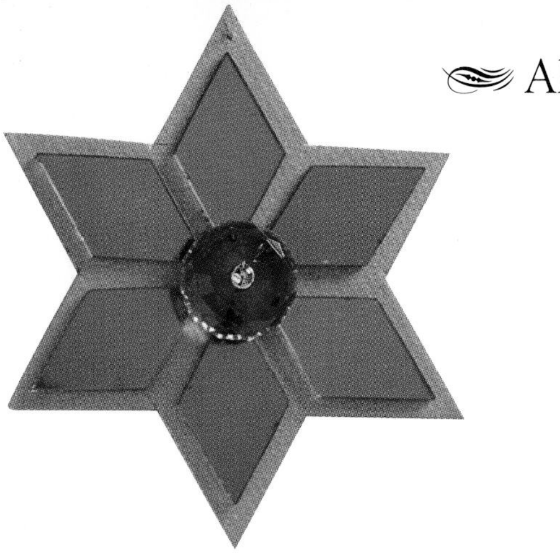

INSTRUCTIONS

Trace star pattern, *below*, onto tracing paper and cut out. Trace around pattern onto matboard; cut out. Poke hole through top point and center of star with needle.

Spray both sides of star gold. When dry, spray both sides with acrylic sealer.

Glue mirror to each star point, ⅛ inch in from edges. Slide bead to center of gold thread. Next, thread both gold thread tails onto needle and slide on pink bead until it stops next to gold bead. Push needle through center hole in star from front to back, bringing pink bead up against star front. On back side, thread one tail through each hole in button and knot. Thread needle once again with tails and push through hole in top point of star, from back to front. Knot ends to complete hanging loop.

MIRRORED STAR ORNAMENT

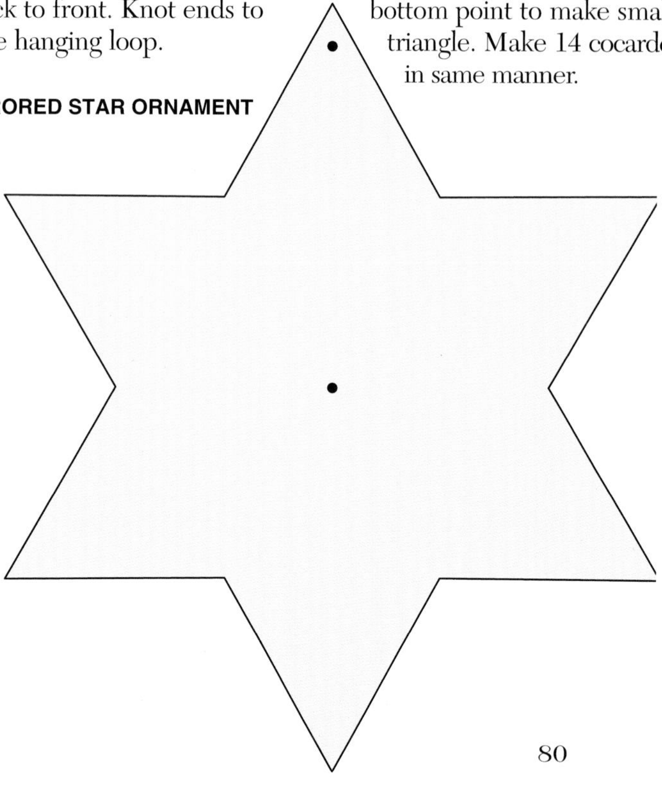

Ribbon Cocarde Ornament

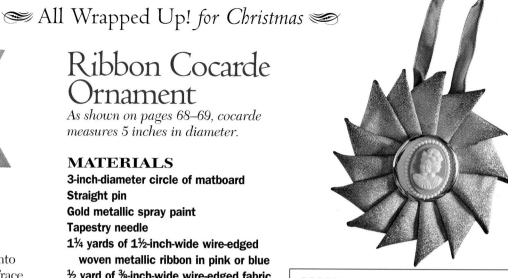

As shown on pages 68–69, cocarde measures 5 inches in diameter.

MATERIALS

3-inch-diameter circle of matboard
Straight pin
Gold metallic spray paint
Tapestry needle
1¼ yards of 1½-inch-wide wire-edged woven metallic ribbon in pink or blue
½ yard of ⅜-inch-wide wire-edged fabric ribbon in pink or blue
Thick crafts glue
Jewel glue
40-mm-diameter gold jewelry "doughnut," or similar jewelry finding
34x26-mm blue or pink plastic cameo or similar jewel

INSTRUCTIONS

Spray back of matboard circle gold; allow to dry. Pierce hole in center with tapestry needle. Cut 1½-inch-wide ribbon into fourteen 3-inch-long pieces.

Referring to Diagram A, *right*, position each ribbon piece with long edges at top and bottom. Fold top corners down to center. Next, fold left bottom point of triangle to right bottom point to make smaller triangle. Make 14 cocarde points in same manner.

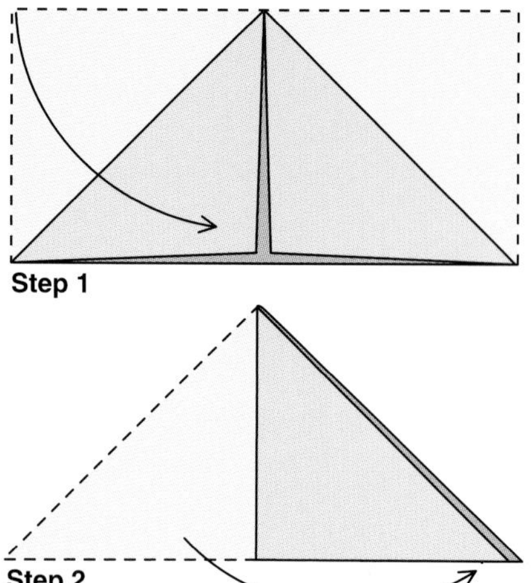

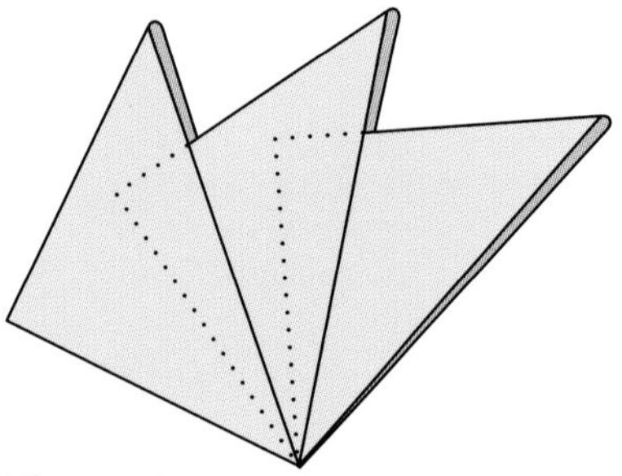

RIBBON COCARDE ORNAMENT

Tie bow in center of ⅜-inch-wide ribbon, leaving long streamers. Spread thick crafts glue over front of circle. Glue streamer ends to circle, approximately 1 inch apart for hanger. Referring to Diagram B, *above*, position cocarde points around circle using center hole as a placement guide, with fold toward outer edge. Tuck each cocarde point slightly inside fold of previous point.

Use jewel glue to glue gold "doughnut" jewelry piece to center, with cameo on top.

Lace-Framed Ornaments

As shown on pages 68–69, each ornament measures 5×7 inches.

MATERIALS

5x7-inch piece of matboard
Gold metallic spray paint
5x7-inch piece of gold gift wrap
Spray adhesive
Tapestry needle
5x7-inch Victorian cotton lace frame, with oval opening
1 yard of 7-mm-wide green or rose silk ribbon
Three ½-inch-diameter gold jingle bells
Jewel glue
Santa cut-out or Victorian scrap to fit 5¼x3¾-inch oval opening in lace frame
18 inches of gold metallic thread

INSTRUCTIONS

Spray back of matboard gold; allow to dry. Affix gold paper to matboard front with spray adhesive. With matboard rectangle positioned lengthwise, pierce hole in each top corner using tapestry needle.

Thread silk ribbon in and out through holes around perimeter of lace frame. Begin and end at center top, leaving tails of equal length. Thread jingle bells onto tails and tie in a bow.

Glue lace to covered matboard front using jewel glue. Center Santa within frame; glue. Thread gold metallic thread end through each hole from front to back. Knot ends at back to complete hanging loop.

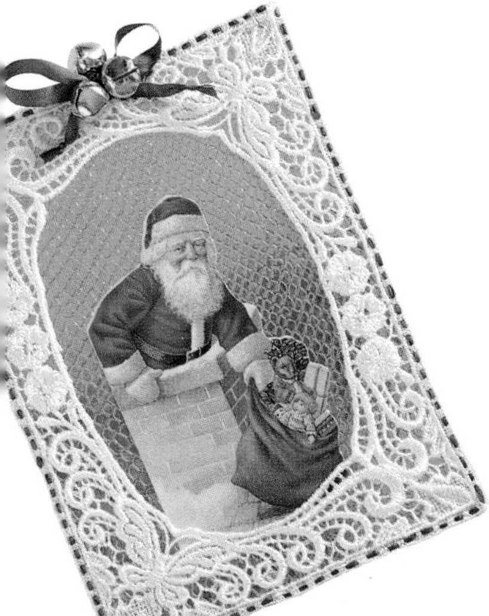

Ribbon Rose Tree Skirt

As shown on page 69, tree skirt measures 44 inches in diameter.

MATERIALS

Graph paper
1⅓ yards of 60-inch-wide pink wool coating fabric
1⅓ yards of 45-inch-wide pink cotton fabric
45x45-inch piece of fleece
Pink sewing thread
10 yards of 1½-inch-wide wire-edged pink-and-green-blend metallic Ombre ribbon
17 yards of 1½-inch-wide wire-edged Ombre ribbon in desired colors for Roses and Primroses
4 additional yards of 1½-inch-wide wire-edged Ombre ribbon in desired color for Roses only
3 yards of 1½-inch-wide wire-edged blue-blend metallic Ombre ribbon for Calla Lilies
8 yards of ⅞-inch-wide wire-edged Ombre ribbon in two different color blends as desired for Leaves
5 yards of ⅞-inch-wide wire-edged pink-and-white-blend Ombre ribbon for flower centers
Fabric glue

INSTRUCTIONS

Enlarge skirt pattern, *right*, onto graph paper and cut out. Cut one skirt each from wool, fleece, and cotton fabric. Layer fleece between wrong sides of cotton fabric and wool; baste layers together. Bind all outside edges with pink-and-green-blend metallic ribbon.

Cut six 18-inch-long pieces of pink and green metallic ribbon. Stitch one end of each of three pieces, evenly spaced, down each side of back opening for ties.

Cut five 14-inch-long pieces of pink and green metallic ribbon. Overlap ends of each piece 1 inch. Make a tuck in center to shape bow. Machine stitch bow to top of each scallop, stitching through center.

To make each Primrose, cut three 5-inch-long pieces of three different

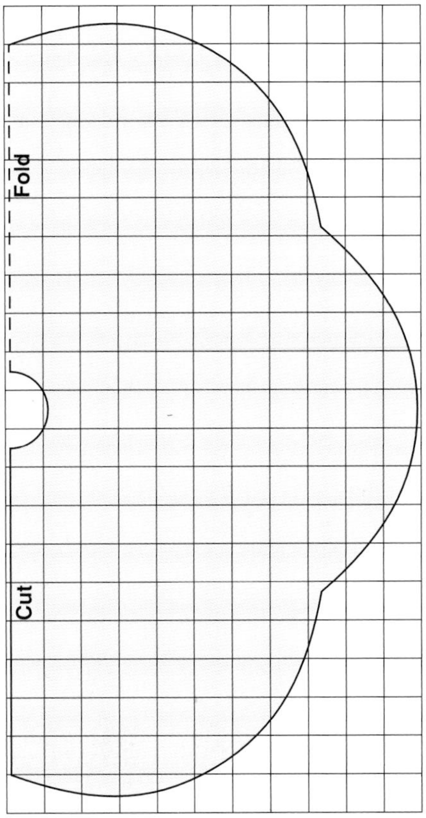

RIBBON ROSE TREE SKIRT **1 Square = 2 Inches (Add seam allowance)**

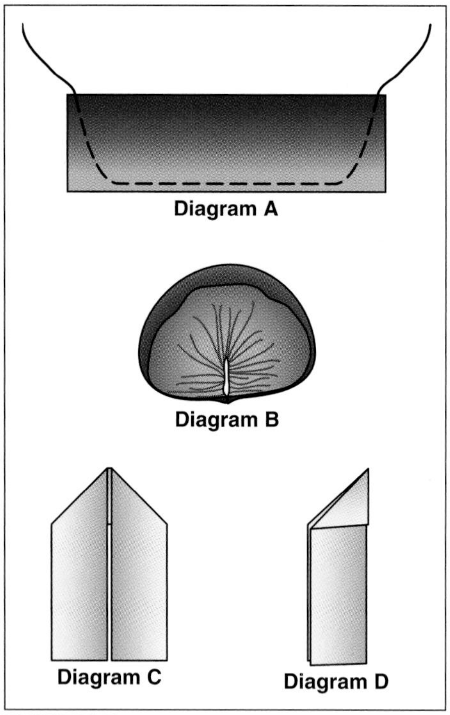

PRIMROSE

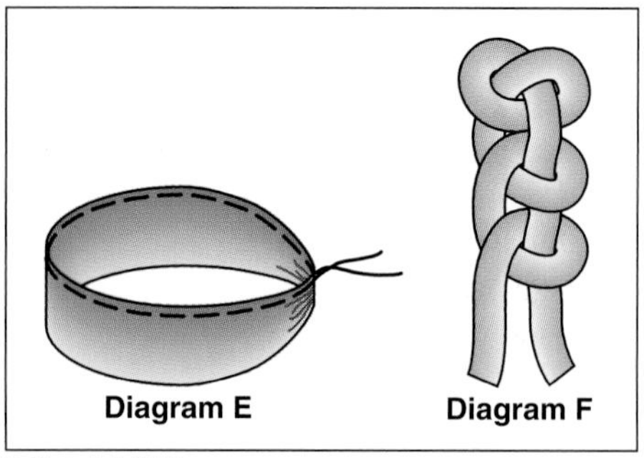

CALLA LILY

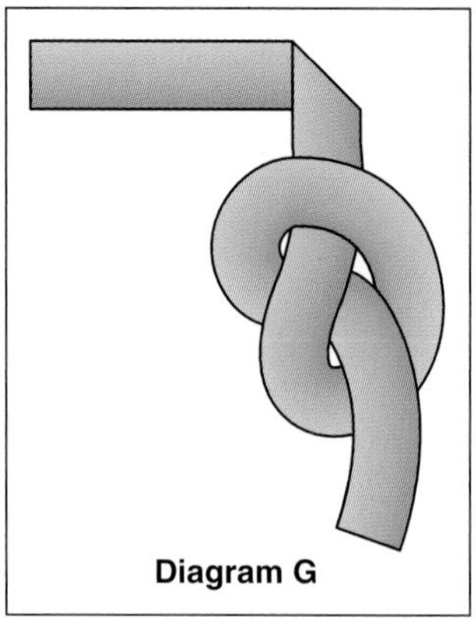

ROSE

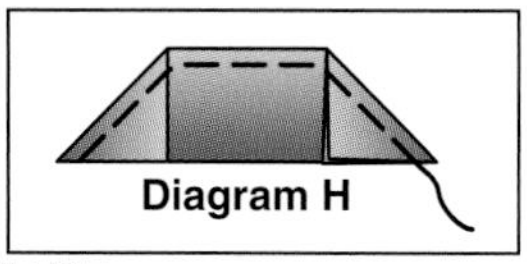

LEAF

color 1½-inch-wide ribbons. On each piece, run a hand gathering stitch as shown in Diagram A, *left*. Pull thread to gather and knot threads at the bottom of petal as shown in Diagram B, *left.* Repeat for two more petals.

For Primrose center, cut a 6-inch-long piece of ⅞-inch-wide pink and white ribbon. Following Diagrams C and D, *below left,* fold ends diagonally down from center, then fold in half lengthwise. Roll ribbon ends toward folded edge.

To finish Primrose, arrange three petals around center; stitch to secure at base. Make 12 Primroses.

To make each Calla Lily, cut 6-inch-long piece of 1½-inch-wide blue-blend metallic ribbon. Fold ribbon in half, matching ends, and run hand gathering stitch across ends. Pull thread to gather; knot. Open out ribbon to resemble circle. Run hand gathering stitch along one long edge as shown in Diagram E, *left;* do not pull thread to gather.

For Calla Lily center, cut 6-inch-long piece of ⅞-inch-wide pink and white ribbon. Tie knot in center. Repeat, tying a total of three knots, as shown in Diagram F, *left.*

To finish Calla Lily, pull threads on blue ribbon to gather around ends of center. Shape flower and stitch to secure at base. Make 12 Calla Lilies.

To make each Rose, cut 1 yard of 1½-inch-wide ribbon in desired color Ombre ribbon. Tie knot in one end, leaving 1-inch-long tail. Referring to Diagram G, *left,* fold down knotted end of ribbon at 45-degree angle, with knot at bottom. Wrap ribbon several times close to knot. Stitch bottom edges of wraps to secure. Fold ribbon diagonally in opposite direction and repeat wrapping and stitching to complete center of rose.

To finish Rose, continue to fold ribbon diagonally, wrap, and make small pleats in bottom secured with stitches. When end of ribbon is reached, gather end and tack to base of rose. Make 11 Roses.

To make each Leaf, cut a 6-inch-long piece of ⅞-inch ribbon in color chosen for Leaves. Fold ribbon in half, matching ends. Fold each doubled end down at 45-degree angle. Referring to Diagram H, *bottom left,* secure thread at folded end and run hand gathering stitches up diagonal, across top, and down opposite diagonal. Pull thread to slightly gather; knot. Open ribbon out; shape leaf. Make 34 Leaves.

Glue flowers and leaves in place on tree skirt, referring to Flower Placement Guide, *below*. Group one Calla Lily with each Primrose and Leaves with flowers as shown.

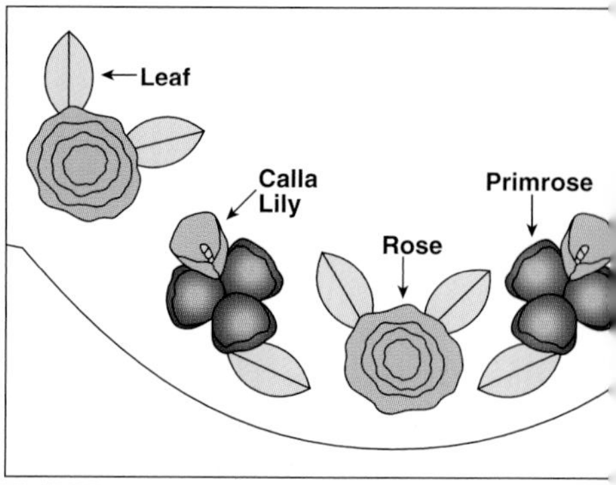

FLOWER PLACEMENT GUIDE

Clever Candy-Cane Containers

As shown on page 74, sizes will vary according to container.

MATERIALS

Colored food container boxes or sacks
1-inch sponge brush
Acrylic paints: red and white

INSTRUCTIONS

Dip the tip of the sponge brush into white paint. Press the tip repeatedly straight down onto the container, following a curved candy cane configuration and leaving spaces for the red paint. Allow to dry. Fill in the spaces with red paint using the same technique.

Spicy Pecans

Pictured on page 74.

INGREDIENTS

- 1 to 1½ teaspoons chili powder
- 1 teaspoon garlic salt
- 1 teaspoon curry powder
- ¼ teaspoon ground cumin
- ¼ teaspoon ground ginger
- ¼ teaspoon ground cinnamon
- 3 tablespoons olive oil or cooking oil
- 1 teaspoon Worcestershire sauce
- ¼ to ½ teaspoon bottled hot pepper sauce
- 3 cups pecan halves

METHOD

Combine the chili powder, garlic salt, curry powder, cumin, ginger, and cinnamon in a large skillet. Stir in oil, Worcestershire sauce, and bottled hot pepper sauce. Cook and stir over low heat for 5 minutes to mellow flavors.

Place pecan halves in a large bowl; add spice mixture. Toss to coat evenly. Spread pecans in a single layer in a 15×10×1-inch baking pan. Bake in a 325° oven for 15 minutes, stirring occasionally. Spread on foil and cool completely. Makes 3 cups.

Sweet Spiced Walnuts

Pictured on page 74.

INGREDIENTS

- 1 egg white
- 1 teaspoon water
- 5 cups walnut halves or pieces
- 1 cup sugar
- 1 teaspoon ground cinnamon
- ½ teaspoon salt
- ¼ teaspoon ground nutmeg
- ¼ teaspoon ground allspice

METHOD

Beat together egg white and water in a large bowl with a fork. Add walnuts; toss to coat. In a small bowl combine sugar, cinnamon, salt, nutmeg, and allspice. Sprinkle sugar mixture over walnuts and toss to coat.

Spread nuts in a greased 15×10×1-inch baking pan. Bake, uncovered, in a 325° oven for 20 minutes. Transfer to waxed paper to cool. Break into clumps. Makes 7 cups.

Grandma's Fudge

Pictured on page 75.

INGREDIENTS

- 4 cups sugar
- 2 5-ounce cans (1⅓ cups total) evaporated milk
- 1 cup butter
- 1 12-ounce package semisweet chocolate pieces
- 1 7-ounce jar marshmallow crème
- 1 cup chopped walnuts
- 1 teaspoon vanilla

METHOD

Line a 13×9×2-inch baking pan with foil; extend foil over edges. Butter the foil; set aside. Butter the sides of a heavy 3-quart saucepan. In it, combine the sugar, milk, and butter. Cook and stir over medium-high heat to boiling. Clip candy thermometer to side of pan. Cook and stir over medium heat to 236°, soft-ball stage (about 12 minutes).

Remove saucepan from heat; remove thermometer. Add chocolate pieces, marshmallow crème, nuts, and vanilla; stir till chocolate melts. Spread into pan. Score into squares while warm. When firm, cut into squares. Store in refrigerator. Makes about 3½ pounds (96 servings).

Marbled Bark

Pictured on page 75.

INGREDIENTS

- ¾ cup semisweet chocolate pieces
- 2 teaspoons shortening
- 4 ounces vanilla-flavored candy coating, chopped
- 2 teaspoons shortening

METHOD

In a small heavy saucepan melt together chocolate pieces and 2 teaspoons shortening. In another small heavy saucepan, melt together candy coating and 2 teaspoons shortening.

Drizzle melted chocolate in a 10-inch-square area on a baking sheet lined with waxed paper. Drizzle melted vanilla coating over chocolate, filling in spaces. Cool slightly. Run a knife or metal spatula through the mixture to achieve a marbled effect. Do not overmix. Chill about 10 minutes or till almost set. Cut into desired shapes.

Sweet Holiday Gift Bags

As shown on page 75, each bag measures 10×6¼ inches.

MATERIALS ***for one bag***

FABRICS

12x8-inch piece of 18-count white cotton Aida cloth
22½x7¼-inch piece of velveteen in desired color
22x6¾-inch piece of desired lining fabric

THREADS

Cotton embroidery floss in colors listed in key on page 85
Blending filament as listed in key on page 85

SUPPLIES

Small red jingle bell
3 red seed beads
Tracing paper
Tailors' chalk pencil
Thread to match velveteen
½ yard of ¼-inch-wide decorative gold braid
Fabric glue
Seam ripper
Two 20-inch-long pieces of ¼-inch-wide satin ribbon in desired color
Safety pin

INSTRUCTIONS

Tape or zigzag the edges of the Aida cloth to prevent fraying. Find the center of one chart, *pages 84–85*, and the center of one piece of Aida cloth; begin stitching there.

Use two plies of embroidery floss to work cross-stitches. Work blended needles using one ply of each color

Santa stitch count: *93 high x 63 wide*
Santa finished design sizes:
18-count fabric – 5¼ x 3½ inches
14-count fabric – 6¾ x 4½ inches
11-count fabric – 8½ x 5¾ inches

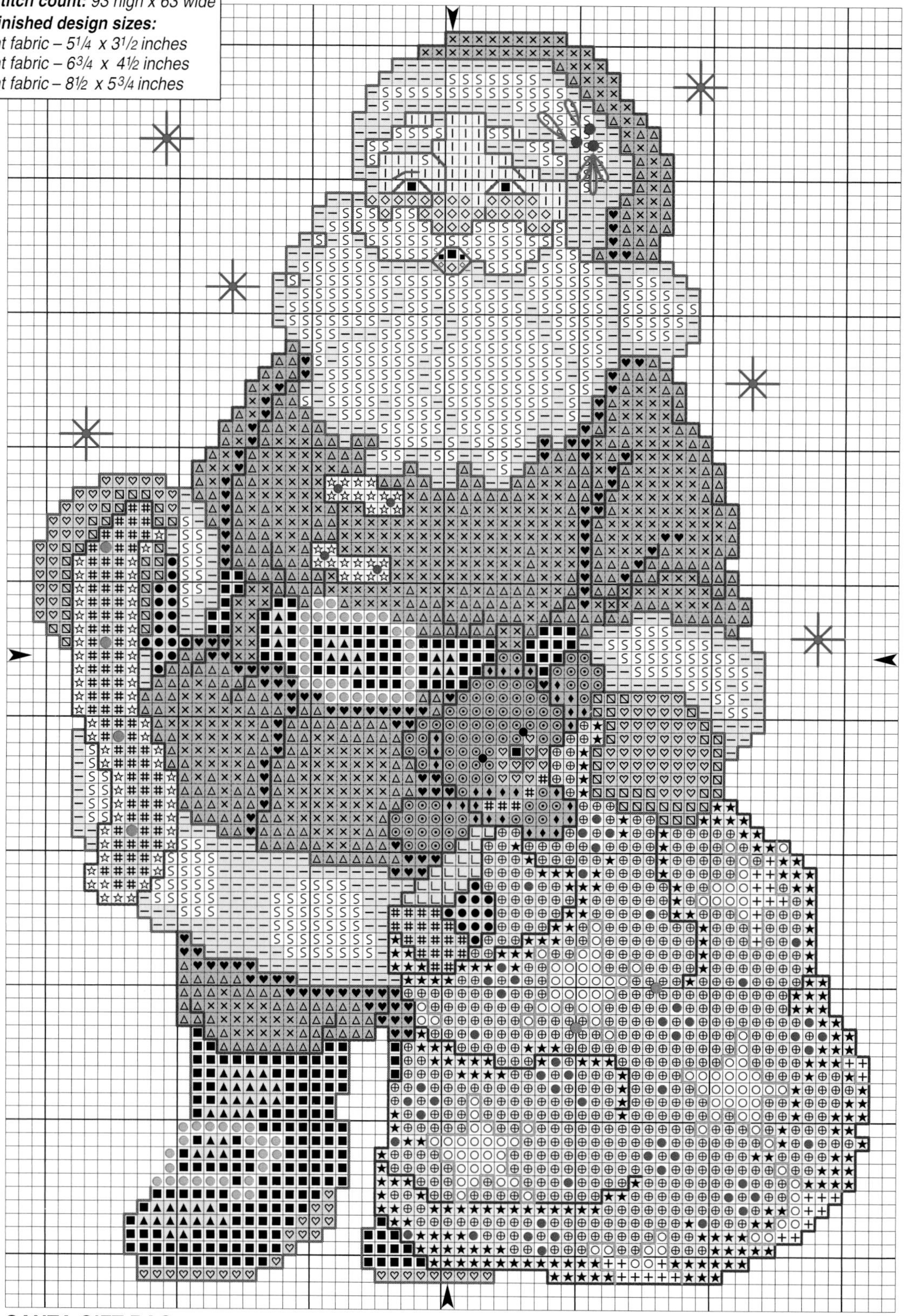

SANTA GIFT BAG

of embroidery floss as listed in the key on page 85. Work backstitches, lazy daisy stitches, and French knots using one ply of embroidery floss or blending filament.

Press stitchery from the back. If stitching reindeer, tack jingle bell to collar as shown on the chart. If stitching Santa, sew beads to hat as shown on the chart.

Trace oval shape from pattern, *page 86*, on paper; cut out. Fabric measurements include ½-inch seam allowances. Sew seams with right sides of fabric facing.

Reindeer stitch count: *87 high x 62 wide*
Reindeer finished design sizes:
18-count fabric – 4⅞ x 3½ inches
14-count fabric – 6¼ x 4½ inches
11-count fabric – 8 x 5⅝ inches

REINDEER GIFT BAG

SANTA AND REINDEER GIFT BAGS

ANCHOR		DMC
002	•	000 White
289	=	307 True lemon
403	■	310 Black
400	▲	317 Pewter
9046	△	321 True Christmas red
009	◇	352 Coral
398	−	415 Pearl gray
290	☆	444 Medium lemon
1005	♥	498 Dark Christmas red
891	♡	676 Old gold
226	#	702 Christmas green
256	L	704 Chartreuse
133	★	796 Royal blue
131	⊕	798 Delft blue
360	⧓	898 Coffee brown
881	I	945 Ivory
355	♦	975 Deep golden brown
035	×	3705 Watermelon
923	●	3818 Emerald
1048	⊙	3826 Dark golden brown
373	⧄	3828 Hazel

BLENDED NEEDLE

002	S	000 White (2X) and 032 Kreinik pearl blending filament (1X)
289	○	307 True lemon (2X) and 028 Kreinik citron blending filament (1X)
290	+	444 Medium lemon (2X) and 028 Kreinik citron blending filament (1X)

BACKSTITCH

400	/	317 Pewter–reindeer's eyes and ear; Santa's coat, beard, face, and boots
360	/	898 Coffee brown–reindeer, bird, teddy bear, Santa's coat
152	/	939 Navy–Santa's bag
298	/	972 Canary–reindeer's blanket
	/	028 Kreinik citron blending filament–stars on Santa's bag
	/	032 Kreinik pearl blending filament–snowflakes

LAZY DAISY

226		702 Christmas green–Santa's hat

FRENCH KNOT

403	•	310 Black–bird's eyes and teddy bear's eyes

SEED BEADS

- 00968 Mill Hill red seed beads–Santa's hat
- 40479 Mill Hill pearl petite beads–snowflakes
- 42011 Mill Hill Victorian gold petite beads–reindeer's blanket and Santa's buckles
- 42013 Mill Hill red petite beads–Santa's bag and coat clasps

JINGLE BELLS

- 1090-01 Darice 6mm gold–reindeer's blanket and ties on Santa's bag
- Red jingle bell–reindeer

Trace around paper oval onto velveteen, centering top of oval 4 inches below one short edge. Cut out oval. Stitch ⅛ inch away from cut edge. Clip to stitching; finger press clipped edge to wrong side.

Draw around the oval pattern onto stitchery, adding ½ inch all around; cut out. Position stitched design inside of the oval from wrong side. Stitch around the oval opening in velveteen close to the edge to secure stitchery.

Fold velveteen rectangle in half to measure 11×6¾ inches. Sew long edges together for bag side seams. Repeat for lining, except leave opening along one side seam; do not turn.

To shape the bottom, fold one corner flat so the bottom and side seams meet. Run row of stitches perpendicular to seam lines, ⅝ inch from fold; trim corner. Repeat for opposite corner and corners of lining.

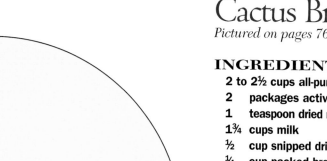

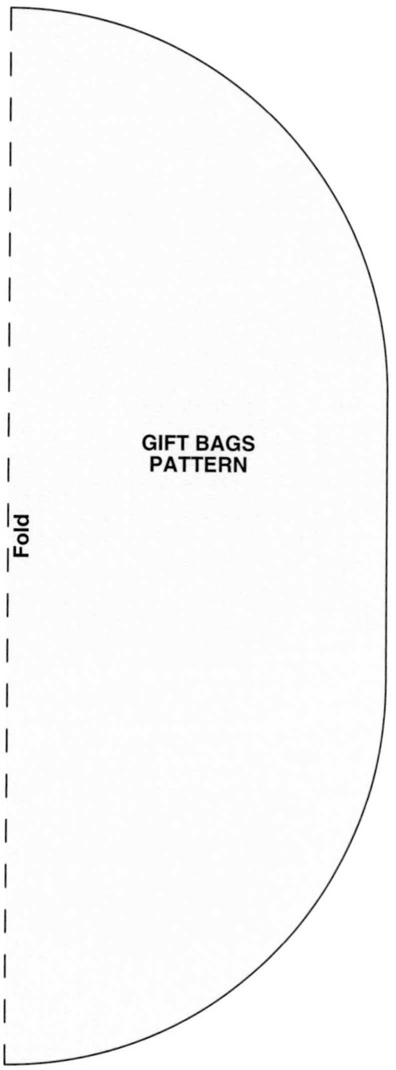

Sew bag to lining around top edge. Turn right side out through opening in lining. Slip-stitch opening closed. Tuck lining into bag. Glue braid around oval opening.

To make casing and drawstring, sew around top of bag 2 inches and again 2⅜ inches below edge. Slit side seam of velveteen between rows of stitching. Using safety pin to catty ribbon, thread one ribbon piece in one side of casing and all the way around between velveteen and lining. Bring ribbon back out same slit; knot ends. Repeat, beginning on the opposite side using the remaining ribbon.

Cactus Bread

Pictured on pages 76-77.

INGREDIENTS

2 to 2½ cups all-purpose flour
2 packages active dry yeast
1 teaspoon dried rosemary, crushed
1¾ cups milk
½ cup snipped dried tomatoes
¼ cup packed brown sugar
3 tablespoons margarine or butter
1 teaspoon salt
2 cups whole wheat flour
½ cup yellow cornmeal
1 slightly beaten egg white
1 tablespoon water
Sunflower nuts

METHOD

In a mixing bowl stir together 1½ cups of the all-purpose flour, the yeast, and rosemary. In a saucepan heat the milk, dried tomatoes, brown sugar, margarine or butter, and salt till warm (120° to 130°) and margarine almost melts. Add to flour mixture. Beat the flour mixture with an electric mixer on low to medium speed 30 seconds. Beat on high for 3 minutes. Stir in whole wheat flour, ½ cup cornmeal, and as much of the remaining all-purpose flour as you can.

On a floured surface, knead in enough remaining all-purpose flour to make a moderately stiff dough that is smooth and elastic (6 to 8 minutes). Shape into a ball. Place in a greased bowl; turn once to grease surface. Cover and let rise in a warm place till double (about 1 hour). Punch dough down. Turn out onto a lightly floured surface. Divide dough in half. Cover; let rest 10 minutes.

Grease two large baking sheets. For single cactus leaves, divide one half of the dough into quarters. Shape each into a leaf about 6 inches long and 4 inches wide. Or, for smaller leaves, divide each quarter in half and shape into smaller cactus leaves. Place on prepared baking sheets. For cactus shape, remove ¼ of the remaining ½ of dough. Shape larger portion into a loaf about 9 inches long. Place on baking sheet. Divide remaining ¼ portion of dough in half. Roll into ropes about 4 inches long and attach to cactus on each side, pinching to seal and curving ends up. Using a sharp knife, make lines down length of loaf and "arms" of cactus about ⅛-inch deep to make lined impressions on cactus. Stir together the egg white and water. Brush over cactus. Arrange sunflower nuts on leaves and cactus to resemble cactus thorns. Cover and let rise till double (about 30 minutes).

Bake in a 375° oven for 20 minutes or till done. Remove and cool on a wire rack. Makes 1 cactus shape with 4 leaves or 8 smaller leaves.

For one large cactus, do not divide dough in half. Remove ¼ of the dough. Shape the larger portion into a 15-inch log. Divide remaining portion in half. Roll each into a rope about 8 inches long. Attach ropes to cactus on each side and continue as above. Makes 1 large cactus.

Western Pots

Shown on pages 76–77, sizes will vary according to pots.

MATERIALS

Clay pots in desired sizes
Plaid Royal Coat decoupage medium
Rubber cement
Plaid Folk Art acrylic paint in desired colors
Sponge brush; crafts glue
Plastic canvas yarn to match paint
Wooden skewer; green cellophane
Oasis; granulated brown sugar

INSTRUCTIONS

Paint each pot with decoupage medium; allow to dry. Apply rubber cement to pots in desired designs, referring to photograph, *pages 76–77,* for ideas. Allow rubber cement to dry. Paint each pot with desired color acrylic paint; allow to dry. Rub off rubber cement to reveal design.

Apply crafts glue all around top edge of each pot. Wrap yarn around top of pot until covered.

Line pot with cellophane. Cut oasis to fit pot. Put large skewer into bread and then into oasis. Fill pot with brown sugar.

For Unto Us A *Child* Is Born

That night so long ago, in the city of Bethlehem, a child was born, filling the world with wonder, hope, and promise. To celebrate the real meaning of Christmas, we have created a collection of crafts that will surely bring the spirit of the season into your heart and home.

Cross-Stitched *Nativity*

Depicting the birth of Christ in the lowly stable, our cross-stitched Nativity is stitched over two threads of 28-count ivory Jobelan fabric using subtle colors and neutral accents. We have finished the pieces to stand in a purchased crèche using taffeta and gold trims. The pieces may also be finished as lovely ornaments by attaching a gold hanger to the top of each piece. Instructions and charts for the Nativity begin on page 94.

Design: Barbara Sestok

Peace on Earth

Folk Art Pillow

The Wise Men came from afar bearing gifts. Our folk art pillow captures the wonder of that eventful night. Able to be worked up quickly, the pillow narrates its tale with rich-hued felts that are appliquéd using running stitches. *Complete instructions begin on page 96.*

Design: Terrece Beesley

Sweet *Advent Angel*

Counting the days until Christmas, our Advent angel holds in her hand the number of days remaining until that very special day. Created from wood and paint, our sweet angel has feather wings. Instructions and full-size pattern are on pages 98-99.

Design: Susan Cage-Knoch

Sparkling *Chrismons*

Portraying symbols of the Christian faith, our chrismons are worked on plastic canvas with metallic needlepoint yarn. These lovely ornaments are sure to be found on huge evergreens celebrating the season in churches everywhere. You can easily make multiples of these quick-to-stitch gems to grace your own Christmas tree. Instructions and charts begin on page 99.

Designs: Joan Green

A Child Is Born
Card and Bookmark

A *Child is born, a Son is given. God's gift is portrayed in this elegant card with a delicate crocheted cross inside. Perfect for Sunday School students or special friends, this card and cross tell the Christmas story beautifully. Instructions for both projects begin on page 100.*

Designs: Crochet Cross, Marie Holmstrand; Card, Carol Dahlstrom

Cross-Stitched Nativity

Pictured on pages 88–89.

MATERIALS

For 1 each of 5 nativity figures

FABRICS

Five 12x11-inch pieces of 28-count
 ivory Jobelan fabric
¼ yard of moiré taffeta fabric in desired
 color
¼ yard of fleece
¼ yard of lightweight fusible interfacing
8x6-inch piece of ivory felt

THREADS

Cotton embroidery floss in colors listed
 in key
Metallic gold thread

SUPPLIES

Fabric marking pencil; tracing paper
Matboard; fabric glue
5 yards of narrow gold metallic flat trim
1 yard of narrow flat or round
 contrasting trim for each figure
 (5 yards total)
Polyester fiberfill
Paper-backed iron-on adhesive

INSTRUCTIONS

Tape or zigzag edges of fabric to
prevent fraying. For each figure, find
center of chart and of one piece of
fabric; begin stitching there. Use two
plies of floss to work cross-stitches
over two threads of fabric. Work
backstitches, straight stitches, and
French knots using one ply. Work
blended needle as indicated on key.
Press finished stitchery from back.

Use marking pencil to outline
design shape, approximately ⅜ inch
from edge of stitching. Cut fleece
piece to cover back of stitching;
baste in place along marked outline.

For angel, use outline, *page 95,* as a
guide to draw pattern on tracing paper;
cut out. Trace shape on matboard; cut
out. Glue layer of fleece to matboard
shape. Trim fleece-lined angel to
¾ inch beyond basting. Clip into seam
allowance and position angel over
matboard; glue allowance to back.
Glue contrasting trim around outside
edge, followed by gold metallic trim.
Using pattern, cut piece from felt and

glue to back. If desired, glue ribbon
to back of angel and tie to crèche.

For remaining figures, use stitched
pieces as guides to cut back pieces
from moiré taffeta. With right sides
facing, stitch figure fronts to backs on
basting line, leaving bottom edge
open. Trim seam allowance to ¼ inch.
Trim away all fleece seam allowance.
Clip curves; turn right side out.

Turn under ¼ inch along bottom
edge and baste. Stuff figure with
polyester fiberfill.

Trace base patterns, *pages 96–97;*
cut out. Cut shapes from matboard.
Fuse taffeta to right side of matboard,
following manufacturer's directions
on iron-on adhesive. Trim fabric
½ inch beyond matboard; clip and
glue to wrong side. Whipstitch bases
to bottoms of figures. Remove basting
threads at bottom edge if visible.

Glue contrasting trim along seam
line of sides and top of each figure.
Repeat with metallic gold trim. Glue
gold trim around bottom edge.

NATIVITY

ANCHOR		DMC	
387	S		Ecru
002	•	000	White
1026	L	225	Pale shell pink
1017	◎	316	Medium antique mauve
978	◇	322	Pale navy
1047	★	402	Pale mahogany
358	O	433	Dark chestnut
310	X	434	Medium chestnut
1046	▽	435	Light chestnut
1045	□	436	Dark tan
362	=	437	Medium tan
933	\	543	Pale beige brown
168	△	597	Light turquoise
392	✗	640	Dark beige gray
891	Φ	676	Light old gold
295	‖	726	Light topaz
890	▣	729	Medium old gold
1016	♡	778	Pale antique mauve
130	⊕	809	True Delft blue
907	◮	832	Medium bronze
945	⌐	834	Pale bronze
379	⊞	840	Medium beige brown
378	⊘	841	True beige brown
1041	⋈	844	Deep beaver gray
897	♥	902	Deep garnet
1035	●	930	Dark antique blue
4146	⋮	950	Light rose beige
360	◆	3031	Deep mocha
903	☆	3032	Medium mocha
391	–	3033	Pale mocha
886	▷	3047	Light yellow beige
292	∾	3078	Pale lemon
382	■	3371	Black brown
896	✳	3721	Dark shell pink
1018	▲	3726	True antique mauve
120	⊠	3747	Pale periwinkle
1009	✚	3770	True ivory
1008	△	3773	Medium rose beige
778	⊏	3774	Pale rose beige
1050	⊞	3781	Dark mocha
899	◎	3782	Light mocha
393	▼	3790	Deep beige gray

ANCHOR		DMC	
1019	◗	3802	Deep antique mauve
851	✣	3808	Deep turquoise
779	★	3809	Dark turquoise
168	◩	3810	True turquoise
890	◆	3829	Deep old gold
	◈	284	Metallic gold thread

BLENDED NEEDLE

| 360 | ◨ | 839 | Dark beige brown (1X) and |
| 905 | | 3021 | Deep brown gray (1X) – cradle |

BACKSTITCH

	╱	284	Metallic gold thread – halos, angel's wings, hair, banner, and bottom of gown
352	╱	300	Deep mahogany – rope on donkey
1019	╱	315	Dark antique mauve – donkey's blanket
358	╱	433	Dark chestnut – shepherd's eyebrows
897	╱	902	Deep garnet – shepherd's mouth and sheep's mouth
1035	╱	930	Dark antique blue – lettering on angel's banner
360	╱	3031	Deep mocha – Mary's hair (2X)
896	╱	3721	Dark shell pink – Joseph's, Mary's, and angel's mouths
382	╱	3371	Black brown – all remaining stitches

STRAIGHT STITCH

| 891 | ╱ | 676 | Light old gold – hay |
| 897 | ╱ | 902 | Deep garnet – Joseph's sash |

FRENCH KNOT

002	•	000	White – donkey's and lamb's eyes
897	•	902	Deep garnet – Joseph's sash
382	•	3371	Black brown – Mary's, baby's, and Joseph's eyes

ALGERIAN EYELET

| | ✳ | 284 | Metallic gold thread – angel's hair |

ANGEL

Angel stitch count: *106 high x 75 wide*
Angel finished design sizes:
28-count fabric – 7 1/2 x 5 3/8 inches
22-count fabric – 9 5/8 x 6 7/8 inches
36-count fabric – 5 7/8 x 4 1/4 inches

Folk Art Pillow

As shown on page 90, pillow measures 18×17 inches.

MATERIALS

17½x18½-inch piece of black felt
16½x17½-inch piece of cranberry red felt
Pinking shears; tracing paper
6x12-inch piece of cinnamon brown felt
7x9-inch piece of dark blue-and-black print cotton fabric
4x8-inch piece of green felt
6x6-inch piece of gold felt
4x4-inch piece of tan felt
2x4-inch piece of cranberry red felt
3x3-inch piece of light heather gray felt
1x3-inch piece of ivory felt
7x9-inch piece of paper-backed iron-on adhesive; straight pins; needle
Sewing threads: black, dark brown, tan, gold, and green
3 gold or brown-toned, ¼- to ½-inch-diameter buttons
16-inch-square pillow form

INSTRUCTIONS

Trim edges of large red and black felt pieces using pinking shears; set aside.

Enlarge patterns, *page 98*, onto tracing paper and cut out. Following manufacturer's instructions, fuse paper-backed adhesive to back of blue-and-black print cotton fabric. Cut sky background piece from blue print. Cut fence boards and camel from brown felt. Cut curved ground pieces from green felt. Cut king's body from red felt. Cut star, crown, and infant's basket from gold felt. Cut cow, king's feet, and infant's and king's heads from tan felt. Cut donkey's head and forelock from gray felt. Cut infant's body from ivory felt.

Position large red rectangle on work surface with 17½-inch measurement running horizontally. Following pattern diagram for placement, and marking center, remove paper backing from blue fabric and fuse in place on felt pillow top. Use placement diagram to position remaining pieces; pin in place. Pin donkey's forelock to top of head.

To sew each piece in place, use doubled strand of sewing thread. Using running stitches ⅛ inch from outer edges, stitch around fused sky

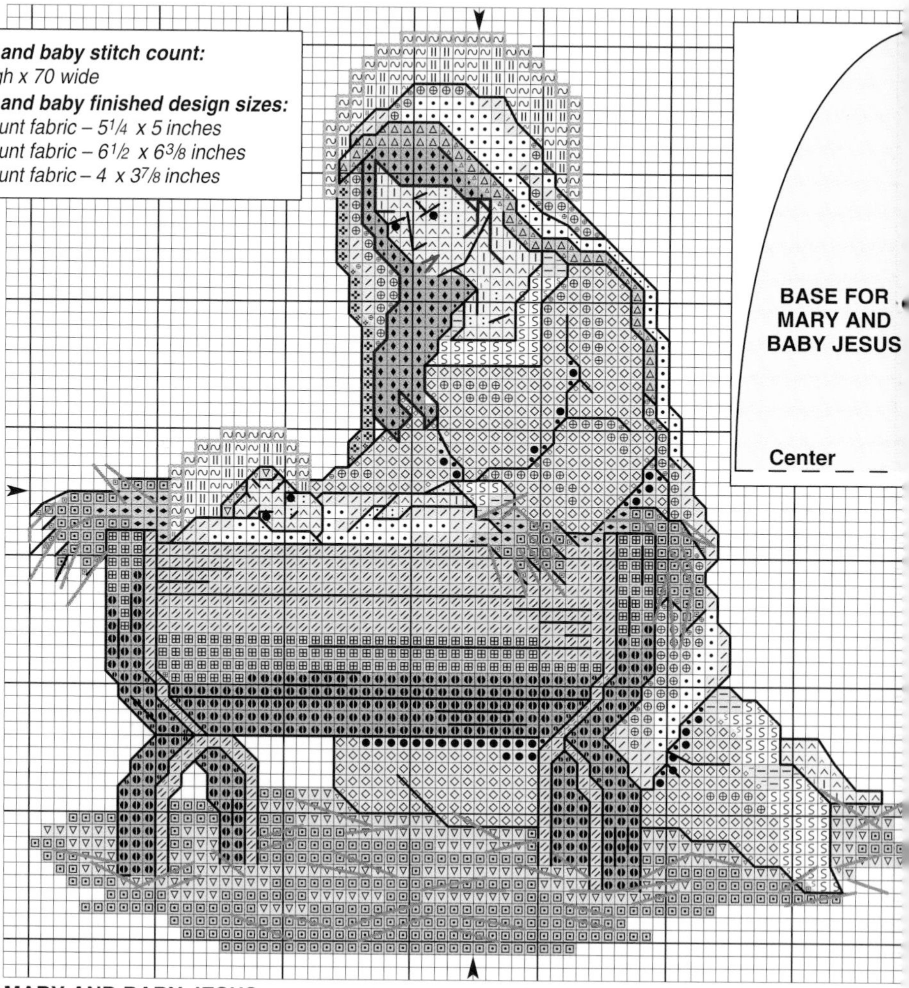

MARY AND BABY JESUS

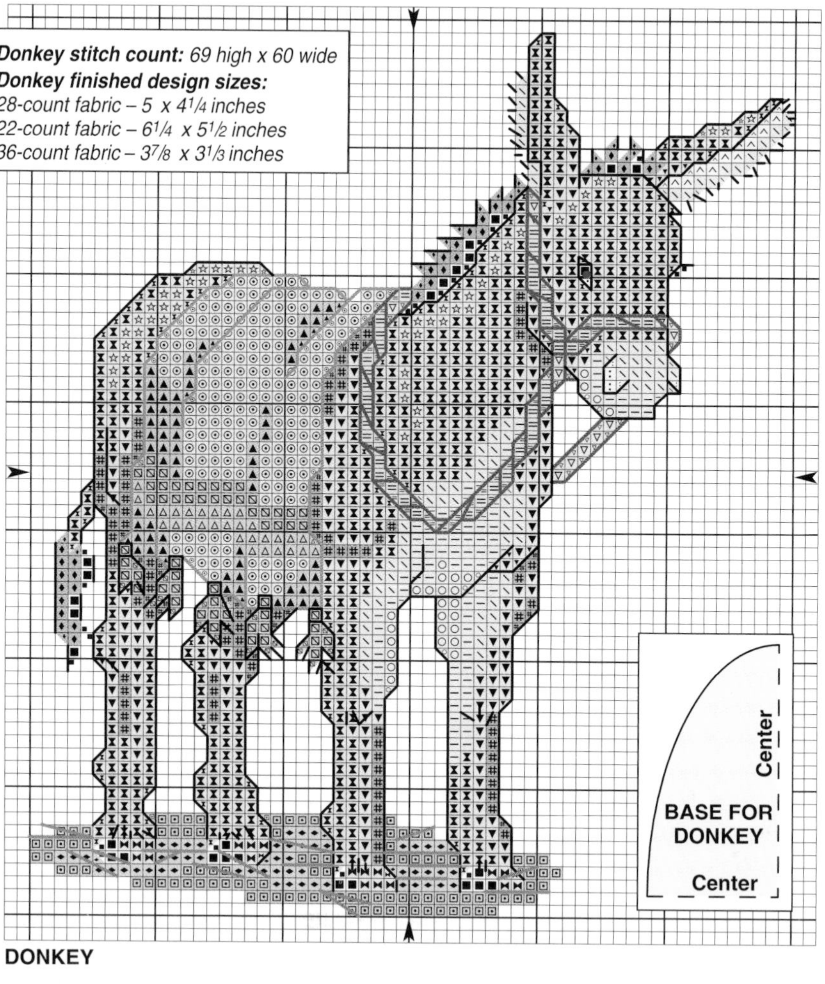

DONKEY

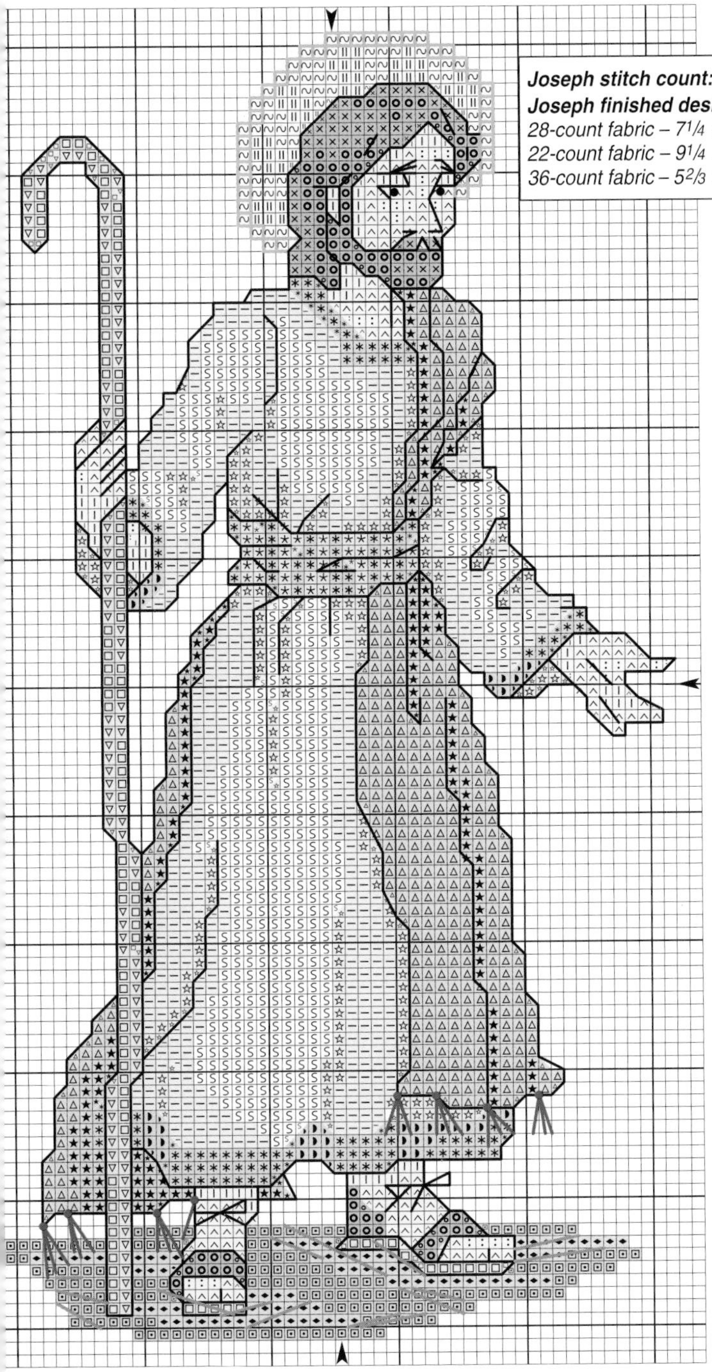

Joseph stitch count: *102 high x 53 wide*
Joseph finished design sizes:
28-count fabric – 7 1/4 x 3 3/4 inches
22-count fabric – 9 1/4 x 4 7/8 inches
36-count fabric – 5 2/3 x 3 inches

SEPH

piece with black thread. With green running stitches, sew green ground pieces in place. Use dark brown running stitches to sew fence boards, camel, king's body, and infant's body in place. Use gray running stitches to sew donkey's head in place, catching forelock along top. Use tan running stitches for cow, infant's and king's head, and king's feet. Sew crown in place with gold running stitches. Use gold buttonhole stitches to sew infant's basket and star in place.

Work face detail on donkey and cow using dark brown thread. Also using dark brown, sew buttons at Xs on star.

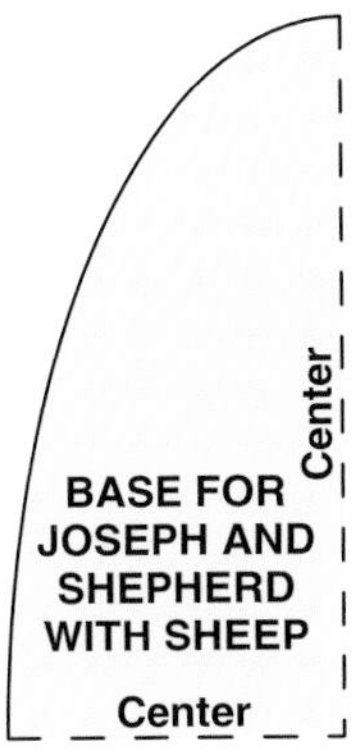

Cut two 1/8×12-inch strips each of green felt, red felt, and dark blue fabric. Treating strands of each color as one strip, braid. Tack top of braid at center top edge of camel's head. Tack again at camel's neck, then to center left edge of king's clothing. Allow unbraided ends to hang.

Center pillow top on black felt pillow back, wrong sides facing. Sew front to back, machine-stitching 1 inch from pinked edge of red felt. Do not leave opening. Slit pillow back vertically between top and bottom stitching. Insert pillow form and hand-sew opening closed.

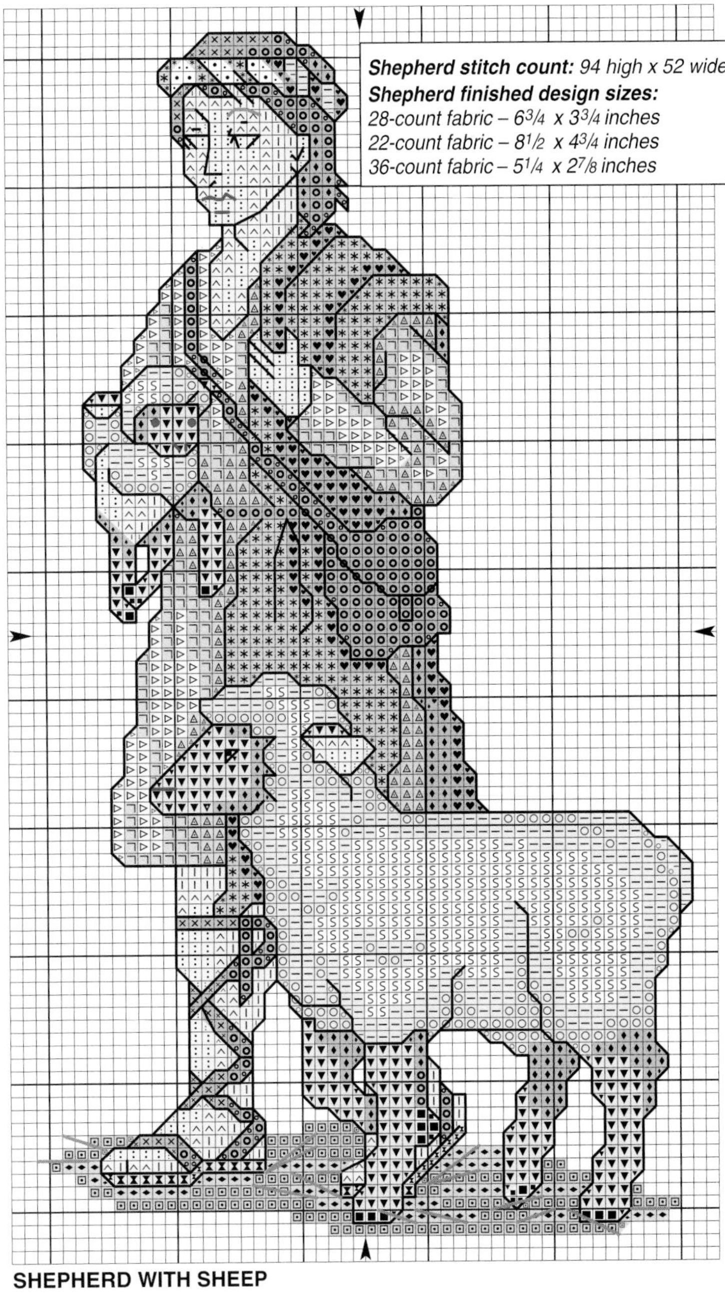

Shepherd stitch count: *94 high x 52 wide*
Shepherd finished design sizes:
28-count fabric – 6 3/4 x 3 3/4 inches
22-count fabric – 8 1/2 x 4 3/4 inches
36-count fabric – 5 1/4 x 2 7/8 inches

SHEPHERD WITH SHEEP

FOLK ART PILLOW

1 Square = 1 Inch

Advent Angel Ornament

As shown on page 91, ornament measures 5¾×4⅞ inches.

MATERIALS

Tracing paper; carbon paper; ballpoint pen
5x5-inch piece of ⅛-inch Baltic birch plywood
8x7-inch piece of ¼-inch Baltic birch plywood
Scroll saw; drill with ⅛-inch bit
Fine grit sandpaper
Delta Ceramcoat acrylic paints: coral, light ivory, green isle, rouge, empire gold, black, sea green, Georgia clay, burnt sienna, and Santa's flesh
Artists' brushes
.01 and .05 black permanent artists' pens
Polyurethane spray
¼-inch-long piece of ⅛-inch-diameter dowel
Crafts glue; ¼-inch screw eye
Two 4-inch-long pieces of ⅛-inch-wide green satin ribbon
12 inches of ¼-inch-wide red satin ribbon
Six 3-inch-long fluffy white feathers

INSTRUCTIONS

Trace pattern, *page 99*, onto tracing paper. Place carbon paper between pattern and larger piece of birch; transfer outlines, omitting fine detail, by tracing over lines with ballpoint pen. Cut out ornament with scroll saw. On smaller piece of birch, mark twenty-four 1×1-inch squares; cut out. Drill holes through center top of each square, ¼ inch from top edge. Drill hole ⅛-inch-deep in center of angel, approximately 1 inch below neck. Sand surfaces smooth.

Paint angel's skin Santa's flesh, dress sea green, shoes green isle, and hair Georgia clay. When dry, transfer basic face detail using carbon paper and pattern. Refer closely to pattern for all remaining fine detail.

Using thinned paint, blend rouge into inside edges of legs, lower edge of each hand, tip of nose, eyelids, and under chin. Blend coral into cheeks and knees. Paint lips coral; shade lower lip with rouge. Shade hair around face with thinned burnt sienna. Paint eyes sea green with black pupils. Paint eyebrows Georgia clay. Add tiny rouge dots at inner and outer corners of eyes.

Shade dress with thinned green isle. Paint holly leaves green isle and berries rouge. Paint star empire gold and heart rouge.

Use .01 black pen to outline and draw all fine detail including hair, eyebrow detail, eyes and lashes, around mouth, and holly and dress detail. Use .05 black pen to write "days until Christmas" across bottom of dress.

Highlight eyes, shoes, tip of nose, holly berries, star, and heart with tiny dots or strokes of light ivory.

Paint front and back of all squares light ivory; let dry. Using numbers at *right* as patterns, paint dates 1 through 24 onto squares using green isle.

Spray all pieces with several coats of polyurethane spray. Ream all holes clean of paint.

Glue ⅛-inch dowel into center hole in angel. Affix screw eye into center top edge of ornament. Thread red ribbon through screw eye and tie in bow. For each shoe, fold green ribbon piece in half; glue middle to inside leg by top edge of shoe at heel. Tie knot at ankle and cut off excess ribbon.

To make wings, hold quills of three feathers together; glue to ornament back so feathers extend past shoulder on one side. Repeat for opposite side.

ADVENT ANGEL ORNAMENT

1 2 3 4 5 6 7 8 9 0

Sparkling Chrismons

Pictured on page 92.

MATERIALS

FABRIC

1 sheet of 7-count plastic canvas

THREAD

Rainbow Gallery Plastic Canvas 7 Metallic Needlepoint Yarn: 26 yards of No. 10 pearl; 24 yards of No. 1 gold

SUPPLIES

Thirty-five 4-mm gold beads

5 yards of fine gold metallic thread

Tapestry needle; manicure scissors

INSTRUCTIONS

Cut pieces from the sheet of plastic canvas using charts, *pages 100–101.* Use small scissors to cut away the inner portions of Chrismons designs where necessary.

Work the continental, long, and straight stitches all using one ply of needlepoint yarn. Overcast all edges using gold yarn.

Use thread to attach beads. If bead symbol lies over an intersection, bring the needle up as for continental stitch, slip bead on needle, then insert the needle back through the canvas as if completing a continental stitch. If the symbol is between stitches, bring the needle up in the hole, slip the bead on, and insert the needle back through the canvas in the same place. Knot all ends, then weave in tails.

Cut a 5-inch length of gold yarn for each ornament and secure at top of ornaments for hangers.

A Child Is Born Card

As shown on page 93, closed card measures 5⅞×4¼ inches.

MATERIALS

5⅞x8½-inch piece of white cardstock paper; purchased dark colored marbled or plain paper
Rubber cement; gold paint marker
Solid color gold metallic paper
Diamond-shaped jewel; X-acto knife
Tracing paper; needle; white thread

INSTRUCTIONS

Fold white paper in half to make card measuring 5⅞×4¼ inches. Cut a piece of dark paper the same size; glue to right half of inside of card using rubber cement. Trace die-cut design, *page 101*, onto tracing paper. Transfer to card front; cut out dark areas and shape at top using an X-acto knife. Cut gold paper to measure 5⅞×4¼ inches; glue behind cutout. Glue jewel to center of die cut, using "X" as a guide.

Transfer lettering, *page 101*, onto front and inside of card, referring to photograph, *page 93*. Trace over the lettering using a gold paint marker.

Use a needle and thread to tack the top of the crocheted cross to inside of the card using two or three loose stitches. (These stitches can be clipped easily so the cross can be removed to use as a bookmark.)

A Child Is Born Bookmark

As shown on page 93, bookmark measures 3½ inches tall.

MATERIALS

Coats Big Ball cotton crochet thread, size 30: 1 ball each of white (001) and ecru (0061)
Size 12 steel crochet hook
Stiffy Fabric Stiffener
Paint brush; waxed paper

INSTRUCTIONS

Beginning at the lower edge with white thread, ch 4.

Row 1 (RS): In fourth ch from hook (3 dc, ch 2, 4 dc); turn.

Row 2: Ch 4, in ch-2 sp (3 dc, ch 2, 3 dc), trc in turning ch; turn.

Rows 3-13: Rep Row 2. Fasten off.

Left Side: With RS facing, counting from top down and along the left-hand side of fabric, sk 3 rows (or, the spaces made by the turning chs), join white thread in next sp with a sl st.

Row 1: Ch 1, sc in same sp as join, in next sp (3 dc, ch 2, 3 dc), sc in next sp; turn.

Cross Pat'ee stitch count: *19 high x 19 wide*
Cross Pat'ee finished design sizes:
7-count fabric–2¾ x 2¾ inches
14-count fabric–1⅜ x 1⅜ inches

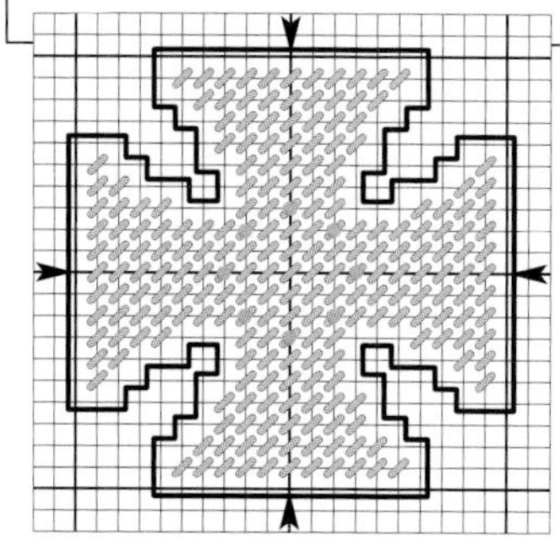

CROSS PAT'EE

Fish stitch count: *21 high x 19 wide*
Fish finished design sizes:
7-count fabric–3 x 2¾ inches
14-count fabric–1½ x 1⅜ inches

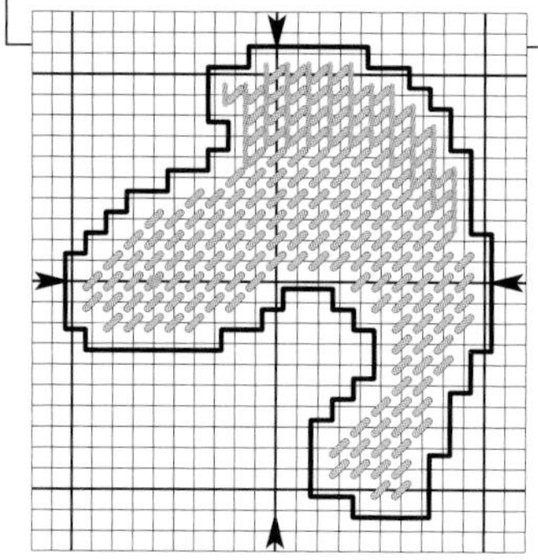

FISH

Cross and Chi stitch count: *26 high x 26 wide*
Cross and Chi finished design sizes:
7-count fabric–3¾ x 3¾ inches
14-count fabric–1⅞ x 1⅞ inches

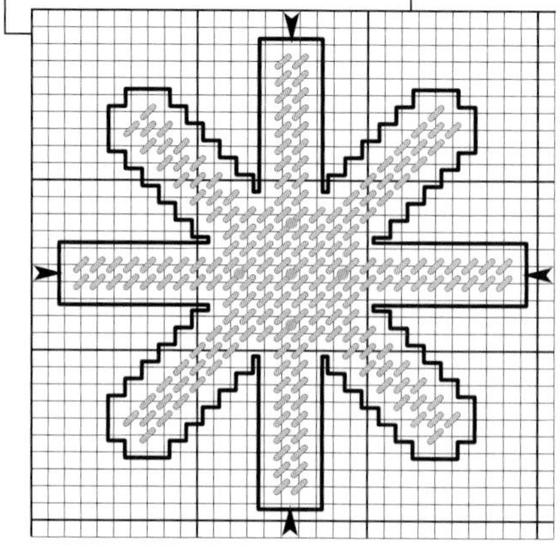

CROSS AND CHI

NEEDLEPOINT CHRISMONS
07 Rainbow Gallery Metallic gold plastic canvas yarn
10 Rainbow Gallery Metallic pearl plastic canvas yarn
STRAIGHT STITCH
07 Rainbow Gallery Metallic gold plastic canvas yarn – crown, fish, descending dove
BEADS
Gold beads–1/8- inch diam

Chi-Rho stitch count: *33 high x 17 wide*
Chi-Rho finished design sizes:
7-count fabric–4¾ x 2⅜ inches
14-count fabric–2⅜ x 1¼ inches

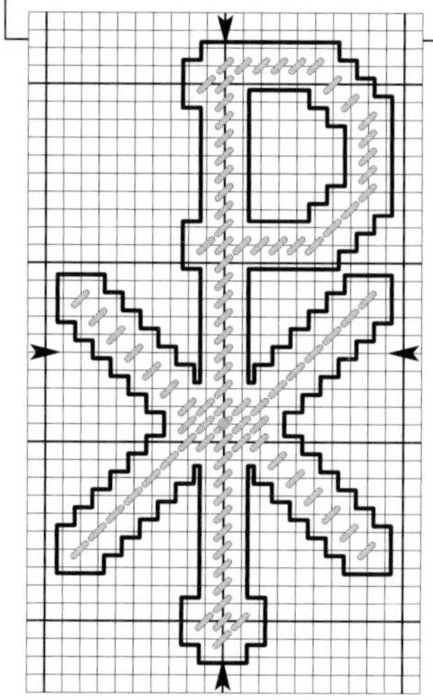

CHI RHO

Decending Dove stitch count: *28 high x 21 wide*
Decending Dove finished design sizes:
7-count fabric–4 x 3 inches
14-count fabric–2 x 1½ inches

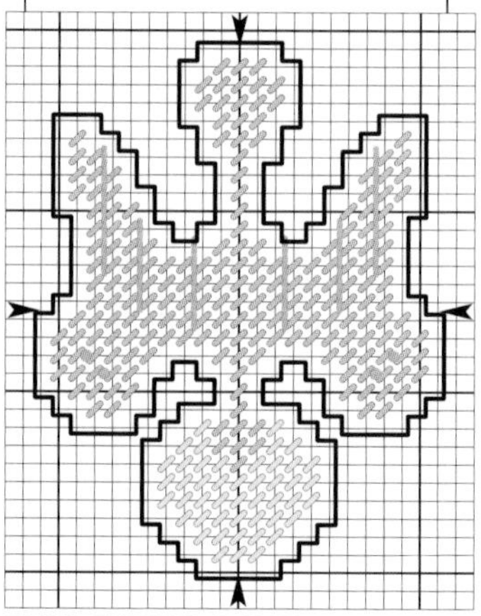

DESCENDING DOVE

Triangle and Trefoil stitch count: *22 high x 24 wide*
Triangle and Trefoil finished design sizes:
7-count fabric – 3⅛ x 3⅜ inches
14-count fabric – 1⅝ x 1¾ inches

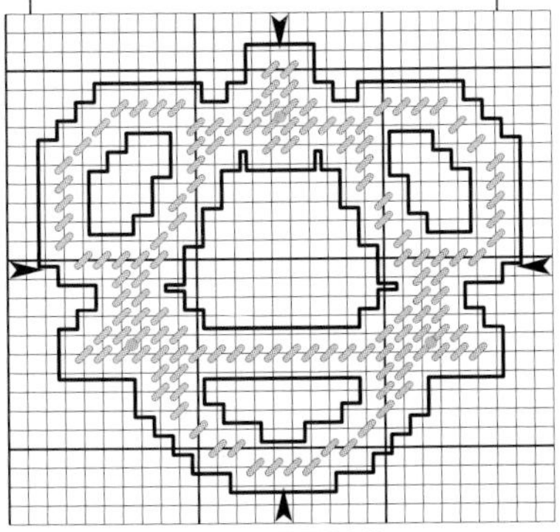

TRIANGLE AND TREFOIL

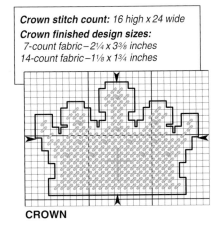

Crown stitch count: *16 high x 24 wide*
Crown finished design sizes:
7-count fabric – 2¼ x 3⅜ inches
14-count fabric – 1⅛ x 1¾ inches

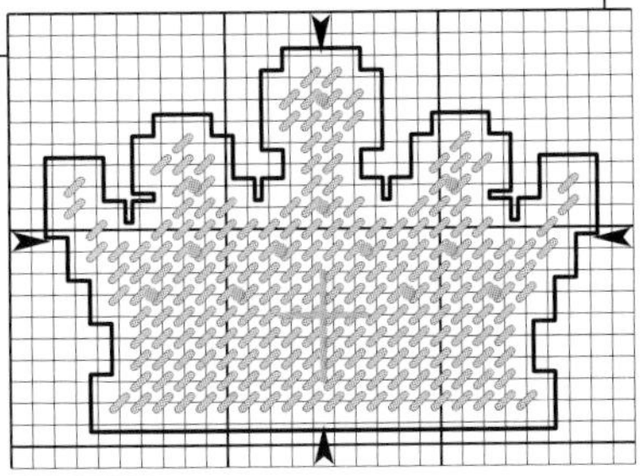

CROWN

A CHILD IS BORN CARD

Row 2: Ch 4, in ch-2 sp (3 dc, ch 2, 3 dc), trc in sc; turn.

Row 3: Ch 4, in ch-2 sp (3 dc, ch 2, 3 dc), trc in turning ch. Fasten off.

Right Side: With the RS facing, counting from first row up 6 rows, join white thread with sl st in seventh sp along right edge. Work Rows 1-3 as for Left Side. Fasten off.

For Edging: With the RS facing, join ecru thread with sl st in top ch-2 sp. Ch 1, in same sp as join (sc, ch 3, sc), sc in each of next 3 dc, [in next sp along side (sc, ch 3, sl st in sc just completed = picot made), 3 sc in same sp] 3 times, 2 sc in next sp; working along Left Side, (3 sc in next sp, picot) twice, sc in each of next 3 dc, picot in ch-2 sp, sc in each of next 3 dc, in each of next 2 sps (picot, 3 sc), 2 sc in next sp, in each of next 5 sps (picot, 3 sc), (picot, sc) in next sp, 3 sc over dc post, picot in ch, 3 sc over dc post, (2 sc, picot) in next sp, in next 5 sps (3 sc, picot), 2 sc in next sp; working along Right Side, in each of next 2 sps (3 sc, pc), sc in 3 dc, picot in ch-2 sp, sc in 3 dc, (picot, 3 sc) in next 2 sps, 2 sc in next sp, (3 sc, picot) in next 3 sps, sc in 3 dc, sl st in first sc. Fasten off.

For Hanging Loop: With the RS facing, join ecru thread with sl st in top ch-3 sp; sc in same sp; ch 50, sl st in sc and fasten off. Cut 11 ecru strands, each 2 inches in length. Holding strands together, fold in half to form a loop. Bring loop through the end of the 50-ch-lp; then, draw ends through loop and pull up to form a knot. Trim ends.

Paint fabric stiffener onto the bookmark and leave on waxed paper until dry.

The Stockings Were Hung by the Chimney

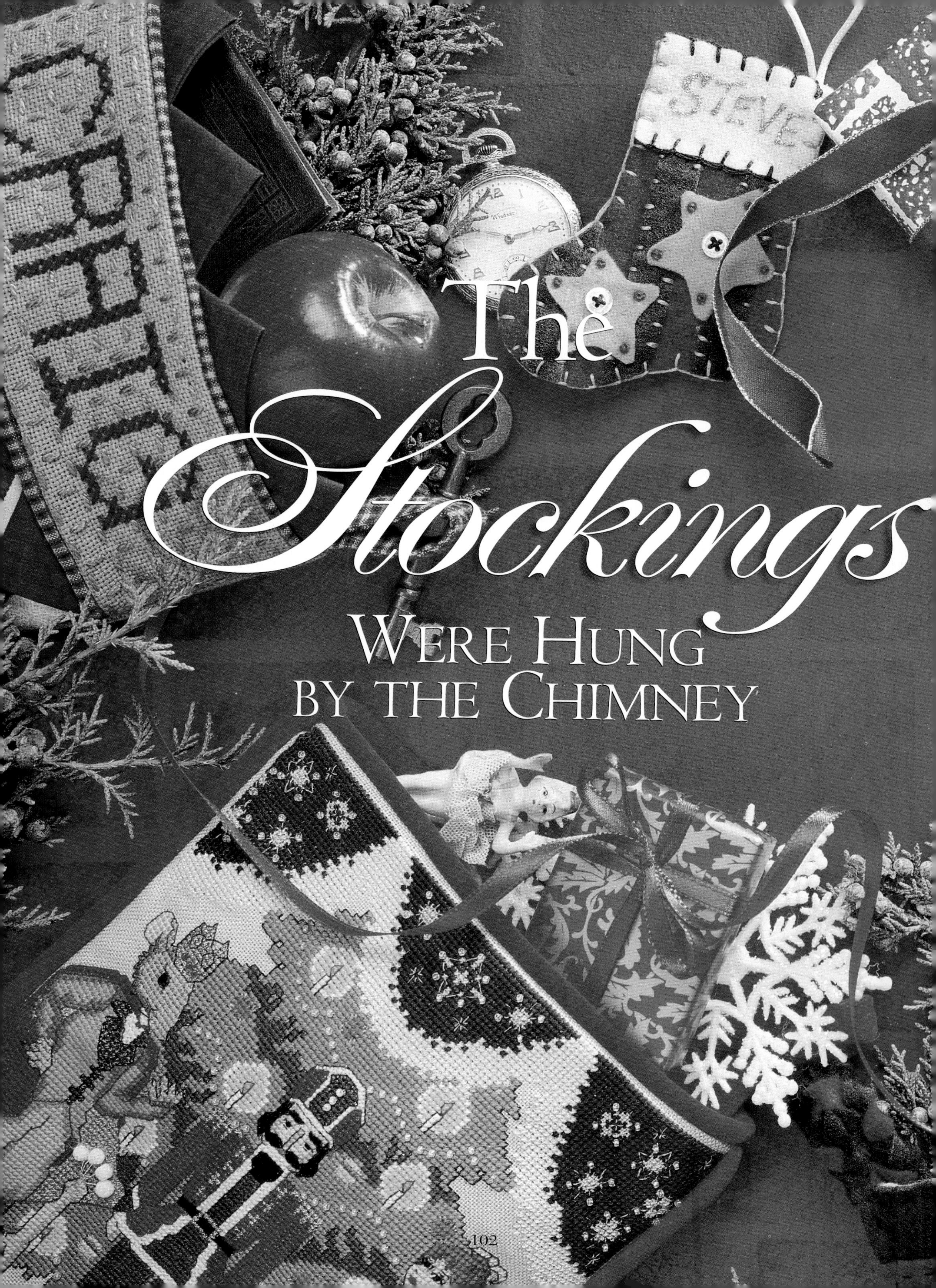

Every child, young and old alike, cherishes that moment of discovery—seeing what Santa has lovingly placed in that special stocking. Whether cross-stitched, crocheted, quilted, or made from felt, these stockings we created for you will please everyone on your list—and Santa, too!

The Enchantment of Christmas Stockings

As the children creep down the stairway, eyes full of wonder, they hope that the great giver of gifts has magically visited once again. And with this sweet anticipation of Santa's long-awaited visit comes another special moment, one that seems to revive heartwarming memories from years gone by—the hanging of each beloved Christmas stocking.

Every Christmas stocking speaks a story of its very own. Some are treasured for the memorable surprises that they once held. Others are cherished for the stockings themselves, tokens from the heart that were lovingly handmade by a dear friend or relative.

The ornate stockings that grace hearths and banisters around the world at Christmastime come in a multitude of designs. Some are pieced from precious fabric scraps adorned with intricate stitches. Others may be embellished with cross-stitched angels, knitted snowflakes, or felt-appliquéd characters that remind us of this magical time of year.

But Christmas stockings weren't always so elaborate. The first Christmas stockings of the early 1800s were simply ordinary stockings from one's dresser drawer. They were hung by the fire with the same hopeful excitement that keeps the tradition alive today.

The custom of hanging one's stocking on Christmas Eve takes us back in time to a tale about Saint Nicholas. There are dozens of variations of the story, but the theme remains the same.

Saint Nicholas was born in Asia Minor, the son of a very wealthy bishop and an extremely holy woman. As he reached adulthood, he became concerned over the great wealth of his parents. Soon after they died, the young saint decided he would give away his money to those less fortunate.

It is said that Saint Nicholas heard of the quandary of three sisters, the daughters of a penniless nobleman. While the nobleman considered selling his daughters into slavery to recover his wealth, the threesome had other concerns. As young girls do, the sisters dreamed of their futures. But with no dowries, they worried they would never marry.

Unselfish Saint Nicholas decided to help them. As the two oldest sisters reached an appropriate age to marry, the generous saint tossed each girl a bag of gold coins through the open window. When the youngest maiden was old enough to marry, she hoped for the same miraculous answer to her prayers. To her delight, Saint Nicholas tossed her bag of gold down the chimney, and it fell into one of the stockings that had been hung near the fire to dry.

Thus, two traditions were born—children began believing that Saint Nicholas was truly the wondrous giver of gifts, and in hopes of receiving their own valuable treasures, wishful people everywhere began to hang their stockings by the chimney with care on Christmas Eve.

In the late 1800s and early 1900s, Christmas stockings became even more popular, and more fanciful renditions began to appear. Soon, the everyday hose and booties returned to bureau drawers, and colorful printed stockings took their place in homes bedecked for the Christmas holiday.

These first commercially made stockings featured festive scenes printed on thin cotton or linen fabrics. Some were premade, and others were designed to be sewn at home with a mother's loving touch. Today crafters and stitchers take great pride in creating personalized stockings for their families to proudly display in their festive holiday homes.

Prefilled stockings were introduced on the market toward the end of the 19th century. These net stockings ranged in size from 8 to 30 inches, costing anywhere from 10 cents to 3 dollars. And because the stockings were transparent, the purchaser could view the surprises inside. The boys' stockings might have held tops, picture books, or Christmas crackers; the version for girls may have included dolls, jewels, fans, or umbrellas.

There was a time, from approximately 1847 to 1880, in which the stocking had a rival. Saint Nicholas was asked to leave presents by a small Christmas tree placed on the family table. Supposedly, this enabled the saint to leave gifts that simply would not fit in the ordinary stockings. But soon the tree tradition faded, and once again it was the stocking that was eagerly hung at Christmastime to catch Saint Nicholas's bounty.

And what does one hope to find nestled in his or her stocking come Christmas morn? Certainly not a black birch rod, a symbol that one has not been good and righteous during the year. And, though one might think that a lump of coal is a sign of bad luck, it actually symbolizes warmth in the years to come. An apple placed in the stocking's toe is a good-health wish; salt sends a message of good luck.

Fruits, candies, and nuts continue to be popular and welcomed stocking fillers. Even more clever and cherished are personal stocking stuffers—handmade or purchased. From tiny stitched keepsakes and hand-written promises to store-bought gems and gift certificates, each stocking surprise reminds us that we are special and very much loved.

Most American families have kept with the tradition of hanging the stockings on the fireplace mantel on Christmas Eve. Still others may choose to place their stockings on the Christmas tree, the foot of a bed, or near the stairs.

Shoes, instead of stockings, are left by the hearth to greet Saint Nicholas in certain regions of France and Germany. As the legend there goes, Saint Nicholas is said to ride a white pony from house to house on December 5, Saint Nicholas Eve. He carries two bags—one with switches to leave for the naughty, the other filled with rewards for the good youngsters.

Dutch children put out their well-worn wooden shoes, too, in hopes that the great gift giver will visit while they are sleeping. They fill their shoes with hay for Saint Nicholas's horse, and if they've been good, in return he fills their wooden shoes with toys and holiday goodies.

In Spain, three celebrations take place at Christmastime. Gift giving on Christmas Eve and Christmas Day is becoming more customary, but some still choose to exchange gifts on the Epiphany, also called the Day of the Three Kings, which falls on January 6. In urban Spain, many families follow the Northern European custom of hanging Christmas stockings on the mantel in anticipation of the arrival of Santa Claus.

In other parts of Europe, stockings adorn the windows on St. Andrew's Eve, which falls on November 29. In Russia, children anxiously await New Year's Eve when Grandfather Frost visits with his bag of surprises.

But no matter what month or day, no matter where the stockings are placed, and no matter what the magical gift bearer is called from country to country, the great night always comes. The ritual of hanging treasured stockings continues to enrich the season and fill children around the world with the wonderment and spirit of Christmas.

St. Nick *Stocking*

Simply and stunningly constructed from felt, our St. Nick stocking is sure to be a holiday favorite. Created using five country colors, the Santa motif is sewn onto the stocking using blanket stitches and cross-stitches with contrasting embroidery floss. For complete instructions and full-size pattern, see pages 111–113.

Design: Terrece Beesley

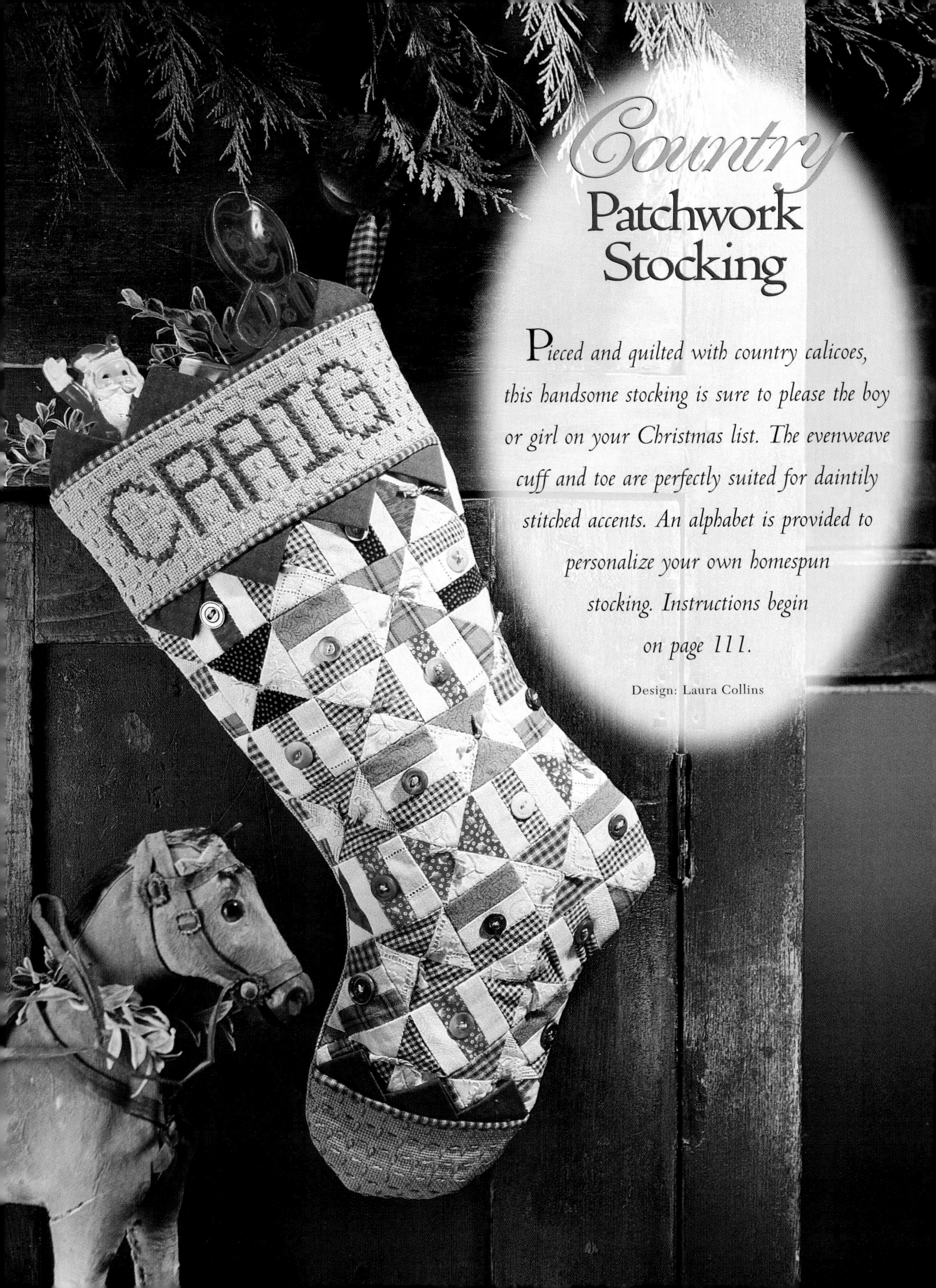

Country Patchwork Stocking

Pieced and quilted with country calicoes, this handsome stocking is sure to please the boy or girl on your Christmas list. The evenweave cuff and toe are perfectly suited for daintily stitched accents. An alphabet is provided to personalize your own homespun stocking. Instructions begin on page 111.

Design: Laura Collins

Festive Hardanger Stocking

Hardanger and simple appliqué combine to create this one-of-a-kind stocking. Tiny symbols of the season are embroidered on the stocking, and the open work of the Hardanger cuff displays a satin lining. *Instructions and chart for this elegant piece begin on page 115.*

Design: Lynne Hermanson

Nutcracker Ballet Stocking

Visions of the Snow Princess and Clara come to mind and the music seems to play as this cross-stitched treasure is displayed on the mantel. Worked on 28-count Jobelan fabric, this magnificent work of art is embellished with beads and metallic threads. Instructions and chart begin on page 119.

Design: Barbara Sestok

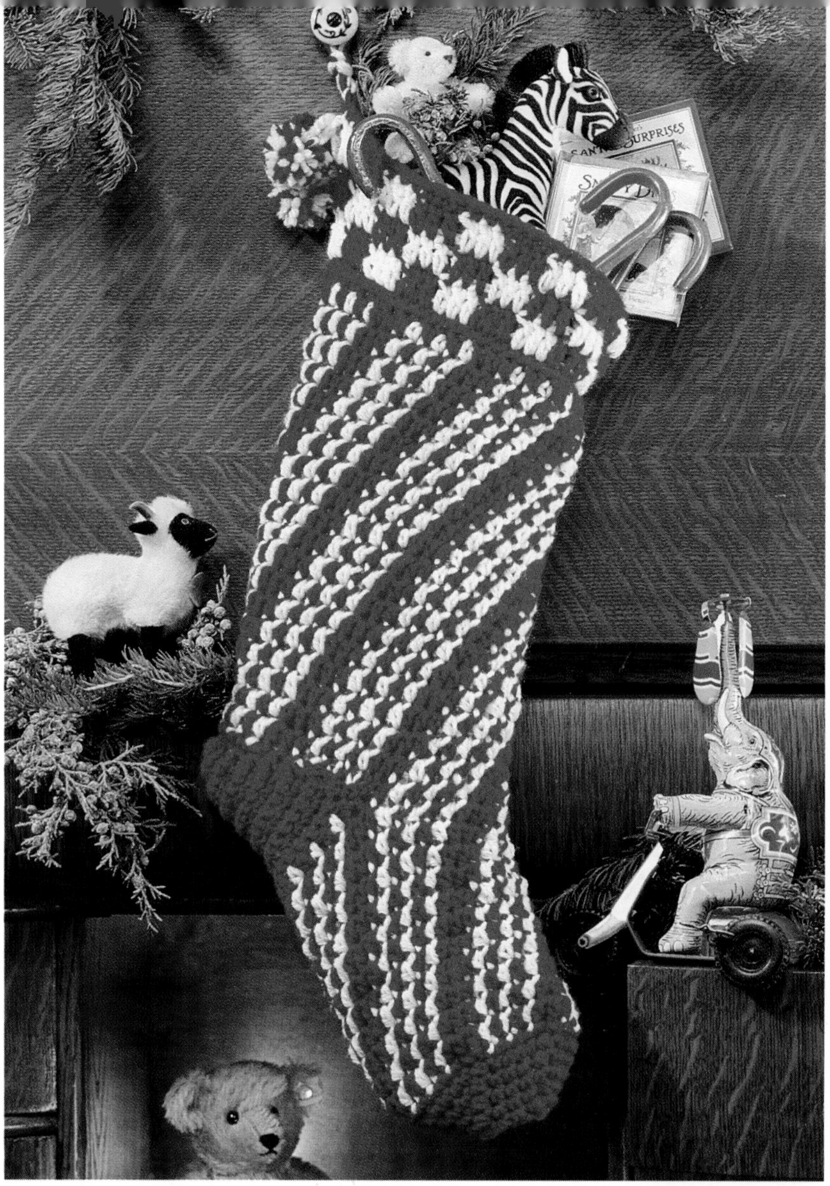

Crocheted Candy-Cane Stocking

Stripes of red and white combine to create this sweet candy-cane stocking crocheted with soft acrylic yarn. The bold stocking design, worked in half double crochet stitches, can be passed down for generations to come. Instructions begin on page 122.

Design: Ann Smith for Monsanto Designers of America

Tiny Felt *Stockings*

Just big enough for a tiny treasure and a lot of love, these felt stockings work up quickly. We've shown them displayed as a centerpiece filled with something special for everyone at the table. Hung on a banister or on the tree, these fun felt stockings are at home almost anywhere. Instructions and full-size patterns begin on page 123.

Designs: Kathy Wirth

St. Nick Stocking

As shown on page 106, stocking measures 14½×7½ inches.

MATERIALS

Tracing paper
½ yard of 45-inch-wide cream felt
5x11-inch piece of hunter green felt
5x6-inch piece of ivory felt
3½x8-inch piece of cranberry red felt
2x2½-inch piece of tan felt
5x5-inch piece of cranberry red print fabric
5x5-inch piece of blue and black print fabric
Paper-backed iron-on adhesive
Cotton embroidery floss: dark brown, ivory, and red
Embroidery needle
Three ½-inch-diameter ivory buttons
Two ⅝-inch-diameter brown buttons

INSTRUCTIONS

Trace one full stocking and each individual piece from pattern, *pages 112–113*, onto tracing paper.

Cut two stockings from cream felt. Cut heel and top border from green felt; scallop border and hearts from red felt; beard, mustache, and brim from ivory felt; and face from tan felt. In addition, cut a 1½×1-inch tassel strip from ivory felt.

Draw around circle, hat, and toe patterns onto paper side of iron-on adhesive. Reverse hat and toe patterns to allow for proper direction after fusing. Following the manufacturer's instructions, fuse double-sided adhesive to backs of blue with black print and red print fabrics. Cut out toe pieces.

Remove paper backing from circle, hat, and toe pieces. Referring to stocking pattern, center circle 2½ inches below stocking top; fuse. Fuse toe piece over toe of stocking and hat in place atop circle.

Pin face, beard, and then hat trim in place. Using two plies of red embroidery floss and blanket stitches, sew the brim to the stocking. Space stitches approximately 3/16 inches apart. Use brown floss and buttonhole stitches to secure the outside edge of the beard and the edge to the left of the face. Also using brown floss, work eyes with large cross-stitches and backstitch the nose.

Attach mustache with ivory floss running stitch through vertical center.

For tassel, cut ⅛-inch-wide fringe 1 inch deep across one long edge of tassel strip. Roll strip, and wrap with ivory floss ¼ inch down from uncut rolled edge. Tack tassel to the tip of the hat.

Pin top border and scallop border in place, allowing scallop border to overlap bottom of top border. Using two strands of brown floss, sew along sides and tops of both borders using running stitches. Using ivory floss, sew cream button to each scallop at dot.

Work large cross-stitches along top edge of toe piece using two plies of brown floss. Tack hearts in place using brown buttons sewn with brown floss.

Cut two 12×¼-inch strips from green felt and one 12×¼-inch strip from red felt. Braid strips to make hanging loop. Fold strip in half, stack ends, and tack to backside of stocking front at outer top corner. Pin the stocking front to back, wrong sides facing. Using buttonhole stitch and two plies of brown floss, sew front to back, securing hanging loop.

Country Patchwork Stocking

As shown on page 107, finished stocking is 16½ inches long.

MATERIALS

Tracing paper
Template plastic or cardboard
Water-soluble marking pen
9x9-inch piece of 18-count beige-gray Davosa evenweave fabric
6x18-inch piece of dark burgundy fabric
¾ yard of assorted burgundy print cotton fabrics
⅛ yard of assorted dark green print cotton fabrics
¼ yard of assorted ecru cotton fabrics or select areas from embroidered garments, handkerchiefs, and doilies
18x24-inch piece of muslin
12x18-inch piece of cotton quilt batting
12x18-inch piece of desired backing fabric
Threads to match fabrics; embroidery hoop
Embroidery and crewel needles
Deep garnet (DMC 902) cotton embroidery floss
#3 Dark beige-gray (DMC 640) pearl cotton
⅔ yard of piping cord
16 assorted ½-inch-diameter buttons

INSTRUCTIONS

Trace pattern pieces, *page 114*, enlarging stocking shape; cut out. Cut prairie point and triangle patterns from template material. Trace around cuff and toe patterns onto evenweave fabric using marking pen, keeping pattern pieces on straight of grain. Mark seam lines; do not cut out.

Cut 11 prairie point squares from a dark burgundy print fabric. From another burgundy print, cut two hanging loops and one 1×24-inch strip for piping.

For each triangle-pieced block, you will need two matching colored triangles and two matching ecru triangles. From burgundy and dark green fabrics, cut a total of 72 triangles, 36 of each color, in pairs of matching fabrics. From assorted ecru fabrics, cut a total of 72 triangles.

For striped blocks, cut 1×20-inch strips as follows: three from assorted burgundy fabrics, three from assorted dark green fabrics, and six from assorted ecru fabrics.

Cut two stocking shapes from muslin for lining and one stocking shape each from cotton batting and backing fabric.

Sew pieces together with right sides facing, using ¼ inch seam allowances unless otherwise indicated. Press all seams open.

To piece triangle block, sew a colored triangle and an ecru triangle together along one short edge to form a larger triangle (see diagram, *page 115*); make two, matching fabrics. Sew larger triangles together

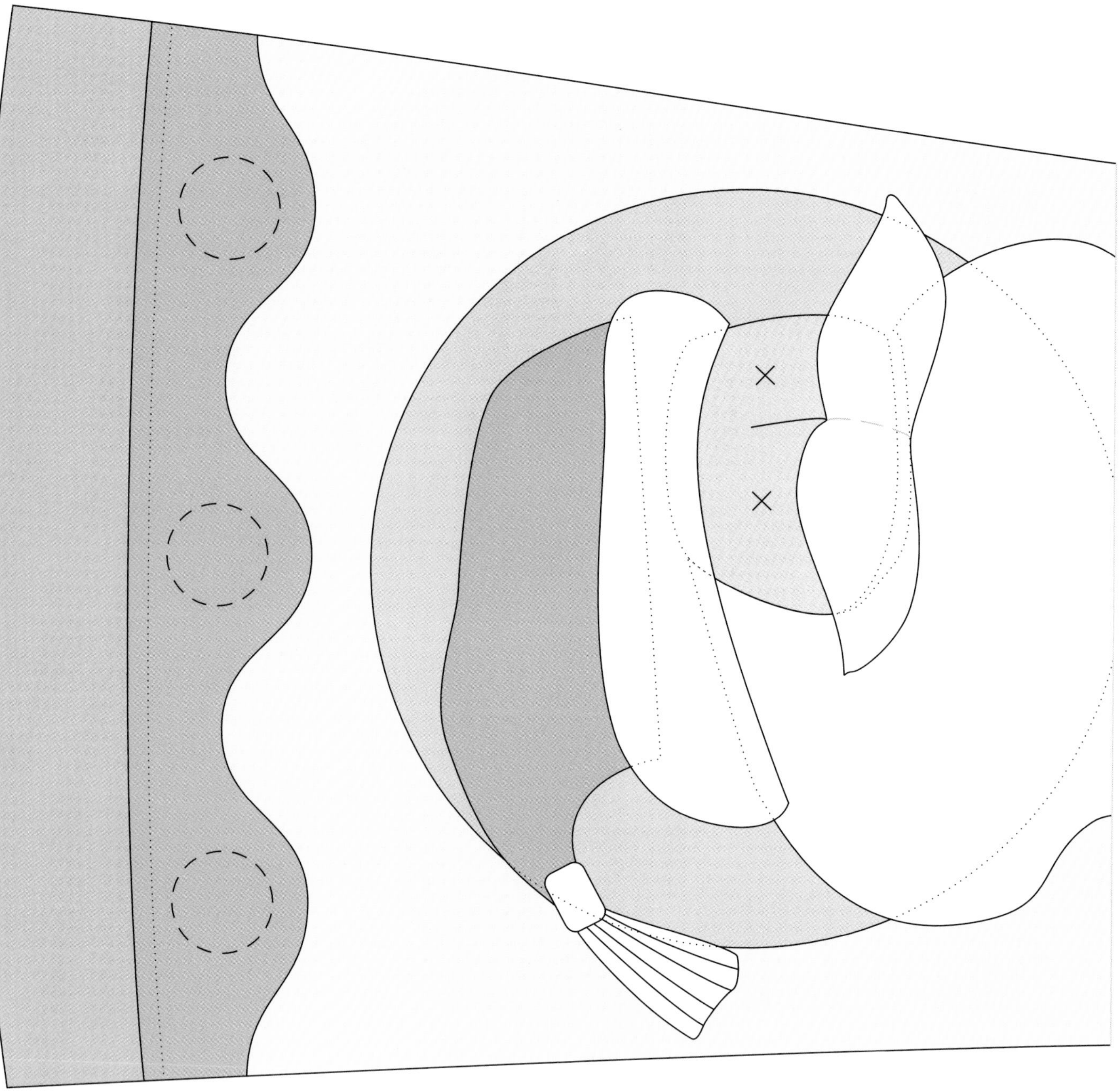

along long edge to complete block. Make 36 blocks.

To piece striped blocks, join three 1×20-inch strips together along long edges as follows: sew one dark green strip to each side of an ecru strip, one burgundy strip to each side of an ecru strip, one ecru strip to each side of a dark green strip, and one ecru strip to each side of a burgundy strip. Cut striped pieces into ten 2-inch-wide blocks.

Arrange blocks in nine rows of eight blocks each, alternating striped and triangle-pieced blocks and referring to diagram, *page 115*, for placement. Four striped blocks will be leftover. Sew blocks into rows, then sew rows together to complete pieced fabric.

Trace a second stocking pattern onto tracing paper, omitting the cuff and toe and adding ¼-inch seams to edges. This is the patchwork front pattern.

Position patchwork front pattern even with the top edge of the pieced fabric. Trace around the shape and cut out.

Cross-stitch name or initials on cuff if desired, using alphabet, *page 115,* and three plies of deep garnet floss. Work running stitches in grid pattern over cuff and toe as shown on chart, *page 115*. Cut out both shapes. Zigzag stitch edges to prevent raveling.

To assemble stocking front, press one prairie-point square in half on diagonal, then press in half again, matching folded edges. Make a total of 11 prairie points. Referring to

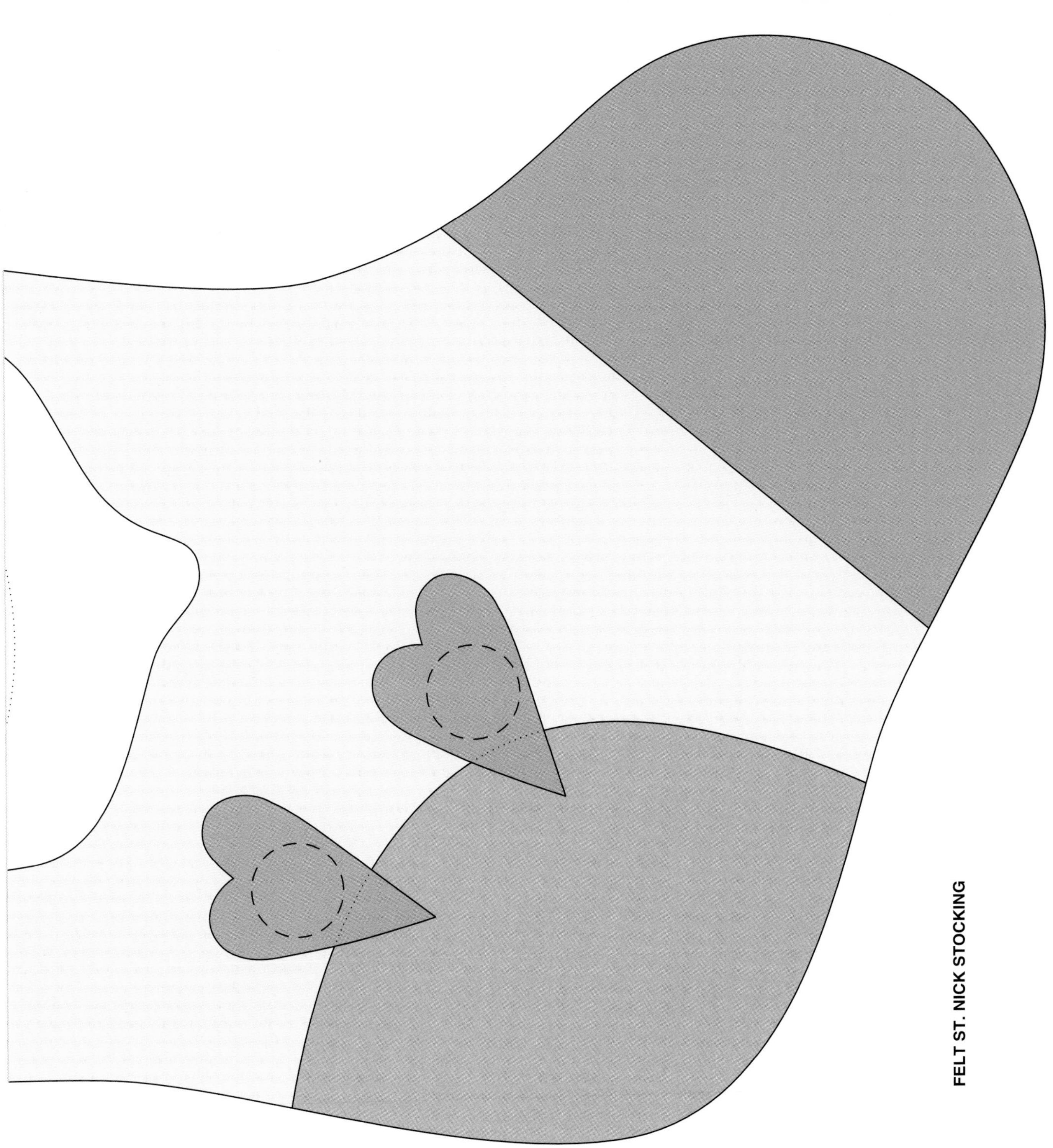

photograph, *page 107*, position four prairie points along top edge of pieced stocking front and three along toe edge, slightly overlapping them and placing points facing toward center of stocking. Baste in place.

Center cording lengthwise on wrong side of piping strip. Fold fabric around cording, raw edges even. Use zipper foot to sew through both fabric layers close to cording. Cut self-covered piping into two 9-inch-long pieces and one 6-inch-long piece. Sew one long piece to top edge of pieced stocking front and short piece to toe edge. Trim excess piping. Sew remaining piece of piping to top edge of cuff; press seam allowances to inside. Referring to photograph, pin remaining prairie points to wrong side of cuff along top edge. Topstitch in place on seam line between piping and cuff. Sew toe and cuff to pieced stocking front.

To assemble stocking, baste batting to wrong side of stocking front. Sew button to center of each striped block; tie center of each triangle-pieced block using pearl cotton thread. With right sides facing, sew stocking front to backing, leaving top edge open. Clip curves, turn stocking right side out; press.

Sew lining shapes together along curved edge, using a ⅝-inch seam allowance. Trim seam; press under ¼ inch along top edge. Slip lining inside stocking; pin to stocking along top edges.

Continued on page 115

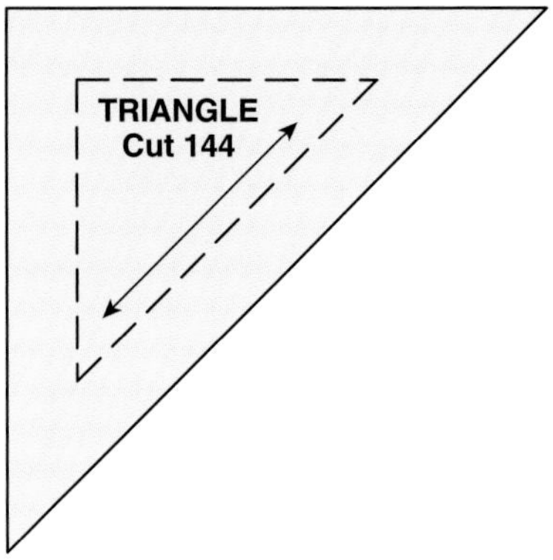

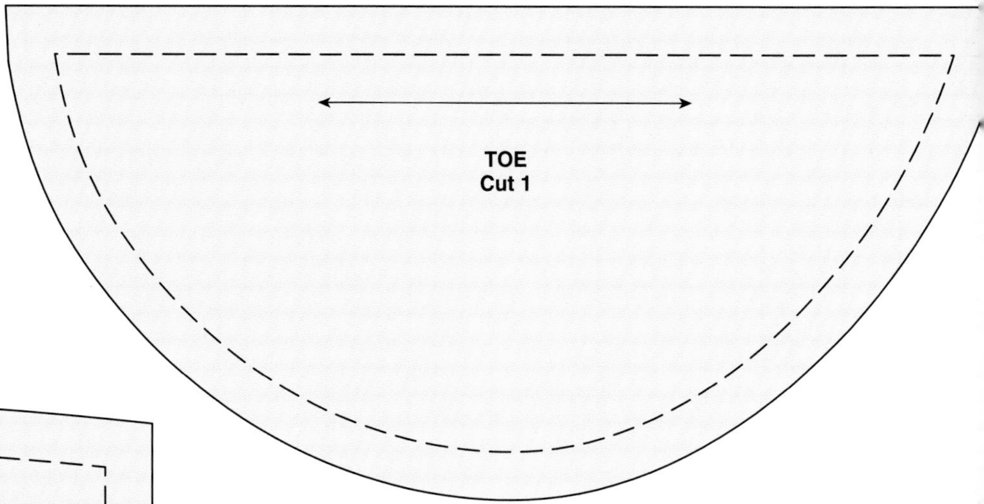

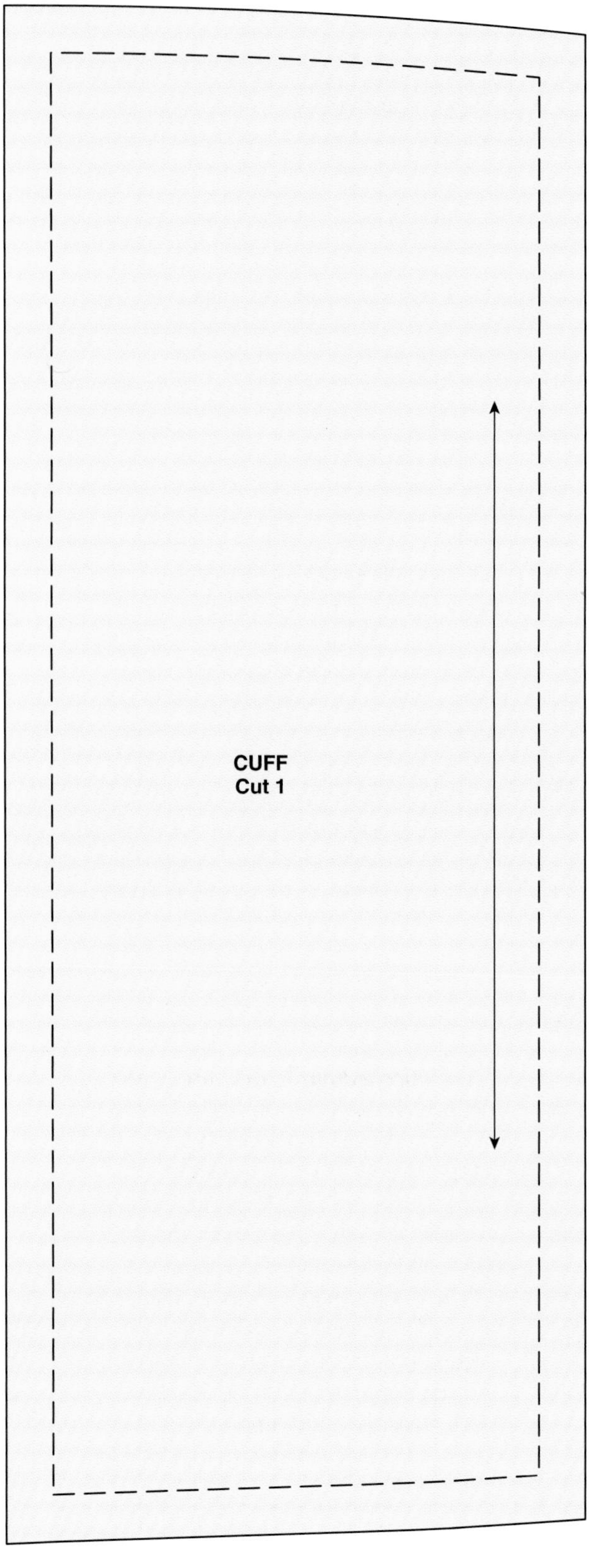

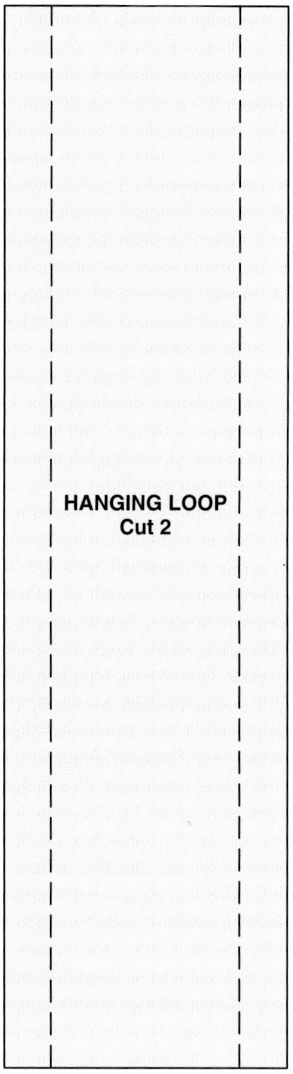

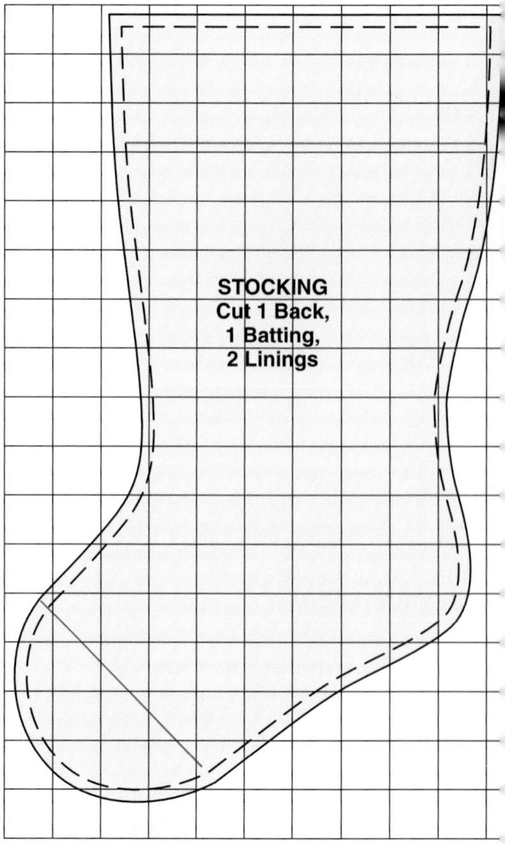

COUNTRY PATCHWORK STOCKING 1 Square = 1

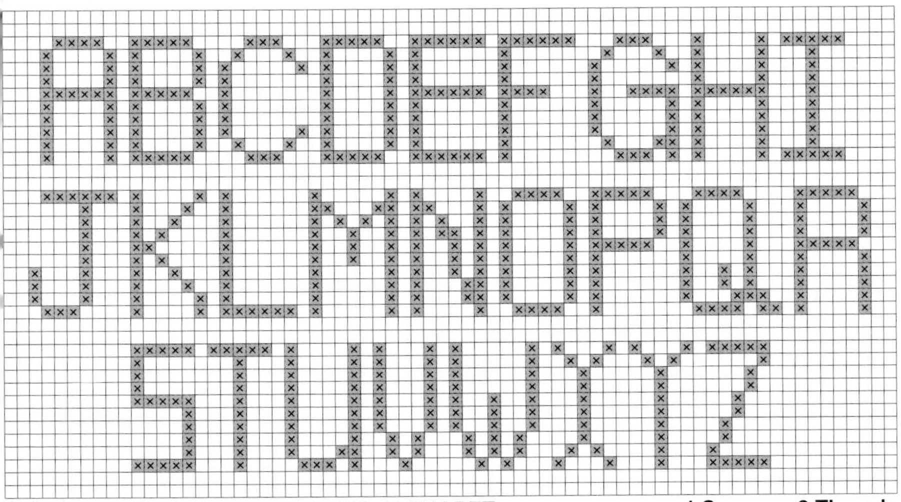

COUNTRY PATCHWORK STOCKING ALPHABET

1 Square = 3 Threads

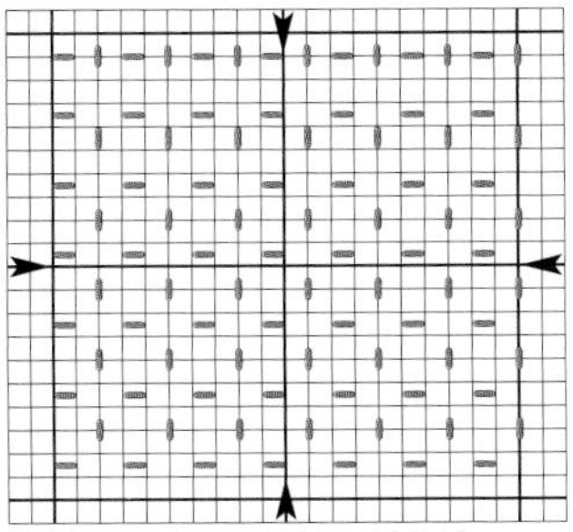

COUNTRY PATCHWORK STOCKING CUFF AND TOE
1 Square = 3 Threads

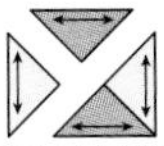

TRIANGLE BLOCK

PATCHWORK STOCKING		
ANCHOR		DMC
897	☒	902 Garnet
RUNNING STITCH		
903	/	640 Beige-gray #3 pearl cotton – background

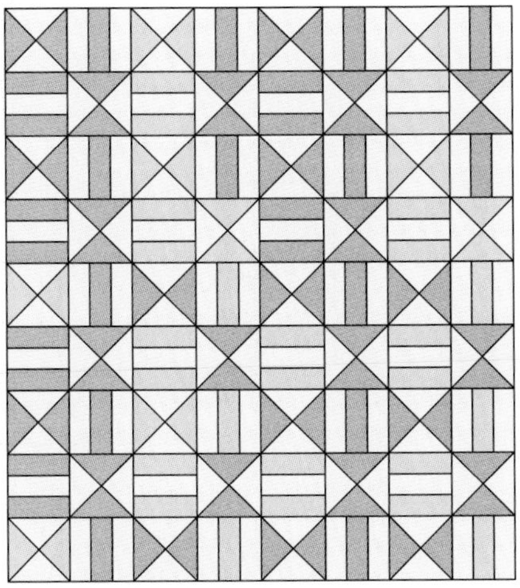

COUNTRY PATCHWORK ASSEMBLY DIAGRAM

For hanging loop, join long edges of strips. Turn right side out; fold in half widthwise. Run gathering stitches ½ inch from raw edges; pull to gather loop end. Slip end between lining and stocking at back seam. Slip-stitch lining to stocking top edge, securing loop.

Hardanger Stocking

As shown on page 108, stocking measures 18½x11¾ inches.

MATERIALS

FABRICS

25x18-inch piece of 20-count white Jobelan fabric
8x14-inch piece of 20-count white Jobelan fabric
½ yard of 45-inch-wide lightweight white twill fabric
½ yard of fusible knit interfacing
¼ yard of 45-inch-wide forest green cotton fabric
⅛ yard of red polyester or rayon jacquard

THREADS

#5 and #8 white pearl cotton
003 Kreinik red #4 braid
009 Kreinik green #4 braid
Sewing threads: white and red

SUPPLIES

Needle; embroidery hoop
9 red seed beads
5 yards of ⅛-inch-wide green satin ribbon
Tracing paper
Water-soluble fabric marking pen
Tailors' chalk pencil

INSTRUCTIONS

Tape or zigzag edges of Jobelan fabric to prevent fraying. To begin stocking front, measure 6½ inches from top and 3 inches in from left edge of 25x18-inch piece of fabric. Using #5 pearl cotton, begin first vertical row of four-sided backstitches there. For all stitches, refer to diagrams, *pages 116–118.*

Work all vertical and horizontal rows of block stitches. Referring to chart, *pages 116–117,* work basic Hardanger candy canes, wreaths, stars, trees, flowers, and gingerbread men using satin stitches and #5 pearl cotton. When satin stitch designs are completed, add red backstitch stripes to candy canes, green lazy daisies and red straight stitch star "flowers" to wreaths, green eyelets to stars, green and red straight stitch star "ornaments" and red treetop star to trees, red cross-stitches to flowers, green cross-stitch eyes, red backstitch mouth, and green backstitch "icing" trim to gingerbread men. Work red and green lazy daisy leaves and straight stitch star "flowers" as desired in partial squares along curved edges. Sew three red seed beads down front of gingerbread men for buttons.

Cut nine 2x2-inch squares of red fabric. Press under ⅛ inch along all edges. Using an appliqué stitch, hand-sew one red square to each unstitched square on stocking front.

Thread needle with green ribbon. Thread ribbon under horizontal and vertical rows of four-sided backstitches as on chart. Weave ribbon top to bottom and left to right, alternating horizontal and vertical rows. Leave 1-inch-long tails extending beyond each row.

Trace stocking outline, *pages 116–117,* onto tracing paper; cut out. Position tracing paper pattern atop stitchery, leaving approximately ⅝ inch between stitches and pattern along left and right edges. Trace around pattern using fabric marking pen. Stitch around stocking perimeter just inside marked outline. Cut out along outline; set stocking front aside.

For stitched cuff front, use 8x14-inch piece of Jobelan fabric and refer to chart, *page 118.* Measure 2½ inches in from 14-inch-long top edge and 2½ inches in from 8-inch-long left edge; begin stitching kloster blocks there. Use one ply of #5 pearl cotton to complete all kloster blocks and buttonhole edge around bottom of design. Work eyelets alternating green and red braid; give each a gentle tug to open hole.

Continued on page 118

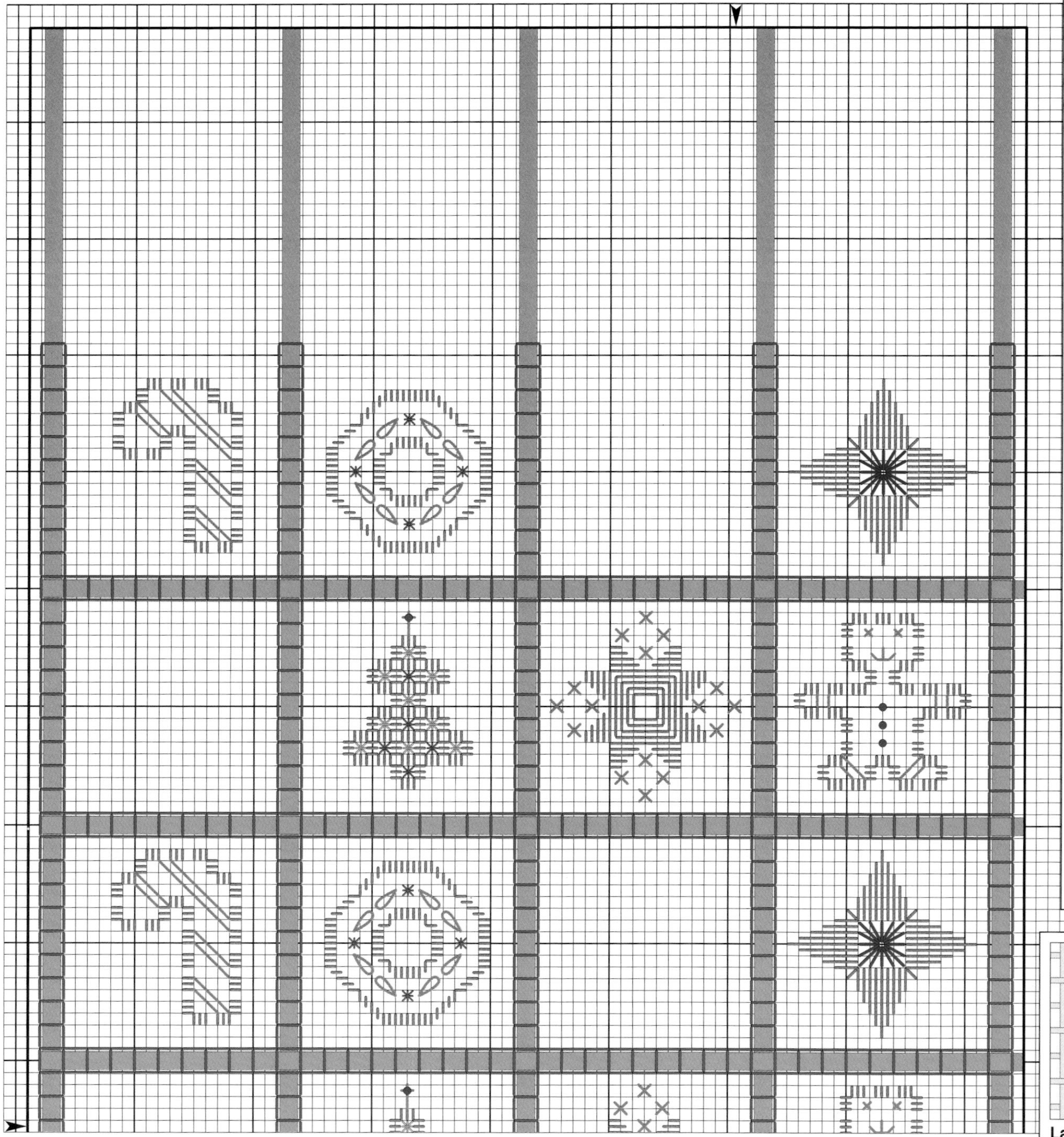

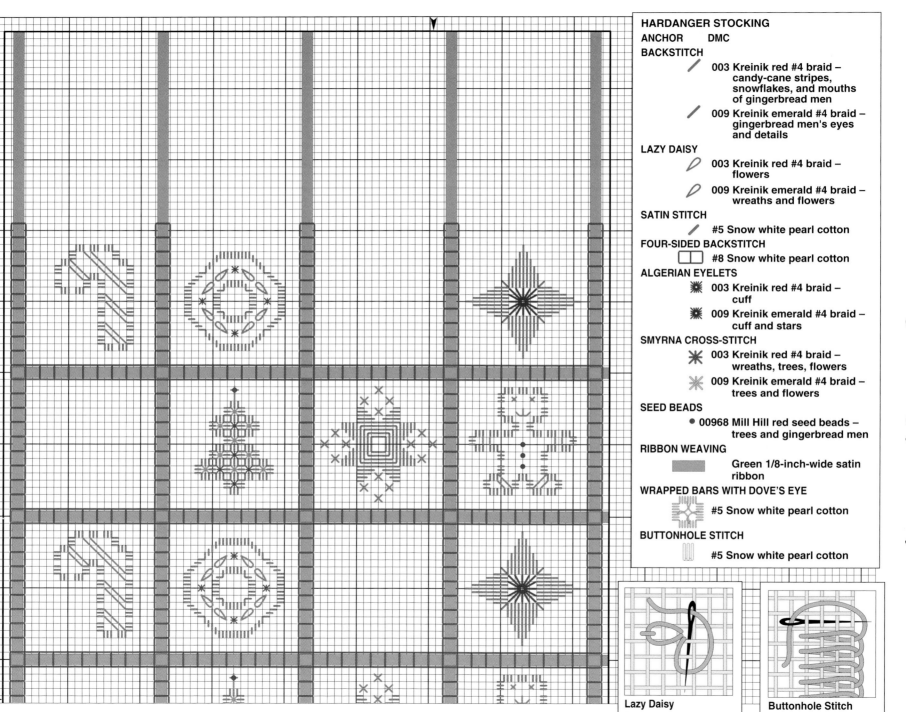

HARDANGER STOCKING

ANCHOR	DMC	
BACKSTITCH		
	003 Kreinik red #4 braid – candy-cane stripes, snowflakes, and mouths of gingerbread men	
	009 Kreinik emerald #4 braid – gingerbread men's eyes and details	
LAZY DAISY		
	003 Kreinik red #4 braid – flowers	
	009 Kreinik emerald #4 braid – wreaths and flowers	
SATIN STITCH		
	#5 Snow white pearl cotton	
FOUR-SIDED BACKSTITCH		
	#8 Snow white pearl cotton	
ALGERIAN EYELETS		
	003 Kreinik red #4 braid – cuff	
	009 Kreinik emerald #4 braid – cuff and stars	
SMYRNA CROSS-STITCH		
	003 Kreinik red #4 braid – wreaths, trees, flowers	
	009 Kreinik emerald #4 braid – trees and flowers	
SEED BEADS		
	00968 Mill Hill red seed beads – trees and gingerbread men	
RIBBON WEAVING		
	Green 1/8-inch-wide satin ribbon	
WRAPPED BARS WITH DOVE'S EYE		
	#5 Snow white pearl cotton	
BUTTONHOLE STITCH		
	#5 Snow white pearl cotton	

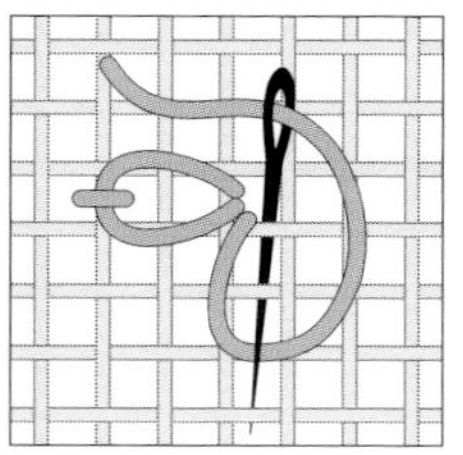

Lazy Daisy

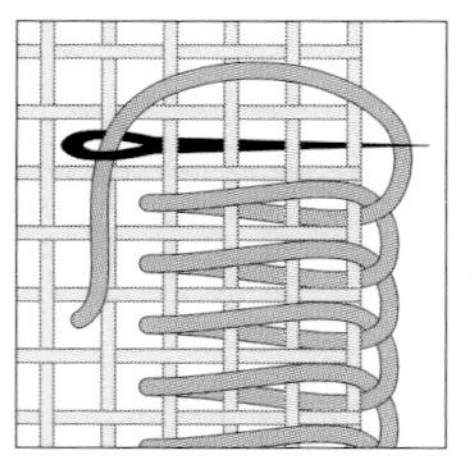

Buttonhole Stitch

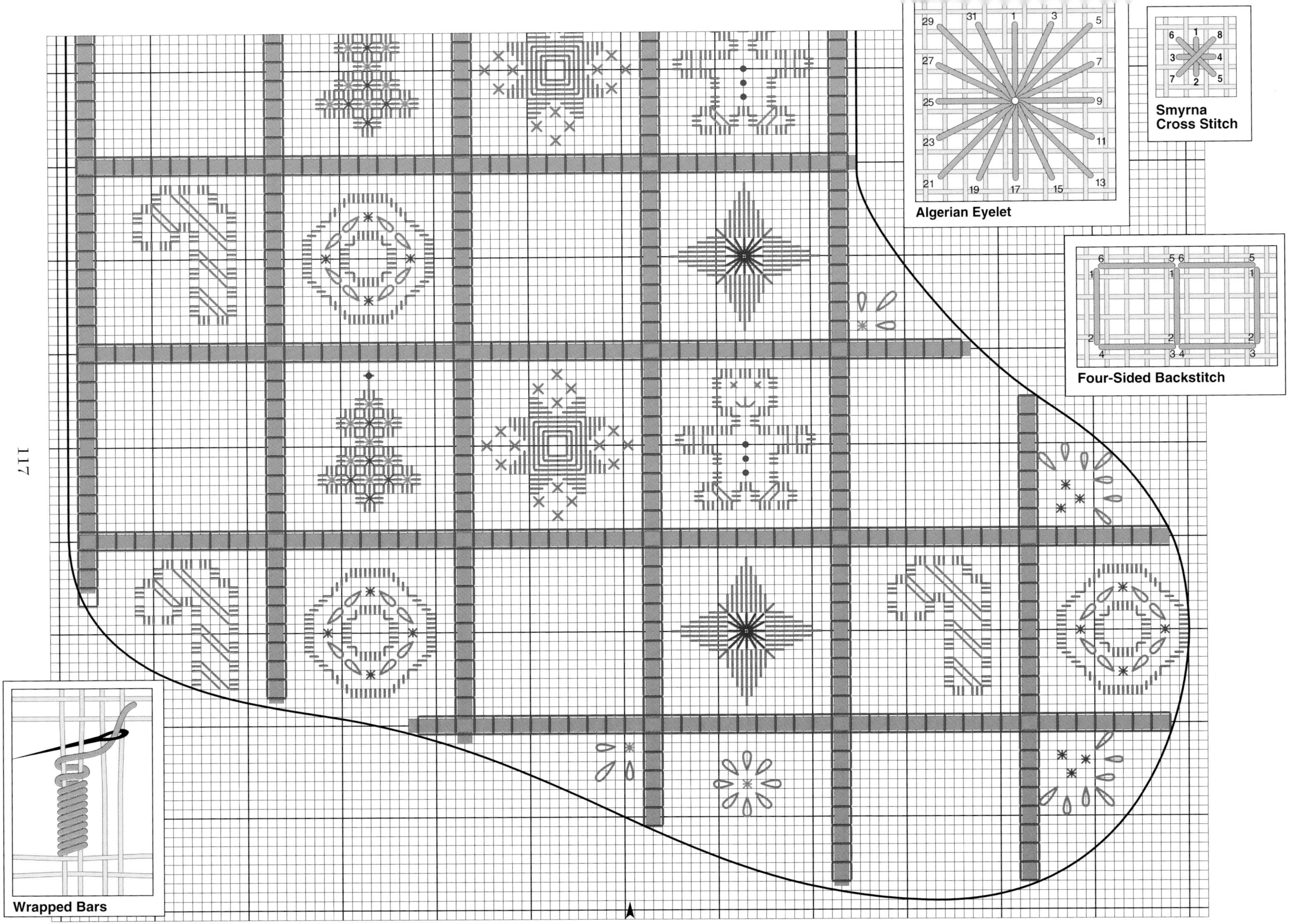

HARDANGER STOCKING

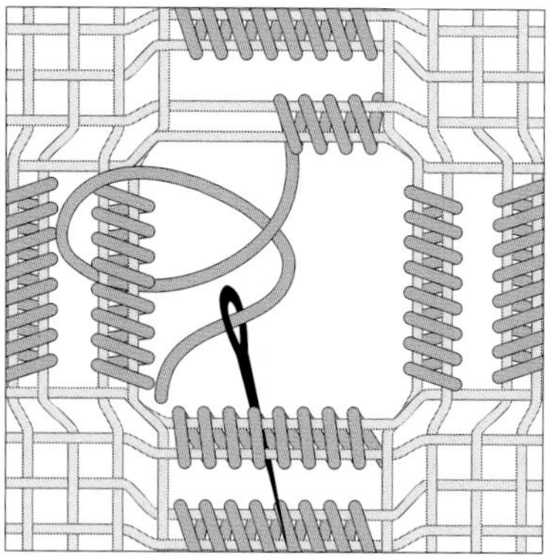

Wrapped Bars with Dove's Eye

Zigzag both edges of cuff as indicated on chart. Cut and remove threads between kloster blocks, referring to chart. Thread needle with one ply of #8 pearl cotton; wrap remaining threads, making divided wrapped bars with dove's eyes. Trim fabric along bottom edge, close to stitching.

Prewash white twill and green cotton fabrics. Soak the interfacing in warm water for 10 minutes to relax the fabric and remove excess fusing adhesive. Lay stocking front right side up atop adhesive side of interfacing and doubled thickness of twill fabric. Cut out interfacing and twill fabric to match stocking front. Fuse the interfacing to the wrong side of the stocking front, following the manufacturer's instructions.

Layer stocking front between right sides of twill pieces. Using zipper foot and shortened stitch length, join the pieces using an approximate ½-inch seam allowance. Sew alongside stitching on straight side edges. Turn the stocking right side out and check seamline; adjust if necessary. Turn the stocking wrong side out once again; trim seams to ¼ inch. Serge or zigzag seams to reduce bulk.

For cuff front lining, cut two pieces of green fabric slightly larger than Hardanger cuff piece. Layer green fabric with right sides facing. Pin Hardanger, wrong side up, atop green fabric. On green fabric, mark Hardanger cuff bottom outline using chalk pencil. Using tiny machine stitches, sew along the outline. Trim the seam allowance to ⅛ inch; trim and clip corners. Turn right side out and press. Pin the Hardanger cuff, right side up, atop green cuff lining and trim the top and sides of lining to match.

For cuff back, cut 7×9¼-inch piece of white twill. Fold in half to measure 3½×9¼ inches; press. Pin the lined cuff front to cuff back, with right sides facing and raw edges matching. Sew side seams and zigzag or serge edges.

Place cuff inside stocking, matching fronts to backs, with right side of cuff facing wrong side of stocking. Sew cuff to stocking; finish seam. Turn cuff out and press.

For hanging loop, cut a 1×8-inch-long strip of green fabric. Sew long sides together using a ¼-inch seam allowance; trim seam and turn right side out. Match ends and tack to inside of stocking along seam, allowing loop to extend 1½ inches beyond top of stocking.

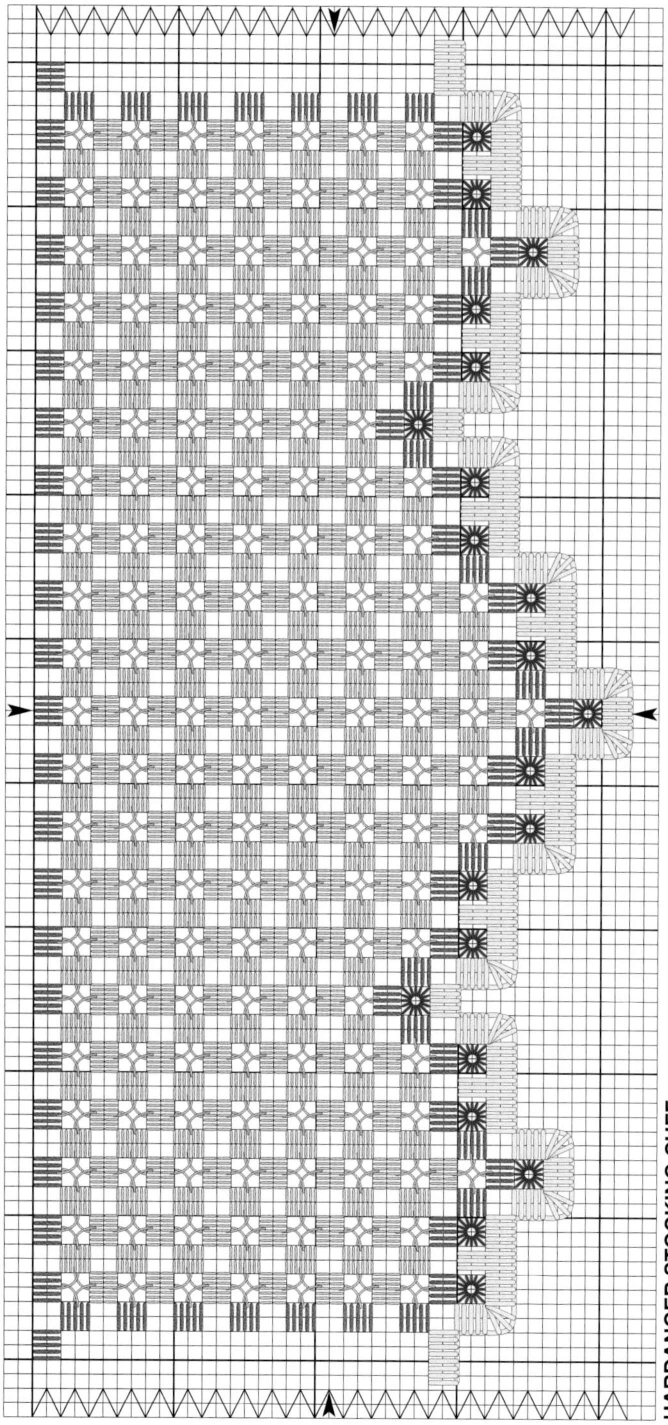

HARDANGER STOCKING CUFF

Nutcracker Stocking

As shown on page 109, the stocking is 16 inches tall.

MATERIALS

FABRICS

22x16-inch piece of 28-count tan Jobelan fabric
½ yard of green velvet
½ yard of desired lining fabric
14x20-inch piece of fusible fleece
½ yard of red velvet

THREADS

Cotton embroidery floss in colors listed in key
Blending filament in colors listed in key
Metallic threads in colors listed in key
Braid in colors listed in key

SUPPLIES

Needle
Embroidery hoop
Water-soluble fabric marker
50 inches of ¼-inch-diameter cotton cording
Seed beads in colors listed in key
Pom-poms in colors listed in key
Hot-glue gun; hot-glue sticks

INSTRUCTIONS

Tape or zigzag edges of Jobelan fabric to prevent fraying. Find center of chart and of fabric; begin stitching there.

Use two plies of embroidery floss or blending filament or one ply of metallic thread or braid to work all stitches over two threads of fabric, unless otherwise noted in key. Attach beads using one ply of coordinating floss. Press the finished stitchery from the back.

Use fabric marker to draw outline around stitched area as indicated on chart, *pages 120–121*. Follow manufacturer's directions to fuse fleece to back of stitchery. Cut out stitched stocking front ½ inch beyond outline. Using stocking front as pattern, cut one green velvet back and two lining pieces. Cut a 6×2½-inch piece of red velvet; set aside. From remainder, cut

Continued on page 122

NUTCRACKER BALLET STOCKING

ANCHOR	DMC
002	000 White
403	310 Black
400	317 Pewter
399	318 Steel
9046	321 Christmas red
288	445 Light lemon
055	604 Cranberry
891	676 Light old gold
226	702 Christmas green
890	729 Medium old gold
314	741 Tangerine
128	775 Baby blue
310	780 Deep topaz
307	783 Christmas gold
359	801 Coffee brown
043	815 Garnet
164	824 Deep bright blue
161	826 Medium bright blue
204	913 Nile green
881	945 Ivory
1001	976 Medium golden brown
246	986 Forest green
292	3078 Pale lemon
060	3688 Medium mauve
049	3689 Light mauve
035	3705 Watermelon
1008	3773 Rose beige
874	3822 Straw
363	3827 Pale golden brown
	001C Kreinik Silver cord
	002 Kreinik Gold #8 braid
	032 Kreinik Pearl blending filament
	127 Kreinik Yellow orange #8 braid

BLENDED NEEDLE

ANCHOR	DMC
002	000 White (1X) and 001C Kreinik Silver cord (1X)
002	000 White (1X) and 100 Kreinik White blending filament (1X)
002	000 White (1X) and 091 Kreinik Star yellow blending filament (1X)
002	000 White (1X) and 032 Kreinik Pearl blending filament (1X)
289	307 True lemon (1X) and 091 Kreinik Star yellow blending filament (1X)
9046	321 Christmas red (1X) and 003C Kreinik Red cord (1X)
305	725 True topaz (1X) and 028 Kreinik Citron blending filament (1X)
162	825 Dark bright blue (1X) and 051C Kreinik Sapphire cord (1X)
205	911 Medium emerald (1X) and 008 Kreinik Green blending filament (1X)
060	3688 Medium mauve (1X) and 093 Kreinik Star mauve blending filament (1X)
049	3689 Light mauve (1X) and 093 Kreinik Star mauve blending filament (1X)
923	3818 Deep emerald (1X) and 008 Kreinik Green blending filament (1X)

BACKSTITCH

ANCHOR	DMC
403	310 Black–Nutcracker's hair, mustache, and chin, girl's eyes
9046	321 Christmas red– mouths of girl, ballerina, dancer, and jester
359	801 Coffee brown– mouse king's jacket and pants, girl's hair, jester's hat, shirt, and pants, dancer's hat, belt, and pants, candle flames
043	815 Garnet– mouse king's cape
161	826 Medium bright blue– ballerina's eyes
236	3799 Charcoal– all remaining stitches

BLENDED BACKSTITCH

ANCHOR	DMC
400	317 Pewter (1X) and 019 Kreinik Pewter blending filament (1X)– ballerina's outfit
9046	321 Christmas red (1X) and 003C Kreinik Red cord (1X)– jester's collar, belt, cuffs, and shoes, trim on dancer's shirt, Nutcracker's outfit
128	775 Baby blue (1X) and 019 Kreinik Pewter blending filament (1X)– girl's nightgown
162	825 Dark bright blue (1X) and 051C Kreinik Sapphire cord (1X)– Nutcracker, trim on jester's clothing
218	890 Pistachio (1X) and 008 Kreinik Green blending filament (1X)– tree, mouse king's jacket, dancer's shirt and shoes

STRAIGHT STITCH

ANCHOR	DMC
002	000 White–snowflakes above tree
403	310 Black–eyes
236	3799 Charcoal–mouse king's whiskers
	001C Kreinik Silver cord – ballerina's headpiece (2x)
	001P Kreinik Silver cable – ballerina's pom-poms (1X)

BLENDED STRAIGHT STITCH

ANCHOR	DMC
400	317 Pewter (1X) and 019 Kreinik Pewter blending filament (1X)– ballerina's slippers
9046	321 Christmas red (1X) and 003C Kreinik Red cord (1X)– jester's belt fringe

DIAMOND EYELET

ANCHOR	DMC
002	000 White–snowflakes above tree

SATIN STITCH

ANCHOR	DMC
403	310 Black–mouse king's eye (2X)

COUCHING

284 DMC Metallic gold embroidery thread (2X)

SMYRNA CROSS

001C Kreinik Silver cord (2X)

POM-POMS

5mm Red–jester
5mm White–ballerina's wands

SEED BEADS

00161 Mill Hill Crystal glass beads
00479 Mill Hill White glass beads
02003 Mill Hill Peach creme glass beads
5118 Wichelt Whimsy Cranberry glass beads

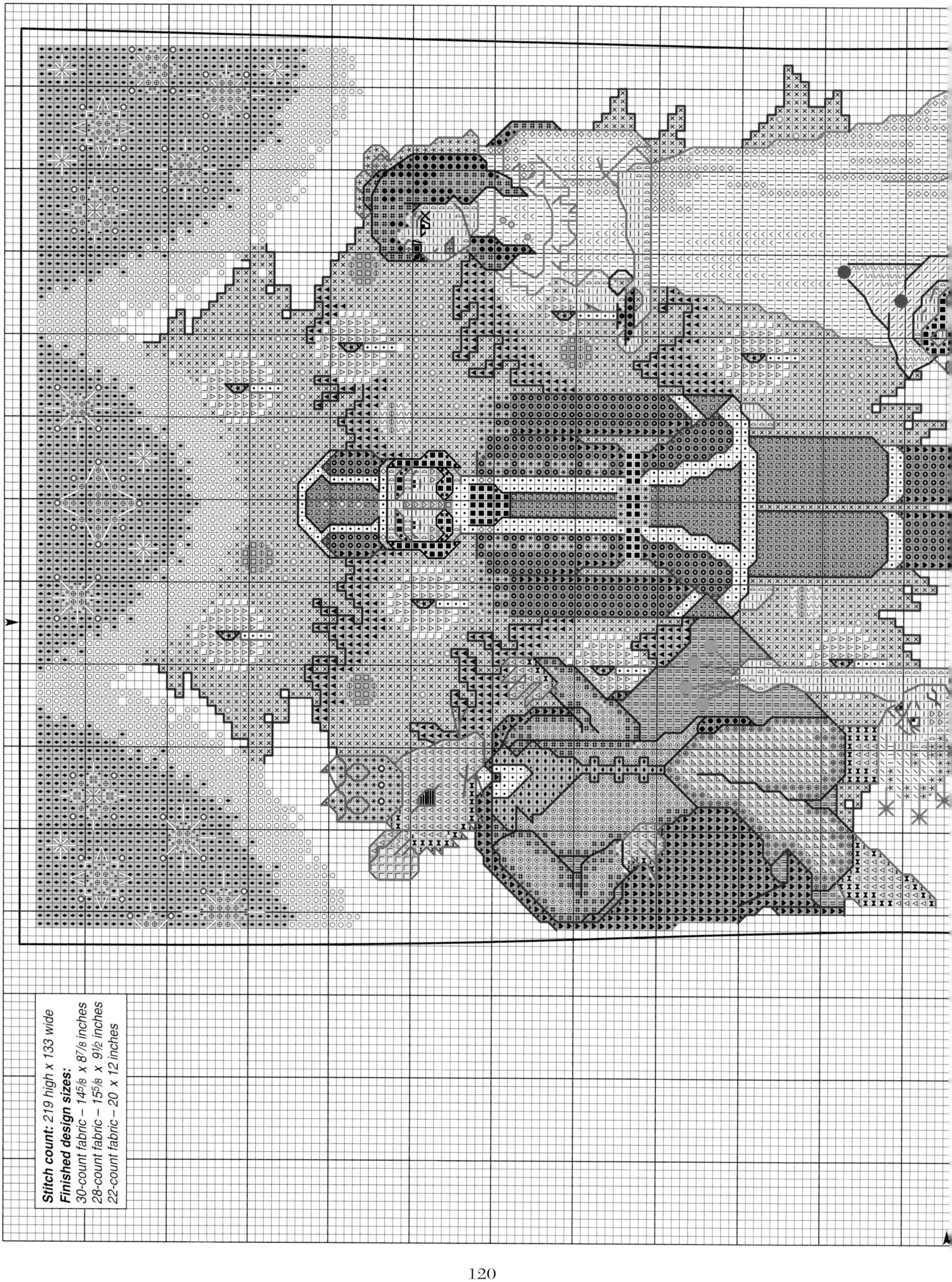

Stitch count: *219 high x 133 wide*
Finished design sizes:
30-count fabric – 14 5/8 x 8 7/8 inches
28-count fabric – 15 5/8 x 9 1/2 inches
22-count fabric – 20 x 12 inches

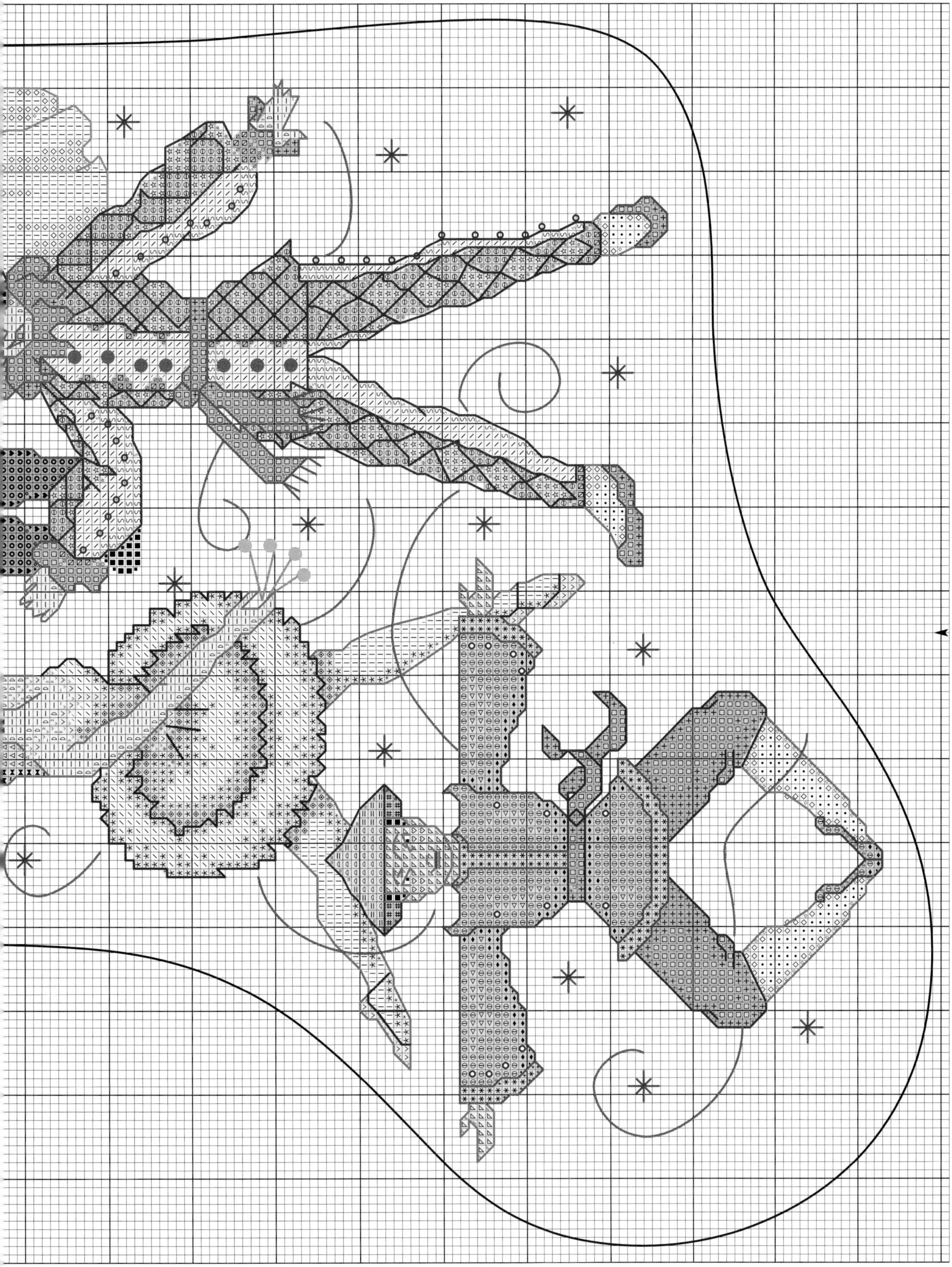

2-inch-wide bias strips to total 55 inches. Sew bias strips end to end. Center cording lengthwise on wrong side of velvet strip. Fold fabric around cording, raw edges together. Use zipper foot to sew through both layers, close to cord. Trim seam allowance to ¼ inch.

Baste piping around stocking front along sides and bottom edges. Sew stocking front to back, leaving top open, using ½ inch seam allowance. Trim and clip seam; turn right side out.

Sew 8-inch-long piece of piping around top edge of stocking. Butt ends at stocking back; secure ends with hand stitches.

Turn under ½ inch along long sides of 6×2½-inch velvet hanging loop piece. Fold strip in half lengthwise and stitch close to folded edges. Sew hanging loop to piping at back seam of stocking.

Sew lining front to back, leaving an opening along bottom edge for turning. Slip the stocking into the lining, right sides facing. Turn under raw edge of lining and stitch to top of stocking. Pull stocking through lining opening; slipstitch opening closed. Tuck stocking into lining. Attach the pom-poms to finished stocking using hot glue.

Crocheted Candy-Cane Stocking

As shown on page 110, stocking measures about 20 inches long.

MATERIALS

Berella "4", "100% Monsanto acrylic" worsted-weight yarn (3.5-oz/100-gm. skein): one skein each of geranium (8929) and winter white (8941)

Size 8/H (5.00 mm) aluminum crochet hook or size to obtain gauge

GAUGE: In hdc stripes, 13 sts and 9 rows = 4 inches.

INSTRUCTIONS

Note: The striped pattern is worked in hdc. To change color in hdc, yo and draw up a lp with present color in last st before change, with new color, yo and draw through all 3 lps on hook. The checked cuff is worked in dc; to change color in dc, with present color make a dc in last st before change until 2 lps rem on hook; with new color, yo and draw through both lps on hook.

STOCKING

Beginning at top and below the cuff, with red, ch 49. Sc in second ch from hook and each ch across = 48 sts; keeping this row untwisted, join with sl st in first sc.

Rnd 1: With red, ch 2 (counts as hdc), hdc in each of next 2 sts changing to white; * (1 white hdc, 1 red hdc) twice, 1 white hdc **, 3 red hdc); rep from * around, ending last rep at **; join with sl st in second ch of beginning ch-2.

Rep Rnd 1 for candy cane pat until piece measures 9 inches from beginning. Fasten off colors.

Heel: With the RS facing, join red with sl st in tenth st to right of joining. Ch 1, sc in same st as join and in each of next 19 sts; turn.

Row 2: Ch 1, sc in 13 sts; turn.

Row 3: Ch 1, sc in 6 sts; turn.

Row 4: Ch 1, sc in 7 sts; turn.

Row 5: Ch 1, sc in 8 sts; turn.

Row 6: Ch 1, sc in 9 sts; turn.

Rows 7-17: Cont as est, working one more sc at end of every row = 20 sts after Row 17. Fasten off.

Sole: With the RS facing, join red with sl st in fifteenth sc from right edge of heel. Ch 2 (counts as hdc), with red, hdc in next 2 sts and change to white; 1 white hdc, 1 red hdc, 1 white hdc; sk first 4 sts along side of stocking, then work hdc around as follows: (1 red, 1 white, 3 red, 1 white, 1 red, 1 white) twice, 1 red, 1 white, 2 red, sk 4 sts along side of stocking, working on rem heel sts work 1 red, (1 white, 1 red) twice, 1 white, 3 red, (1 white, 1 red) twice, 1 white; join = 40 sts.

Rnds 2-12: Work around in striped pat. After Rnd 12, fasten off white.

Toe: Ch 1, sc in each hdc around, dec 4 sts evenly spaced = 36 sts; join.

Rnd 2: Ch 1, (sc in 4 sc, sc 2 tog) around = 30 sts; join.

Rnd 3: Ch 1, (sc in 3 sc, sc 2 tog) around = 24 sts; join.

Rnd 4: Rep Rnd 2 = 20 sts.

Rnd 5: Rep Rnd 3 = 16 sts.

Rnd 6: Ch 1, (sc in 2 sc, sc 2 tog) around = 12 sts; join.

Rnd 7: Ch 1, (sc in sc, sc 2 tog) around = 8 sts; join.

Rnd 8: (Sc 2 tog) around = 4 sts.

Leaving an 8-inch tail, fasten off. Weave tail through sts and pull up to close opening. Secure in place.

Cuff: With the RS facing and working along opposite edge of foundation ch, join red with sl st in first ch. Ch 3 (counts as dc), 1 red dc in each of next 2 ch and change to white; * 1 white dc in each of next 3 ch ** and change to red, 1 red dc in each of next 3 ch and change to white; rep from * around, ending last rep at **; join with sl st in third ch of beg ch-3.

Rnd 2: With white, ch 3 (counts as dc), 1 white dc in each of next 2 dc; * 3 red dc, 3 white dc; rep from * around, ending with 3 red dc; join.

Rnd 3: With red, ch 3 (counts as dc), 1 red dc in each of next 2 dc; * 3 white dc, 3 red dc; rep from * around, ending with 3 white dc; join. Fasten off white.

Rnd 4: With red, ch 1, sc in each dc around; join.

Rnd 5: Ch 1, sl st in each sc around and fasten off.

Finishing: Close openings at heel and cuff. For hanging loops; join white with sl st at top seam; ch 20; remove hook. Join red with sl st at top seam; ch 20; remove hook. Twist chs around each other; insert hook into last ch of each color and join to top of cuff with sl st; fasten off.

Pom-poms (make two): Holding red and white yarns tog, wrap around palm of hand fifteen times. Tie a separate strand tightly around center; clip lps at each edge. Trim to form.

With the RS facing, join white near hanging lp; ch 20 and fasten off. Rep with red. Tie a pom-pom to each ch and twist chs around one another. Attach a third pom-pom to toe of stocking, if desired.

Tiny Felt Stockings

As shown on page 110, each stocking measures 4½×3½ inches.

MATERIALS

Tracing paper
10x12-inch piece of antique white felt
8x10-inch piece of dark denim blue felt
8x10-inch piece of mustard yellow felt
6x6-inch piece of cranberry red felt
3½x5-inch piece of hunter green felt
3x2½-inch piece of cinnamon brown felt
Cotton embroidery floss: mustard yellow, brick red, hunter green, medium brown, ecru, and black
Size 20 chenille needle
Nine ¼-inch-diameter white 4-hole buttons
Hot-glue gun
Two 16-mm gold acrylic stars
12 inches of ⅛-inch-wide green metallic ribbon
Paint pens: gold glitter, dark green, and dark red
1½ yards of ivory rattail cord

INSTRUCTIONS

Trace one full stocking and each individual piece from patterns, *right and page 124*, onto tracing paper; cut out.

For Starry Night Stocking, cut two blue stockings, cuff and bottom large star from antique white, top large star from yellow, and small star from red felt.

For Gingerbread Stocking, cut two yellow stockings, cuff from antique white, and gingerbread from brown.

For Snowperson Stocking, cut two blue stockings, large snowman shape from yellow, and cuff, snow, and smaller snowman shape from antique white.

For Present Under the Tree Stocking, cut two antique white stockings, large tree shape from yellow, smaller tree shape from green, and cuff and present from red.

For Stars and Stripes Stocking, cut two red stockings, stripes from green, stars from yellow, and cuff from antique white.

Use six plies of floss threaded through chenille needle for all stitching. Refer to patterns on this page and page 124 as a guide for positioning the pieces on the stocking fronts.

For Starry Night Stocking, stitch top yellow star in place using evenly spaced ecru straight stitches. Stitch antique white star in place with red blanket stitch. Secure red star in place with a yellow French knot in each point. Sew button at each X, using green floss. Work a green running stitch circle around each button. Work French knots over remainder of stocking front at dots. Position stocking front to back, with cuff in place. Use ecru floss to sew pieces together, leaving stocking top open. Personalize cuff with paint pen. Hot-glue rattail ends together inside outer edge of stocking for hanging loop.

For Gingerbread Stocking, decorate gingerbread man with black French knot eyes, red straight stitch mouth, yellow French knot buttons, and yellow straight stitches across feet and hands. Sew figure to stocking front using evenly spaced ecru straight stitches. Sew button at each X, using brown floss. Work a green running stitch circle around each button. Sew cuff, front, and back together using brown blanket stitches and add hanging loop as for Starry Night Stocking. Personalize the cuff with paint pen.

For Snowperson Stocking, decorate white snowman figure with green French knot eyes and buttons and a red straight stitch mouth. Sew figure to larger yellow snowman using evenly spaced ecru straight stitches. Sew snow to stocking front bottom using green running stitches along top edge only. Blanket-stitch snowman to front with red

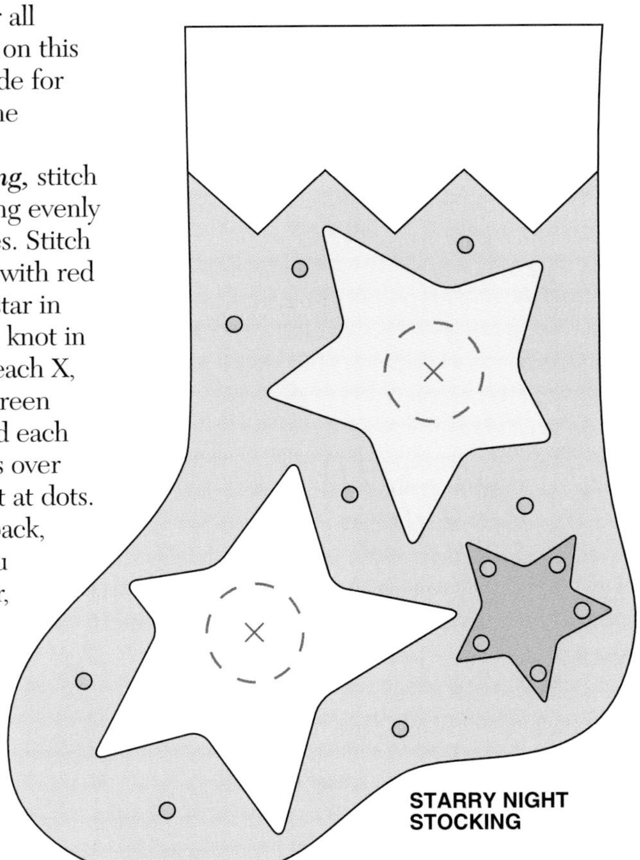

STARRY NIGHT STOCKING

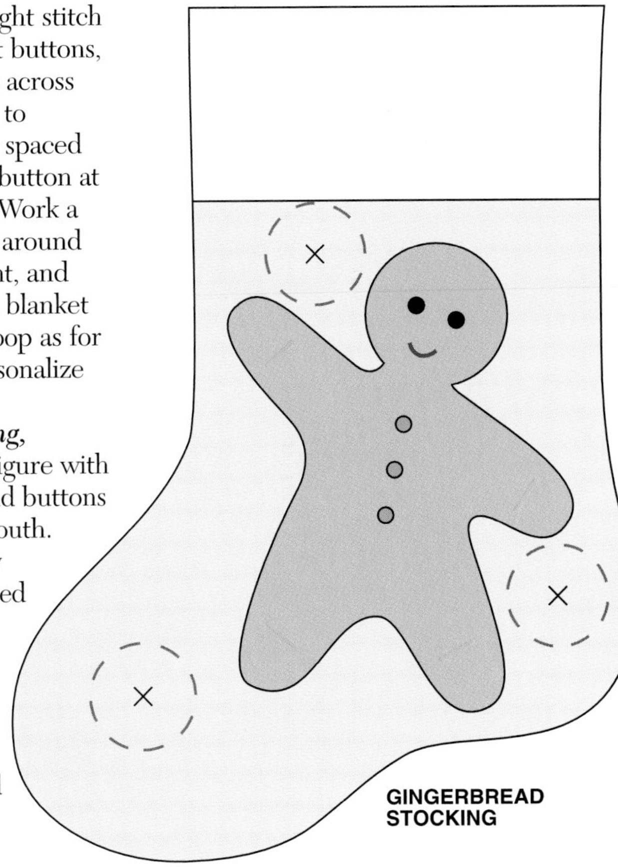

GINGERBREAD STOCKING

floss. Make straight stitch arms and hands using red. Work ecru French knots at dots for snowflakes. Sew cuff, bottom edge of snow, stocking front, and back together using yellow blanket stitches and add hanging loop as for Starry Night Stocking. Personalize cuff with paint pen.

For Present Under the Tree Stocking, affix small tree atop large tree by stitching buttons in place at Xs, using red floss. Add red, white, and gold French knots at dots, using colors randomly. Sew tree to stocking front using evenly spaced red straight stitches. Attach present with running stitches up through center; tie floss bow at top. Sew cuff, front, and back together using green blanket stitches and add hanging loop as for Starry Night Stocking. Glue gold acrylic star to tree top. Personalize cuff with paint pen.

For Stars and Stripes Stocking, sew green stripes in place using evenly spaced yellow straight stitches. Affix stars by stitching a button to each center at X, using green floss. Work a red French knot in each point. Blanket-stitch top and bottom of cuff to stocking front using green floss. Sew front to back using yellow blanket stitches, making sure to catch sides of cuff. Add hanging loop as for other stockings. Personalize cuff with paint pen.

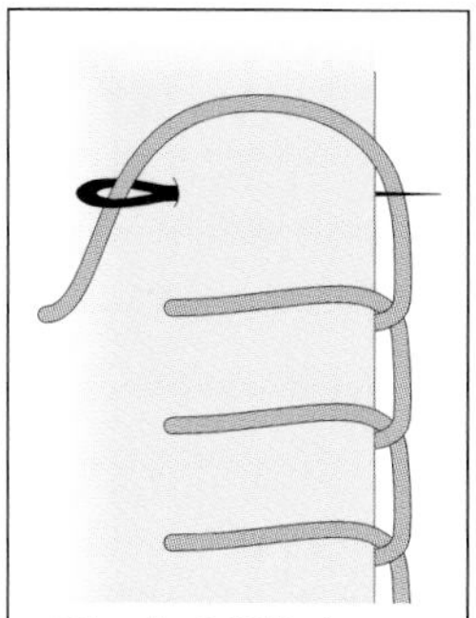

Blanket Stitch

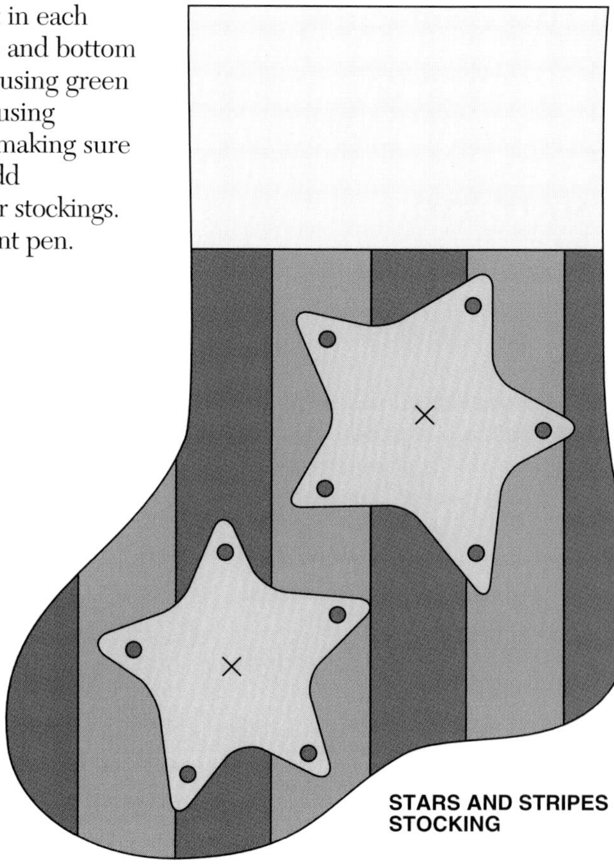

STARS AND STRIPES STOCKING

SNOWPERSON STOCKING

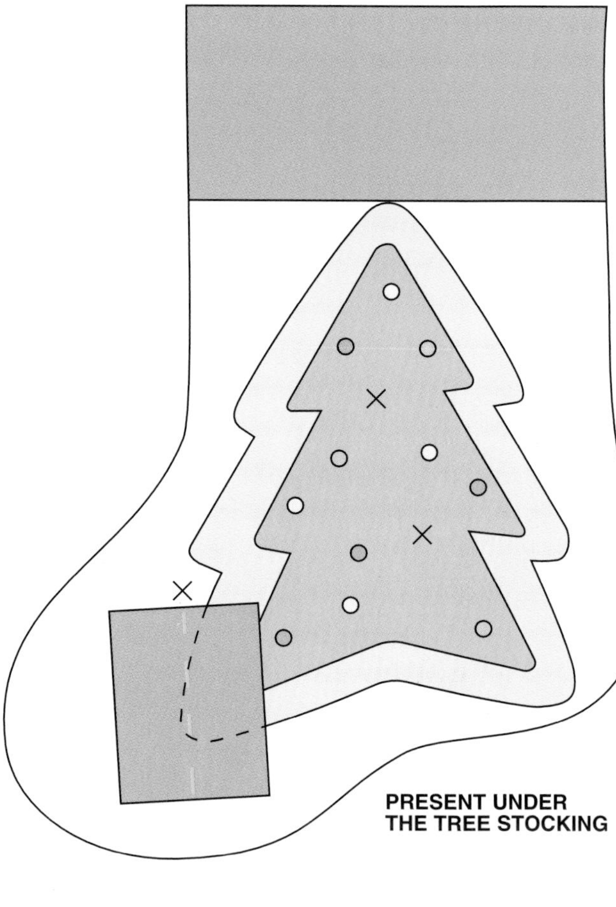

PRESENT UNDER THE TREE STOCKING

All I Want for Christmas

Visions of sugarplums dance in their heads while you're making their dreams come true. In this chapter, you'll find dolls, toys, and goodies for all the little ones on your list—gifts you make that they will treasure and love for a lifetime.

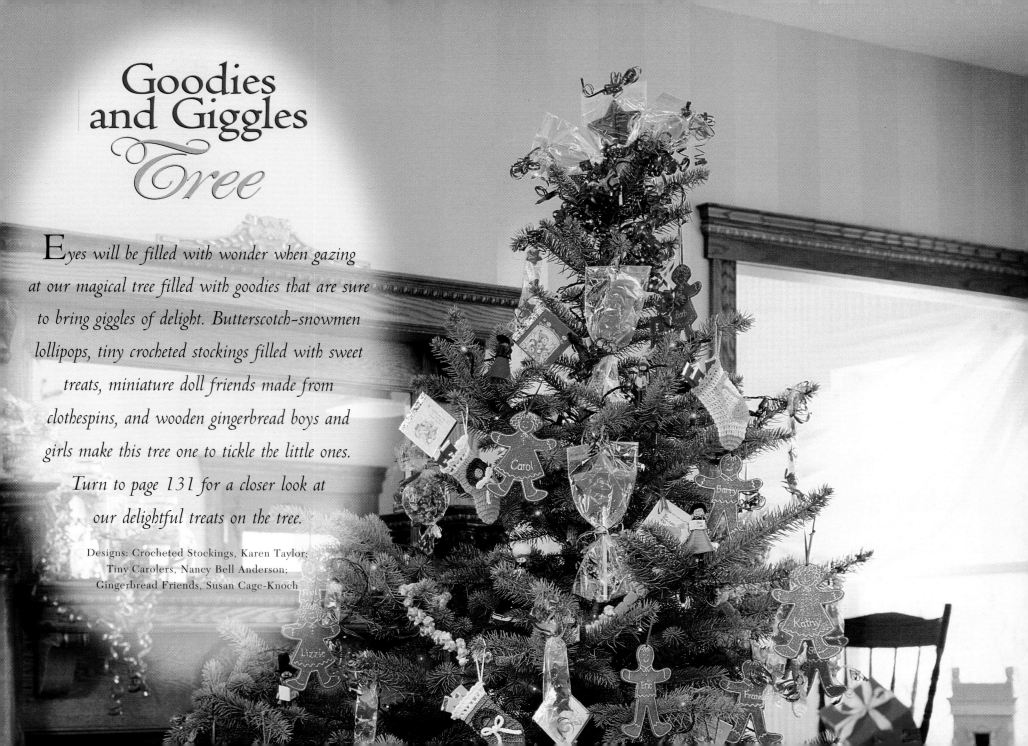

Goodies and Giggles Tree

Eyes will be filled with wonder when gazing at our magical tree filled with goodies that are sure to bring giggles of delight. Butterscotch-snowmen lollipops, tiny crocheted stockings filled with sweet treats, miniature doll friends made from clothespins, and wooden gingerbread boys and girls make this tree one to tickle the little ones.

Turn to page 131 for a closer look at our delightful treats on the tree.

Designs: Crocheted Stockings, Karen Taylor; Tiny Carolers, Nancy Bell Anderson; Gingerbread Friends, Susan Cage-Knoch

Faux Gingerbread *Friends*

Gingerbread people made of wood and paint open their arms to wish that special boy or girl a Merry Christmas. Make these wooden treats even more special by personalizing them with the child's name written with a paint pen. Instructions and patterns are on page 133.

Designs: Susan Cage-Knoch

Christmas Twins

Little Signa and Bjorn are all dressed up for Christmas in their best holiday bib and tucker. The fabric twins are made from cross-stitch fabric with tiny motifs cross-stitched on their sweet removable clothing. Instructions, patterns, and charts begin on page 133.

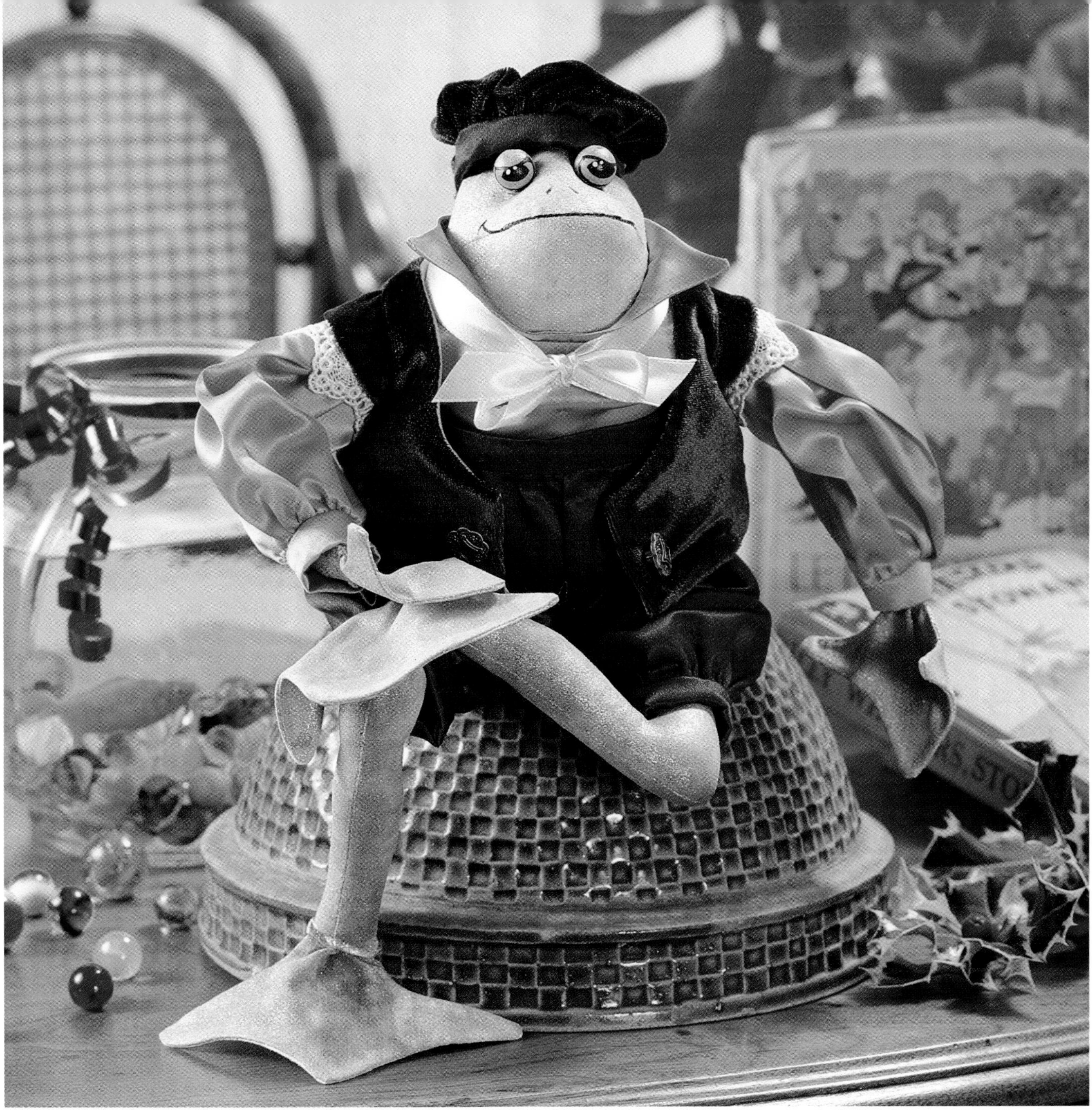

Freddy the *Frog Prince*

Who could resist kissing this magical frog prince? Freddy has personality-plus and is made from muslin, then painted with shimmering green paint. His fancy satin shirt, vest, trousers, and beret make this frog a prince of a fellow. Full-size patterns and instructions start on page 136.

Design: Susan Cage-Knoch

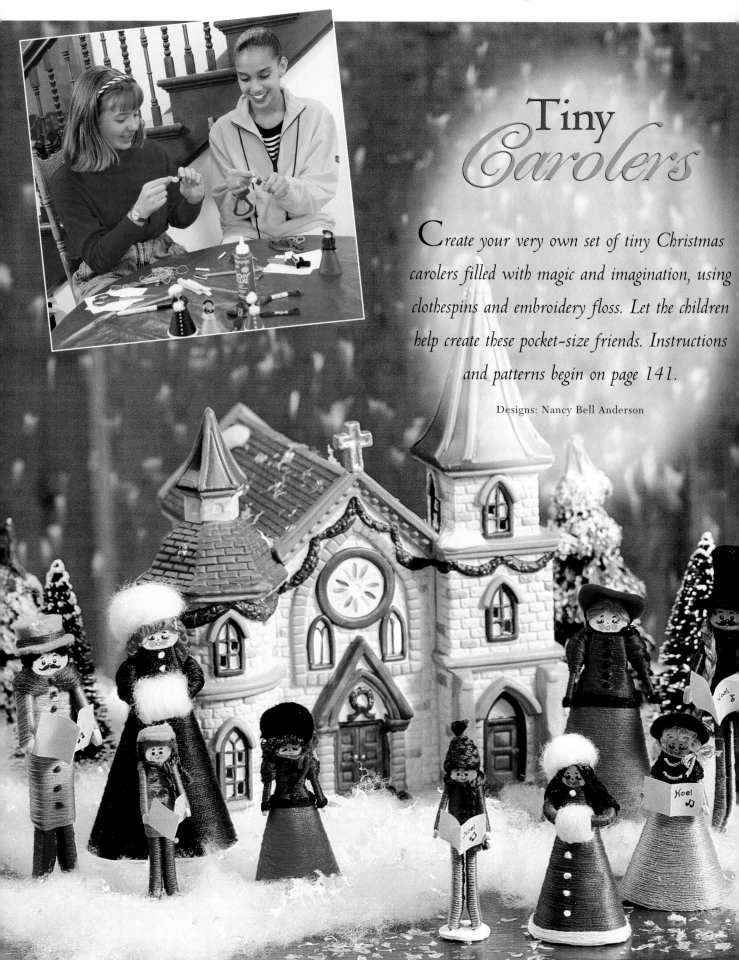

Tiny *Carolers*

Create your very own set of tiny Christmas carolers filled with magic and imagination, using clothespins and embroidery floss. Let the children help create these pocket-size friends. *Instructions and patterns begin on page 141.*

Designs: Nancy Bell Anderson

Butterscotch Lollipops

Shown on pages 126–127.

INGREDIENTS

- **1 cup sugar**
- **¼ cup light-colored corn syrup**
- **2 tablespoons water**
- **1½ teaspoons vinegar**
- **¼ cup butter, cut into 8 pieces**
- **¼ teaspoon vanilla**
- **Lollipop sticks and molds**

METHOD

Butter the sides of a heavy 1-quart saucepan. In the saucepan combine the sugar, corn syrup, water, and vinegar. Cook over medium-high heat to boiling, stirring constantly with a wooden spoon to dissolve sugar. This should take about 5 minutes. Avoid splashing mixture on the sides of pan. Carefully clip candy thermometer to side of pan.

Cook over medium heat, stirring constantly, while adding the ¼ cup butter, two pieces at a time. Continue cooking over medium heat, stirring occasionally, till thermometer registers 300°, hard-crack stage. Mixture should boil at a moderate, steady rate over the entire surface. Reaching hard-crack stage should take 25 to 30 minutes.

Remove saucepan from heat; remove thermometer from saucepan. Stir in vanilla. For each lollipop, insert a lollipop stick into mold. Spoon cooked mixture into mold. Repeat with remaining sticks and cooked mixture. Let stand to cool completely. Makes 24 to 36 lollipops.

Yummy Caramel Corn

Shown on pages 126–127.

INGREDIENTS

- **8 cups popped popcorn**
- **¾ cup packed brown sugar**
- **⅓ cup butter**
- **3 tablespoons light-colored corn syrup**
- **¼ teaspoon baking soda**
- **¼ teaspoon vanilla**
- **1½ cups miniature candy-coated milk chocolate pieces**

METHOD

Remove all unpopped kernels from popped corn. Place popcorn in a greased 17×12×2-inch baking pan. Keep popcorn warm in a 300° oven while making caramel mixture.

Butter the sides of a heavy 1½-quart saucepan. In saucepan combine brown sugar, butter, and corn syrup. Cook and stir over medium heat to boiling. Clip candy thermometer to side of pan. Cook and stir over medium heat to 255°, hard-ball stage (about 4 minutes).

Remove saucepan from heat. Stir in baking soda and vanilla; pour over popcorn. Stir gently to coat. Bake in a 300° oven for 15 minutes; stir. Bake 5 minutes more. Transfer popcorn mixture to a large piece of foil; cool completely. Break into clusters. Toss together with chocolate pieces. Store tightly covered. Makes about 10 cups (10 servings).

Crystal Candies

Shown on pages 126–127.

INGREDIENTS

- **2 cups sugar**
- **1 cup light-colored corn syrup**
- **½ cup water**
- **¼ teaspoon desired food coloring**
- **2 to 4 drops oil of cinnamon or oil of peppermint**
- **Candy molds**

METHOD

Butter the sides of a heavy 2-quart saucepan. In saucepan combine sugar, corn syrup, and water. Cook over medium-high heat to boiling, stirring constantly with a wooden spoon to dissolve sugar. This should take about 5 minutes. Avoid splashing mixture on sides of pan. Carefully clip candy thermometer to side of the saucepan.

Cook over medium heat, stirring occasionally, till thermometer registers 290°, soft-crack stage. Mixture should boil at a moderate, steady rate over the entire surface. Reaching soft-crack stage should take 20 to 25 minutes. Remove the saucepan from heat; remove candy thermometer from the saucepan.

Quickly stir in desired food coloring and flavoring. Immediately pour mixture into oiled molds made for hard candies. Cool 10 minutes or till firm. Invert; twist molds till candies come out. Cool completely. (Or pour mixture into a well-buttered 8×8-inch baking pan. Cool 10 minutes. Score candy with a greased knife or spatula, pressing into candy about ½ inch. Cool completely. Invert pan and remove candy, breaking pieces off with hands.) Store tightly covered. Makes about 1½ pounds.

Crocheted Stockings

As shown on pages 126–127, each ornament measures 4¼-5 inches tall.

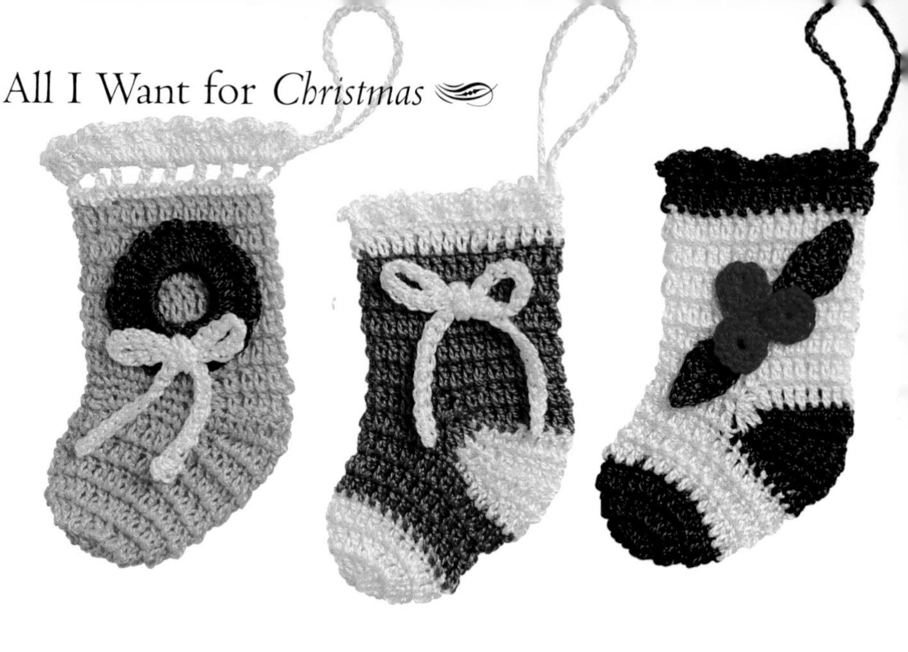

MATERIALS

#5 pearl cotton size [27-yard (24 m) skeins or 53-yard (48 m) ball] in Christmas red (DMC 321), Christmas green, (DMC 909), Canary deep yellow (DMC 444), Blue medium (DMC 797), Violet light (DMC 553), and White
Steel crochet hook size 6; scissors
Blunt-end tapestry needle; crafts glue

INSTRUCTIONS

Note: For the solid color stocking, it takes one whole skein or ½ ball of thread.

Solid Color Stocking: With color of your choice, ch 3. Work 11 dc in third ch from hook; join with sl st in third ch of beginning ch-3. Rnd 2: Ch 3 (counts as dc), * 2 dc in next dc, 1 dc in next dc; rep from * around, ending 2 dc in next dc; join (18 dc). Rnd 3: Ch 3 (counts as dc), dc in next dc; * 2 dc in next dc, dc in next 2 dc; rep from * around; join (24 sts). Rnds 4-5: Ch 3 (counts as dc), dc in each dc around; join. Rnd 6: Ch 3 (counts as dc), dc in each of next 2 dc, * 2 dc in next dc, dc in next 3 dc; rep from * around, ending 2 dc in last dc; join (30 sts). Rnd 7: Ch 1, sc in first 7 sts, hdc in next 2 sts, dc in each of next 12 sts, hdc in next 2 sts, sc in last 7 sts; join with sl st in first sc.

Heel: Ch 1, sc in 7 sc, hdc in 2 hdc, dc in 12 dc, hdc in 2 hdc; turn; * ch 2 (counts as hdc), hdc in next hdc, dc in 12 dc, hdc in 2 hdc *, turn; rep bet *s once again; sc in each of next 7 sc on stocking top; join with sl st in next sc.

Rnd 9: Rep Rnd 7. Rnds 10-15: Ch 3 (counts as dc), dc in each st around; join. Fasten off after Rnd 15.

Top Ruffle: With the RS facing, join yarn with sl st in fifteenth st from Rnd 15 joining. Rnd 1: Ch 1, sc in each st around; join. Rnd 2: Ch 4 (counts as dc, ch 1), * sk 1 sc, dc in next sc, ch 1; rep from * around, ending join with sl st in third ch of beginning ch-4. Rnd 3: In first ch-1 sp (sl st, ch 3, 2 trc, dc), (dc, 2 trc, dc) in each ch-1 sp around;' at end, sl st in 3rd ch of beginning ch-3, ch 30, sl st in same ch. Fasten off.

Two Tone Stocking: With Color A, work as for Solid Color Stocking through Rnd 3. Fasten off. With the RS facing, join Color B with sl st in join; work Rnds 4-6 of Solid Color Stocking. Fasten off Color B. Heel: With the RS facing, join Color A with sl st in join. Row 1: Ch 1, sc in first 2 sts, hdc in next st, dc in 11 sts, hdc in next st, sc in 2 sts; turn. Rows 2-4: Rep Row 1. Fasten off Color A after Row 4.

Top: With the RS facing, join Color B with sl st in ninth st from right edge of heel. Ch 3 (counts as dc), dc in each of next 8 sts; * yo and draw up a lp in first Color A row, (yo and through 2 lps on hook, yo and draw up a lp in next Color A row) 3 times, yo and through 2 lps on hook, yo and through all 5 lps on hook *, continuing along top in the Color B sts, dc in each of next 13 sts; rep bet *s once again, dc in each on next 8 heel sts; join. Rnd 2: Ch 3 (counts as dc), dc in each st around; join (32 sts). Rnds 3-7: Rep Rnd 2. After Rnd 7, fasten off.

Top Border: With the RS facing, join Color A with sl st in join. Ch 3 (counts as dc), dc in each dc around. Rnd 2: Ch 1, sc in first dc, * ch 4, sk 1 dc, sc in next dc; rep from * around, ending sl st in first sc, ch 30, sl st in same sc. Fasten off.

To decorate the stocking, choose from the following designs:

Bow: Ch 51; sc in second ch from hook and in each ch across. Fasten off. Tie into a bow.

Flower: With white or red, ch 4; join with sl st to form ring. Rnd 1: Ch 1, work 10 sc in ring; join. Rnd 2: (Ch 10, sc in next sc) around; fasten off.

Leaves: With green or white, ch 9. Sl st in second ch from hook, sc in next ch, hdc in next ch, dc in 2 ch, hdc in next ch, sc in next ch, sl st in last ch; working along opposite edge, sc in next ch, hdc in next, dc in next 2 ch, hdc in next ch, sc in next ch, sl st in next ch and in first sc. Fasten off.

Holly Berry (make three): With red, ch 2; work 12 hdc in second ch from hook; join with sl st in second ch of beginning ch-2.

Wreath: With green, ch 12; join with sl st to form ring. Rnd 1: Ch 3 (counts as dc); * 3 trc in ring **, dc in ring; rep from * around, ending last rep at **; join with sl st in third ch of beginning ch-3. Fasten off.

Finishing: With a tapestry needle, hide all loose ends on WS of fabric by running thread back into work for a few stitches; press. Glue motifs in place with crafts glue, making sure glue does not go through thread to inside of stocking. If necessary, put a piece of plastic wrap inside stocking to prevent glue from spreading through the stocking.

FAUX GINGERBREAD FRIENDS

Faux Gingerbread Friends

As shown on pages 126–128, each ornament measures 5×3⅞ inches.

MATERIALS

For both ornaments

Tracing paper; carbon paper; ballpoint pen
8x7-inch piece of ⅛-inch Baltic birch plywood
Scroll saw; drill with ⅛-inch bit
Fine grit sandpaper
Delta Ceramcoat acrylic paints: autumn brown and brown velvet
Tulip Crystals fabric paint: icicle crystals
Tulip Slick fabric paint pen: white
¼- and ½-inch paint brushes
Polyurethane spray
12 inches of ⅛-inch-diameter red satin ribbon

INSTRUCTIONS

Trace pattern, *above*, onto tracing paper. Place carbon paper between pattern and wood; transfer body outline, tracing over line with ballpoint pen. Cut out ornament with scroll saw. Drill hole in top for hanger. Sand surfaces smooth.

Paint entire ornament autumn brown. While fronts are still damp, blend velvet brown around edges to resemble baked edges of cookies; let dry. Brush several coats of crystals paint over front. When crystals paint is dry, use white paint pen to draw "icing" detail as desired, using photograph, *page 128*, for ideas.

Thread ribbon through hole in top of ornament; knot ends.

Christmas Twins

As shown on page 128, dolls are 6 inches tall.

MATERIALS

FABRICS *for boy*

Two 8x10-inch pieces of 28-count ivory Jobelan fabric
Two 5x6-inch pieces of 28-count tan Jobelan fabric
5x8½-inch piece of cotton fabric
5½x9-inch piece of red fabric
Two 4¼x3-inch pieces of dark green fabric

FABRICS *for girl*

Two 8x10-inch pieces of 28-count ivory Jobelan fabric
6x10¼-inch piece of 28-count tan Jobelan fabric
4x4½-inch piece of 28-count tan Jobelan fabric
5x9-inch piece of red fabric
1⅞x2½-inch piece of tan fabric
1x26½-inch piece of dark green fabric

THREADS

Cotton embroidery floss in colors listed in key on page 134
Two additional skeins of deep mahogany (DMC 300) embroidery floss

SUPPLIES

Tracing paper
Water-soluble marking pen
Light box or brightly lit window
Embroidery hoop; needle
Threads to match fabrics
3¼-inch-wide piece of cardboard
Polyester fiberfill
Cosmetic blush and small brush
⅛-inch-wide elastic
Four ¼-inch-diameter snaps

Vest stitch count: *13 high x 11 wide*
Vest finished design sizes:
28-count fabric – 1 x ¾ inch
36-count fabric – ¾ x ⅝ inch
22-count fabric – 1⅛ x 1 inches

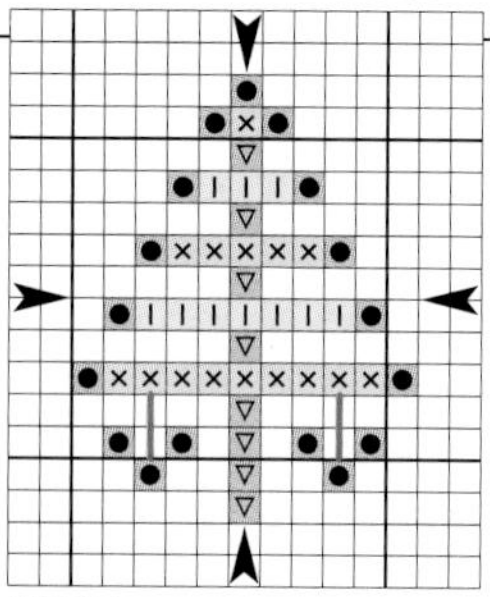

VEST

Face stitch count: *8 high x 12 wide*
Face finished design sizes:
28-count fabric – ½ x ⅞ inch
36-count fabric – ⅜ x ⅝ inch
22-count fabric – ¾ x 1 inch

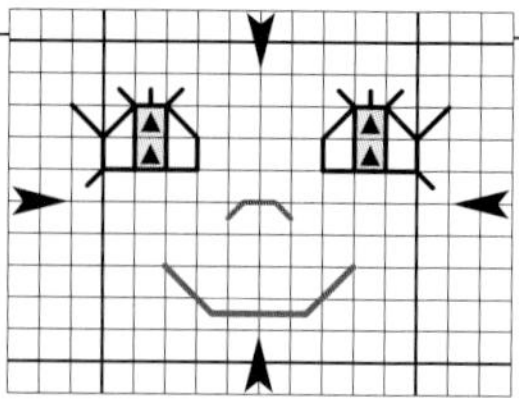

FACE

Pinafore Bib stitch count:
14 high x 13 wide
Pinafore Bib finished design sizes:
28-count fabric – 1 x 1 inch
36-count fabric – ⅞ x ¾ inch
22-count fabric – 1¼ x 1⅛ inches

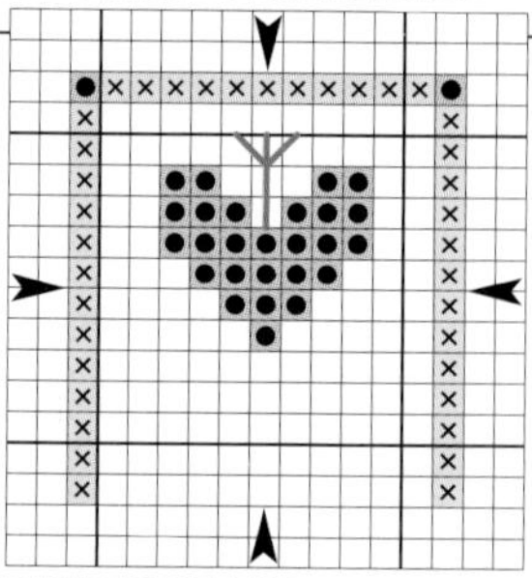

PINAFORE BIB

Pinafore Skirt Border stitch count:
9 high x 46 wide
Pinafore Skirt Border finished design sizes:
28-count fabric – ⅝ x 3¼ inches
36-count fabric – ½ x 2½ inches
22-count fabric – ⅞ x 4⅛ inches

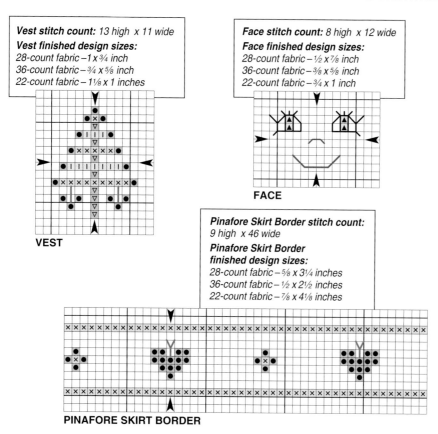

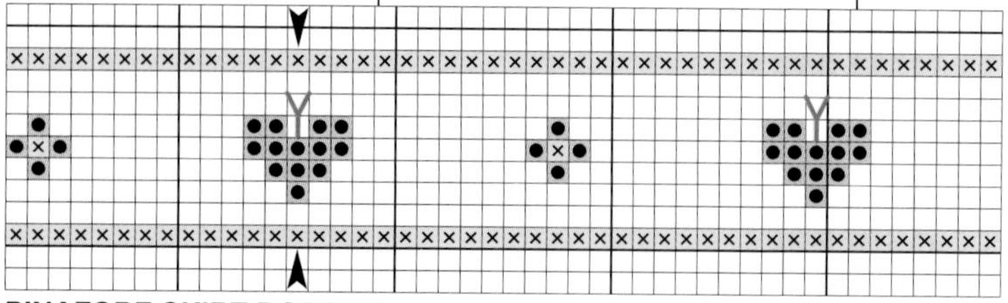

PINAFORE SKIRT BORDER

CHRISTMAS TWINS

ANCHOR		DMC
352	▽	300 Mahogany
1005	●	498 Christmas red
212	✕	561 Dark seafoam
210	I	562 Medium seafoam
132	▲	797 Royal blue
BACKSTITCH		
403	/	310 Black–eyes
914	/	407 Cocoa–nose
1005	/	498 Christmas red–mouth
212	/	561 Dark seafoam–vest, bib, and skirt border

INSTRUCTIONS

Trace body and clothing patterns, *page 135*, onto tracing paper and cut out. Use patterns to cut dress bodice and sleeves from 5×9-inch piece of red fabric, vest back and lining from 5×8½-inch piece of tan fabric, and shirt and shirt sleeves from 5½×9-inch piece of red fabric. Vest fronts are cut after stitching is completed. Patterns for clothes and measurements include ¼-inch seam allowances as necessary. Sew all seams with the right sides of fabric facing. Sew Jobelan fabric using very small machine stitches.

Tape or zigzag raw edges of Jobelan to prevent fraying.

For body, stitch lengthwise center of each 8×10-inch Jobelan piece using contrasting basting thread. Match center of body pattern to basting thread on each piece and mark outline using fabric marker. Holding each fabric piece to light source, marked side up, slide body pattern behind fabric and realign outline. Mark shoe tops and body stitching lines.

Cross-stitch shoes below shoe top lines, making each shoe the same number of rows and stitches. Center nose on body front face, leaving 30 threads between top of nose and top of head. Stitch face according to chart, *above*. Use two plies of floss to work cross-stitches over two threads of fabric. Work backstitches and straight stitches using one ply of floss over two threads of fabric.

For each body piece, match center of pattern to basting thread on wrong side of fabric. Place against light source to trace body lines from right side of fabric to wrong side; remove pattern. Pin fronts to backs with right sides facing. Hold fabric to light source to match centers, lines, dots, and shoe tops.

Sew fronts to backs along outlines, leaving opening for turning. Restitch inner legs and inside curves. Remove basting threads and fabric marker lines; press. Cut bodies a scant ¼ inch beyond stitching, leaving wider seam allowances at opening. Clip curves; turn right side out.

Stuff limbs, leaving top ¾ inch of legs and top ½ inch of arms unstuffed. Stitch across limb tops along dotted lines. Stuff head and body, leaving ½ inch of body bottom stuffed; sew opening closed. Stitch along body bottom dotted lines.

For boy's hair, wrap deep mahogany floss 20 times around 3¼-inch cardboard. Slide loops off card and spread center of wrapped floss to measure 1 inch. Machine stitch across center to make part. Hand-stitch part to head top using floss. Pull loops down; hand-stitch to nape of neck. Spread loops as necessary to cover back of head.

For bangs, use floss from same skein as boy's hair. Wrap floss five times around three fingers. Cut off, tie around center, and cut loops. Use point of pin to separate strands. Hand-stitch bangs to front part; trim to shape.

For girl's hair, spread center of full skein of deep mahogany floss to

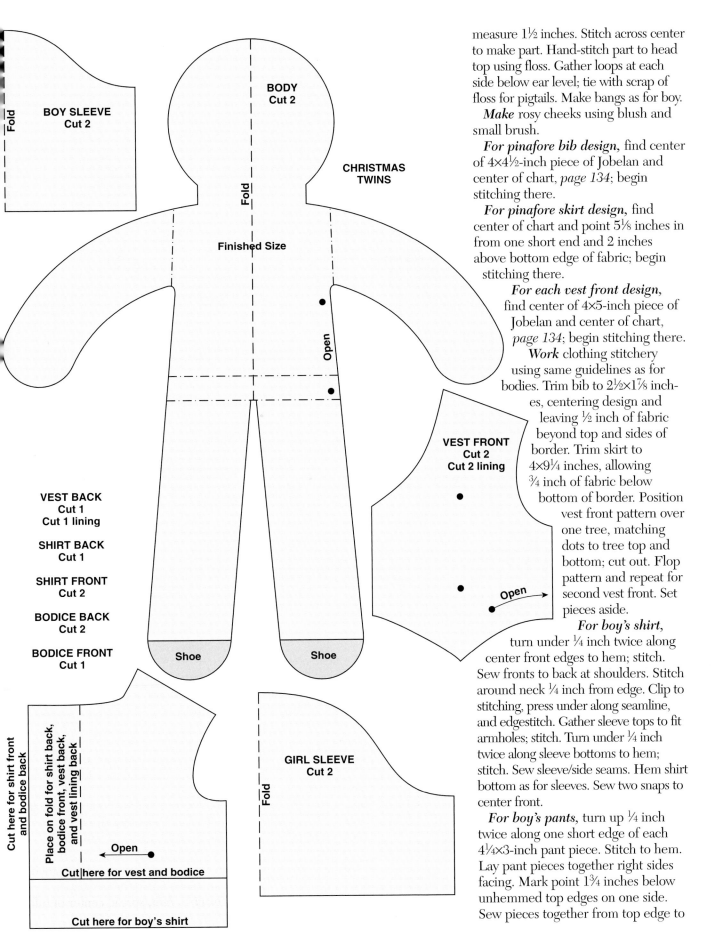

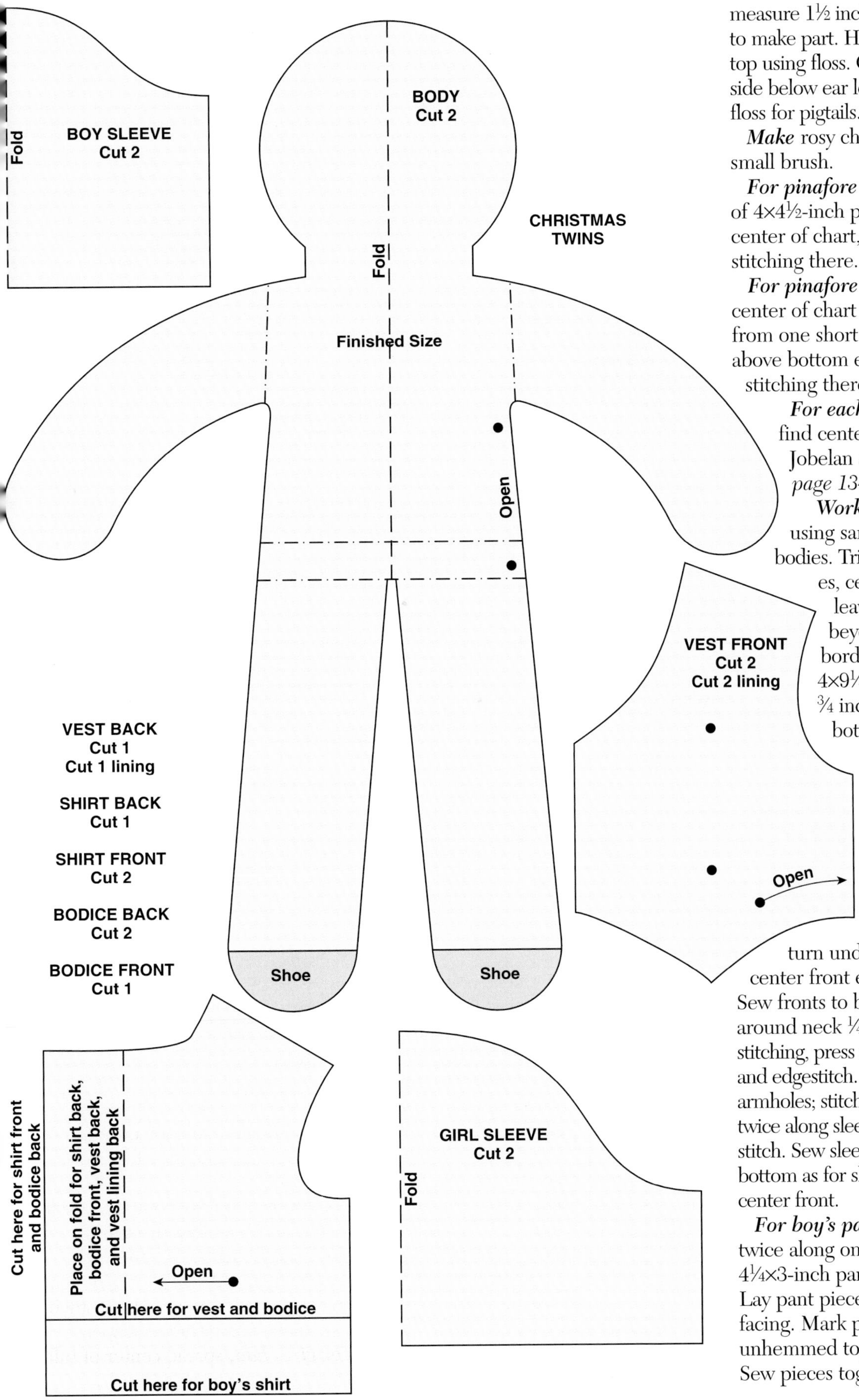

measure 1½ inches. Stitch across center to make part. Hand-stitch part to head top using floss. Gather loops at each side below ear level; tie with scrap of floss for pigtails. Make bangs as for boy.

Make rosy cheeks using blush and small brush.

For pinafore bib design, find center of 4×4½-inch piece of Jobelan and center of chart, *page 134*; begin stitching there.

For pinafore skirt design, find center of chart and point 5⅛ inches in from one short end and 2 inches above bottom edge of fabric; begin stitching there.

For each vest front design, find center of 4×5-inch piece of Jobelan and center of chart, *page 134*; begin stitching there.

Work clothing stitchery using same guidelines as for bodies. Trim bib to 2½×1⅞ inches, centering design and leaving ½ inch of fabric beyond top and sides of border. Trim skirt to 4×9¼ inches, allowing ¾ inch of fabric below bottom of border. Position vest front pattern over one tree, matching dots to tree top and bottom; cut out. Flop pattern and repeat for second vest front. Set pieces aside.

For boy's shirt, turn under ¼ inch twice along center front edges to hem; stitch. Sew fronts to back at shoulders. Stitch around neck ¼ inch from edge. Clip to stitching, press under along seamline, and edgestitch. Gather sleeve tops to fit armholes; stitch. Turn under ¼ inch twice along sleeve bottoms to hem; stitch. Sew sleeve/side seams. Hem shirt bottom as for sleeves. Sew two snaps to center front.

For boy's pants, turn up ¼ inch twice along one short edge of each 4¼×3-inch pant piece. Stitch to hem. Lay pant pieces together right sides facing. Mark point 1¾ inches below unhemmed top edges on one side. Sew pieces together from top edge to mark using ¼-inch seam allowance to make center front seam. Open piece out. Press top raw edge as for hem. Lay elastic within fold and sew casing closed. Secure one elastic end, pull elastic to fit waist, and secure opposite end. Sew center back seam as for center front seam. Sew leg inseams.

For boy's vest, sew fronts to back at side seams. Repeat for lining. Sew vest to lining leaving open between dots. Clip curves and trim seams, leaving wider seam allowance at opening. Turn to right side, press, and sew opening closed. Hand-sew shoulder seams.

For girl's dress bodice, turn under ¼ inch twice along center back edges to hem; stitch. Sew fronts to back at shoulders. Finish neck and sew in sleeves as for shirt. Press sleeve bottoms as for hem. Lay elastic within fold and sew casing closed. On each sleeve, secure one end of elastic, pull elastic to fit arm, and secure opposite end. Sew sleeve/side seams.

To finish dress, hem one long edge of 3¾×13-inch skirt strip in same manner as other hems. Press under ¼ inch on short ends. Gather top edge to fit bodice bottom edge; stitch. Beginning at hem, sew 1½-inch center back seam. Sew snaps to bodice back.

For pinafore, press 1×26½-inch waistband and strap piece in half lengthwise. Press both long raw edges under to meet first fold. Cut 20-inch long waistband and two 3¼-inch-long straps. Hem pinafore skirt sides and bottom in same manner as other hems. Gather top edge to measure 3¼ inches. Center gathered top along waistband and encase edge in fold, allowing waistband ends to extend for ties. Topstitch along waistband, securing skirt. Knot ends of ties.

Sew bib to lining leaving bottom open. Turn, press, and sew opening closed. Position bib bottom edge, centered, behind waistband. Stitch bib to skirt along previous topstitching.

Sew folded strap edges together. Turn ends under and hand-stitch each to wrong side of bib top. Fit straps over shoulders and under waistband, with straps even with skirt backs. Sew straps in place along previous waistband stitching.

Press all pieces lightly and dress the dolls.

Frog Prince

As shown on page 129, frog prince is approximately 13 inches long and sits 7½ inches tall.

MATERIALS

Tracing paper
¼ yard of 45-inch-wide unbleached muslin
¼ yard of 45-inch-wide dark gold satin
¼ yard of 45-inch-wide light gold taffeta
¼ yard of 45-inch-wide purple satin
¼ yard of 45-inch-wide dark purple velvet
1½x13-inch piece of fusible interfacing
Threads to match fabrics
Polyester fiberfill; polyfill pellet beads
Two 12-mm wood beads
Wood putty
Delta Ceramcoat acrylic paints: black and empire gold
Delta Starlite Dye Shimmering Fabric Color: leaf green, ivory, and hunter green
Delta Fabric Dye Brush-On Fabric Color: red
Artists' brushes; large darning needle
Light green carpet thread
Hot-glue gun
Two 16-mm antique gold buttons
4 small snaps
7x1½-inch strip of fusible interfacing

INSTRUCTIONS

Trace patterns, *pages 137–142*, onto tracing paper and cut out. Patterns and measurements include ¼-inch seam allowances. All seams are sewn with right sides of fabric facing, unless otherwise specified. Clip curved seams as necessary.

Cut all frog body parts from muslin fabric.

Cut shirt pieces from gold satin, pants from purple satin, jacket and hat pieces from purple velvet, and jacket and a 5½-inch circle for hat lining from light gold taffeta. In addition, cut two 1½×3¼-inch shirt cuffs from gold satin, two 1½×4½-inch pant cuffs from purple satin, and a 1½×7-inch band and 5 ½-inch circle for hat from purple velvet.

For frog, sew arm seams and legs together in pairs, leaving both ends open. Turn limbs right side out. Sew hands and feet together in pairs leaving top straight edges unstitched; turn and press. Make small tuck in top of each hand and foot; stitch across. Turn under ¼ inch along lower open edge of each arm; insert tucked edge of hand and topstitch, securing hand in arm. Repeat for legs and feet. Stuff limbs firmly with fiberfill; set aside.

Sew darts in head front and back, body front, and throat, using ¼-inch seam allowances. Sew head front to throat piece along mouth edge; sew body front to throat along neck edge. Sew body back center seam, leaving opening for stuffing. Next, join head back to body back at neck.

Sew body front to back around shoulders and head. Put each arm inside body, directly below shoulder, matching raw edges. Sew body side seams, securing arms. Matching raw edges, sew legs in place on body front. Sew base to body with legs and arms inside, taking care not to catch limbs in stitching. Turn body right side out through back opening. Stuff head and then top three-fourths of body firmly with polyester fiberfill. Fill remainder of body with polyfill beads and sew opening closed.

For eyes, fill one hole in each bead with wood putty. When dry, sand smooth. With remaining hole facing down, use eye diagram as a guide to draw eye onto front of each bead. Paint eye leaf green with empire gold irises, black pupils, and black eye outlines. Highlight pupils with dots of white.

Paint frog leaf green. Blend ivory into throat. Blend red into cheeks and knees. Shade approximate spots for eyes and along neckline using hunter green.

Paint thin line along mouth seam for smile, curving line up at corners. Thread needle with a double strand of carpet thread; knot. Stitch back

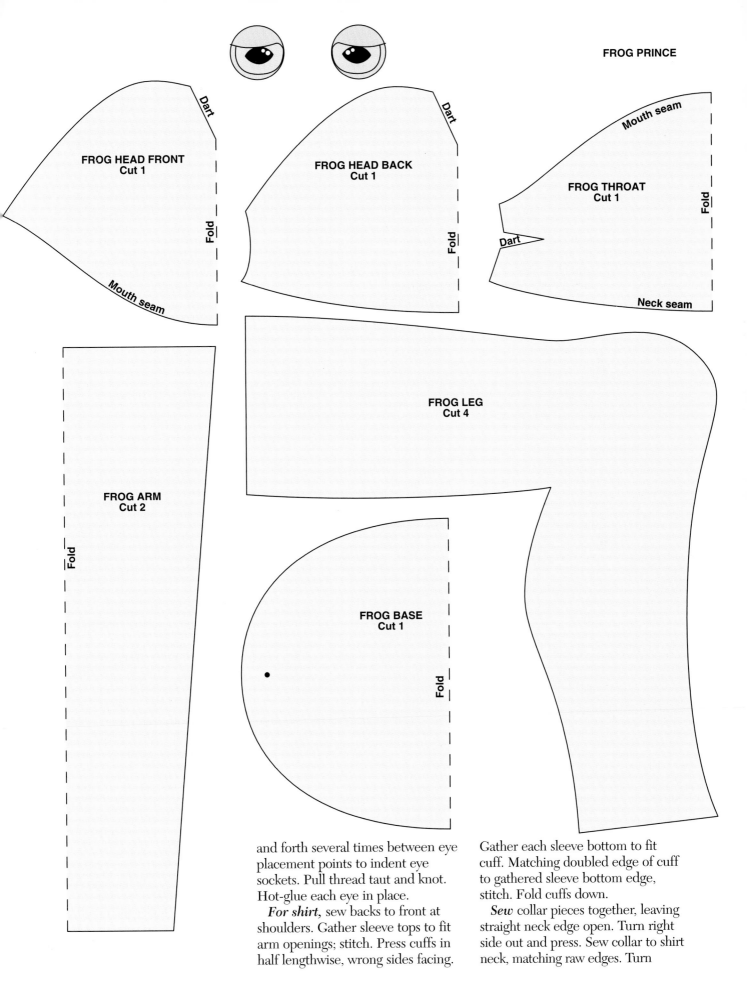

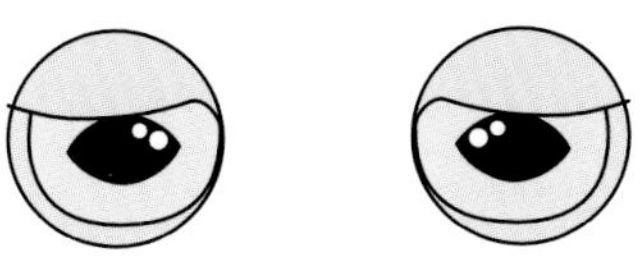

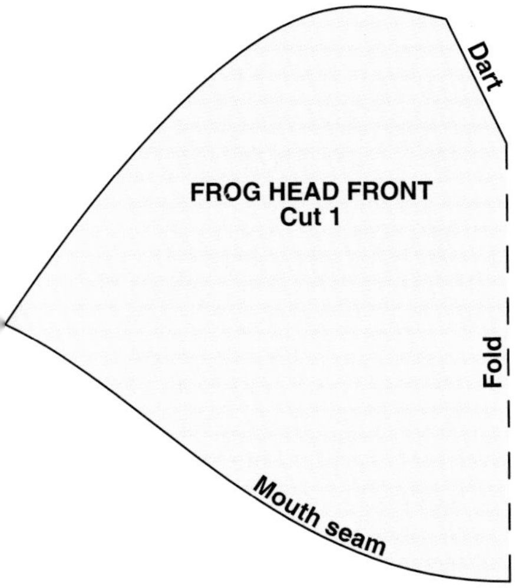

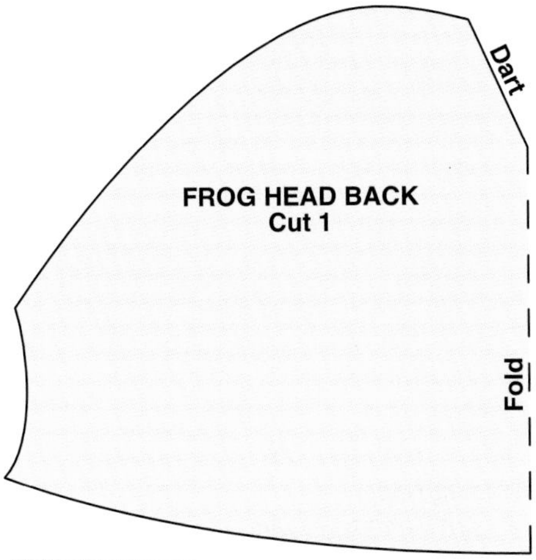

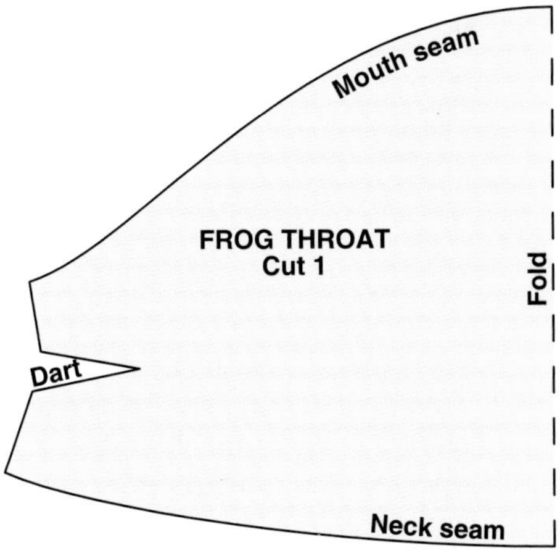

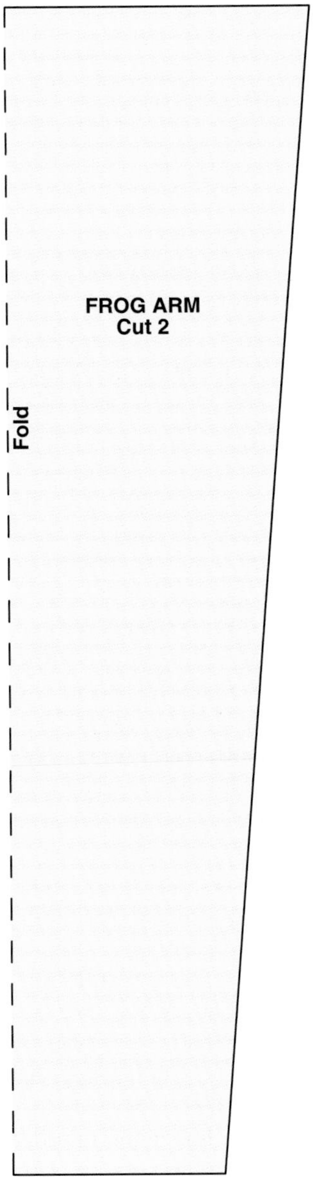

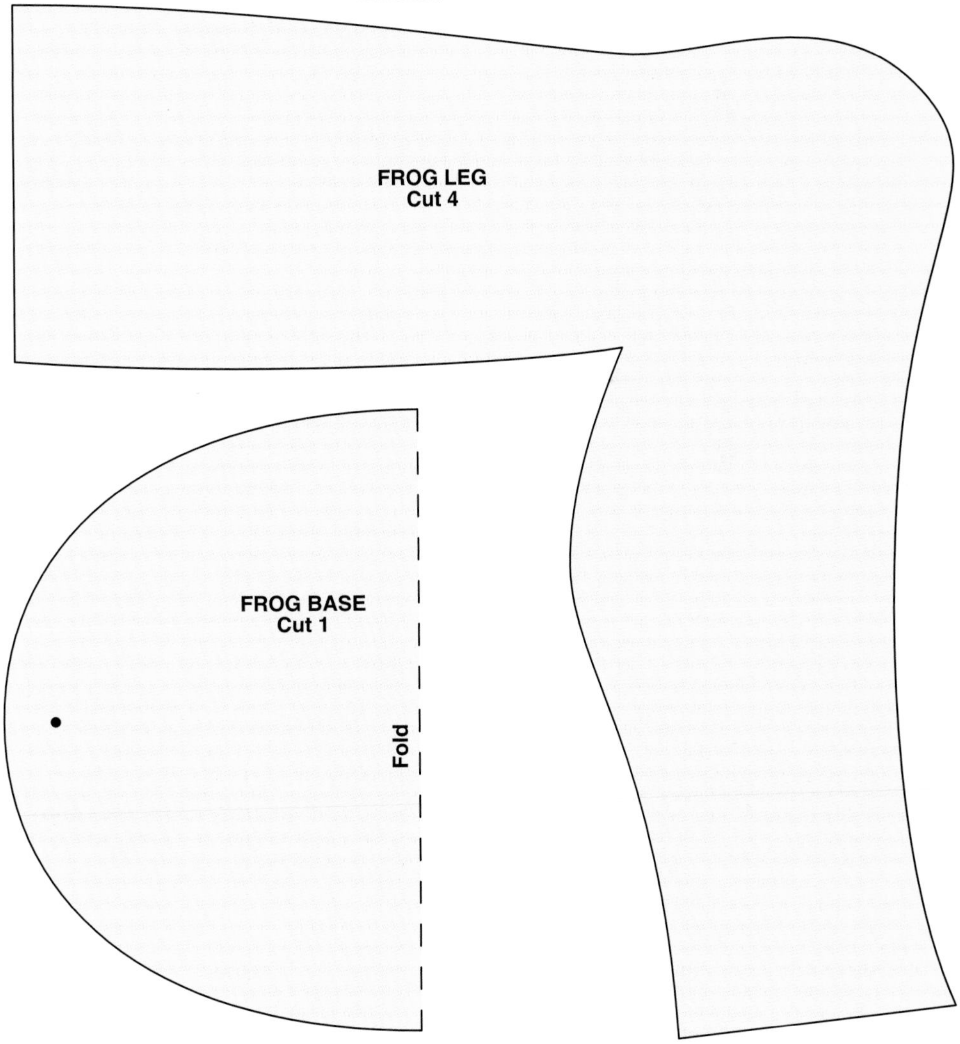

and forth several times between eye placement points to indent eye sockets. Pull thread taut and knot. Hot-glue each eye in place.

For shirt, sew backs to front at shoulders. Gather sleeve tops to fit arm openings; stitch. Press cuffs in half lengthwise, wrong sides facing. Gather each sleeve bottom to fit cuff. Matching doubled edge of cuff to gathered sleeve bottom edge, stitch. Fold cuffs down.

Sew collar pieces together, leaving straight neck edge open. Turn right side out and press. Sew collar to shirt neck, matching raw edges. Turn

FROG PRINCE

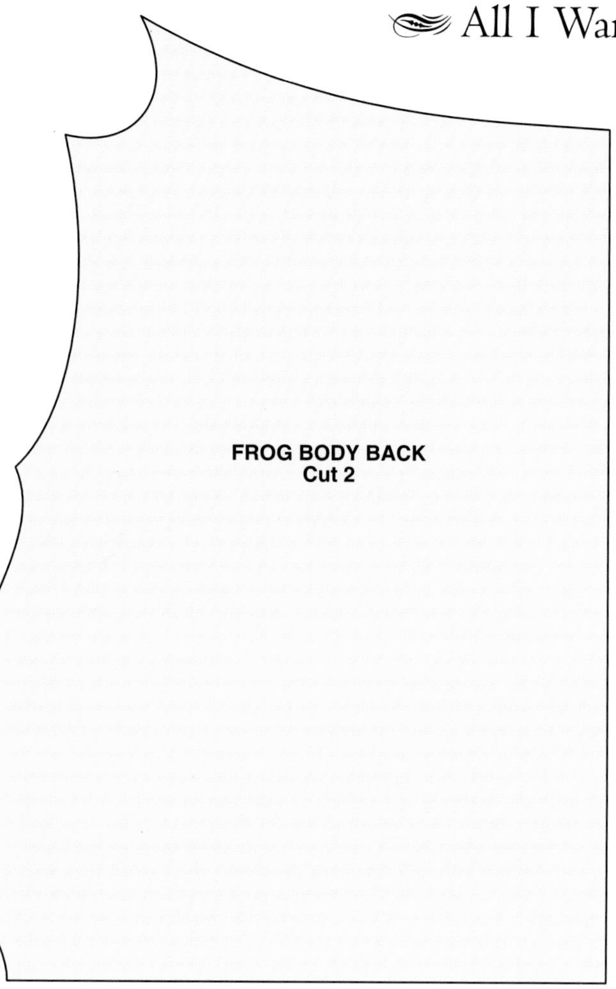

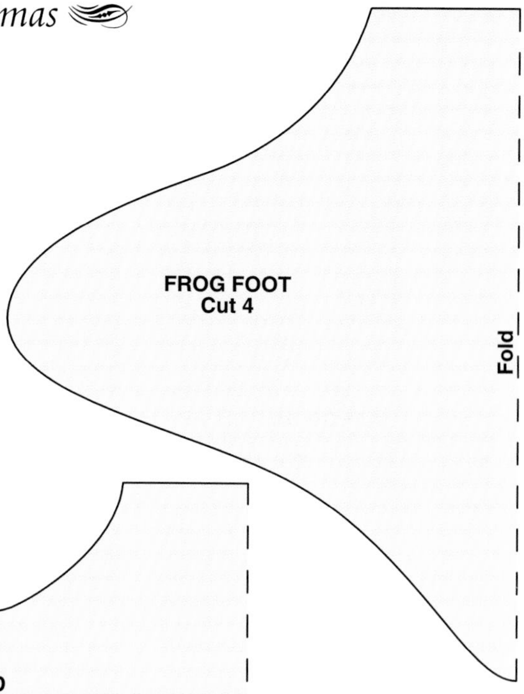

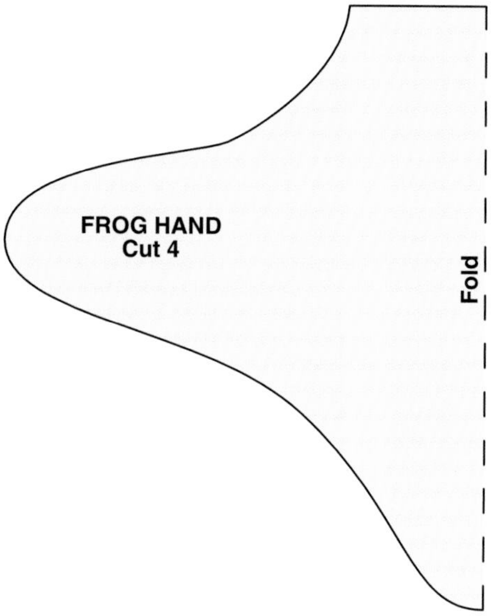

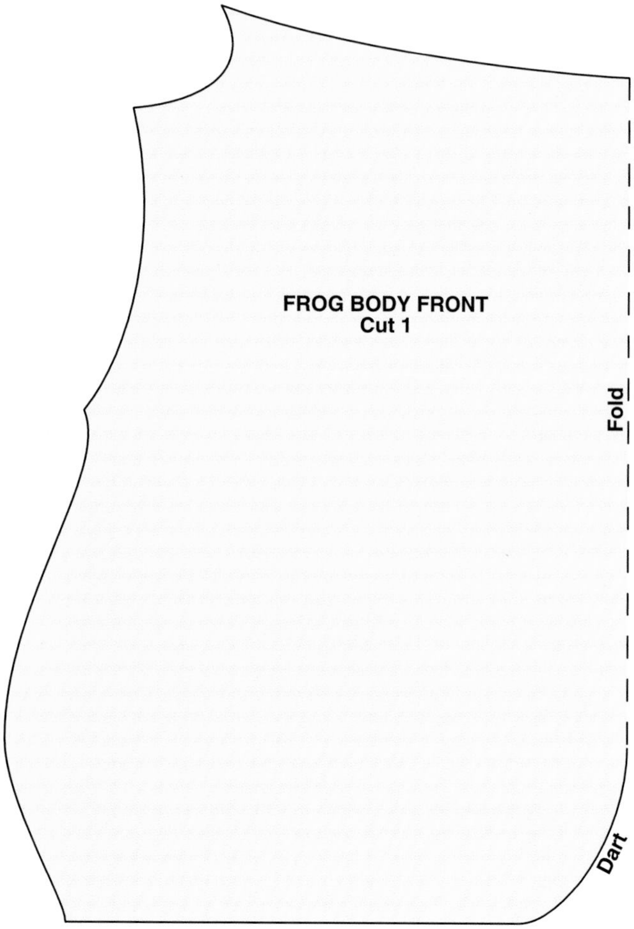

under ¼ inch along outside edge of shirt facing; stitch. Sew facing to neck over collar. Turn facing to inside, with collar standing up, and press.

Sew underarm/side seams. Turn under bottom and back opening edges ¼ inch and stitch to hem. Sew three snaps down shirt back opening.

For pants, sew pieces together along one side from crotch to waist for front seam. Repeat to make back seam, stopping 2 inches below waist to allow for back opening.

Fuse interfacing to wrong side of waistband. Press waistband in half lengthwise, wrong sides facing. Stitch across doubled ends of waistband ¼ inch from edges; turn and press. Gather the pants waist to fit the waistband; stitch.

Press cuffs in half lengthwise, wrong sides facing. Gather pant legs to fit cuffs. Sew cuffs to pant legs as for shirt. Sew inner leg/crotch seam.

FROG PRINCE

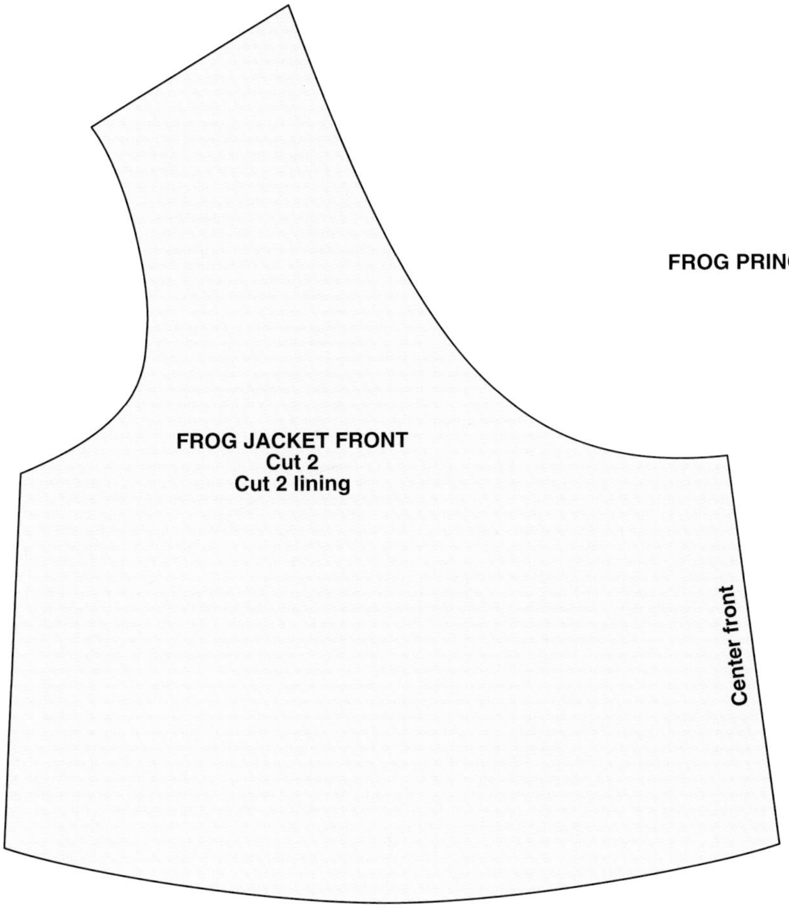

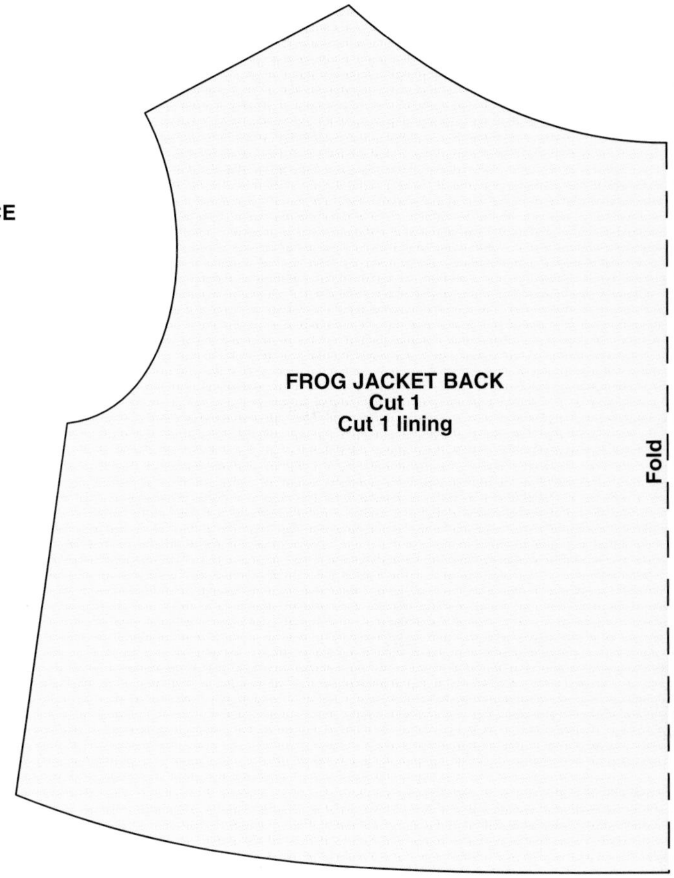

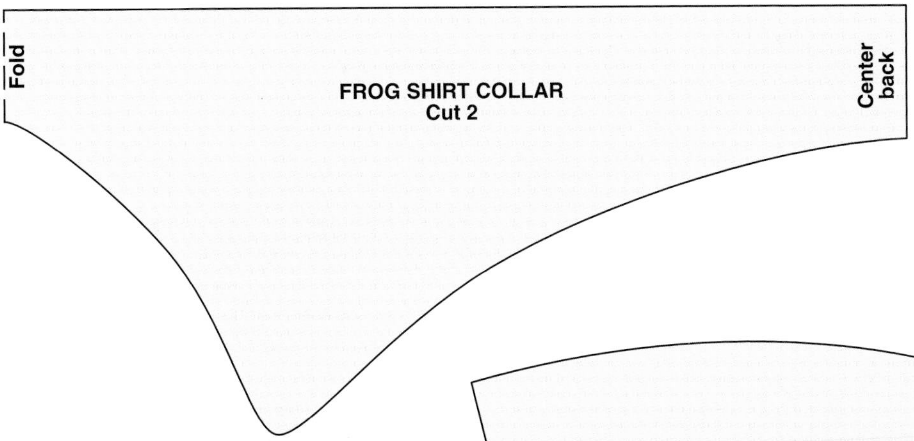

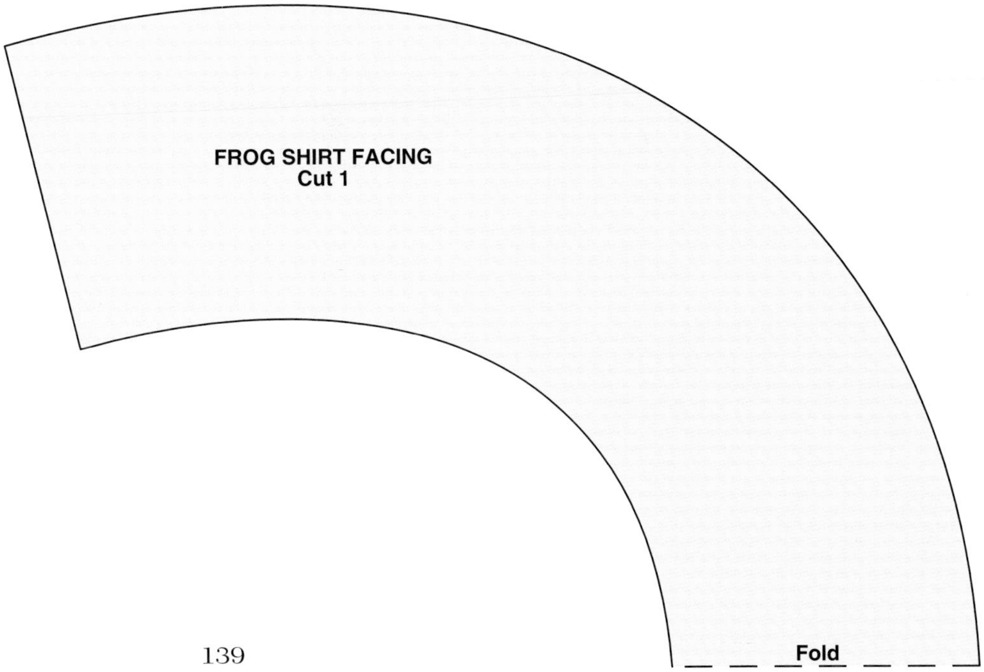

Turn pants right side out. Turn under ¼ inch along back opening edges and stitch to hem. Sew snap to waistband.

For jacket, sew fronts to back at shoulders; repeat for lining. Sew cap sleeve lining to each cap sleeve along straight edge; turn and press with lining side up. Sew cap sleeves to jacket arm openings. Before folding cap sleeves out to extend from arm opening, stitch lace around each opening along same seam line, with cap sleeve between lace and body of jacket. Turn sleeves out, with lace

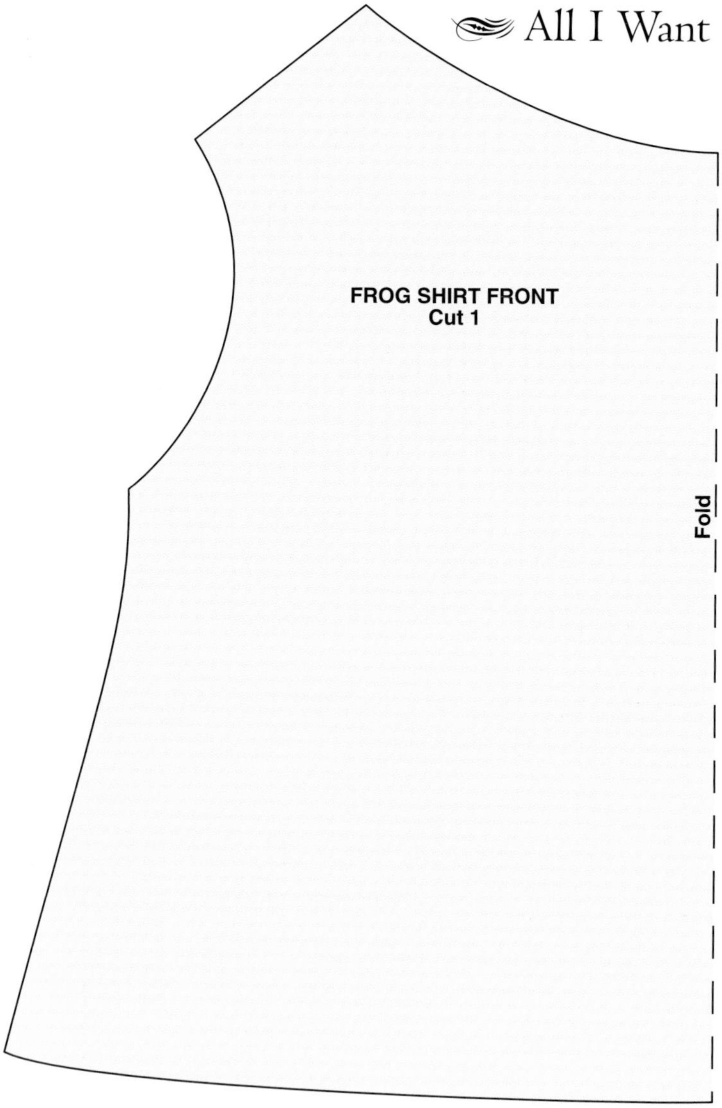

Full-size frog patterns continued on pages 141–142.

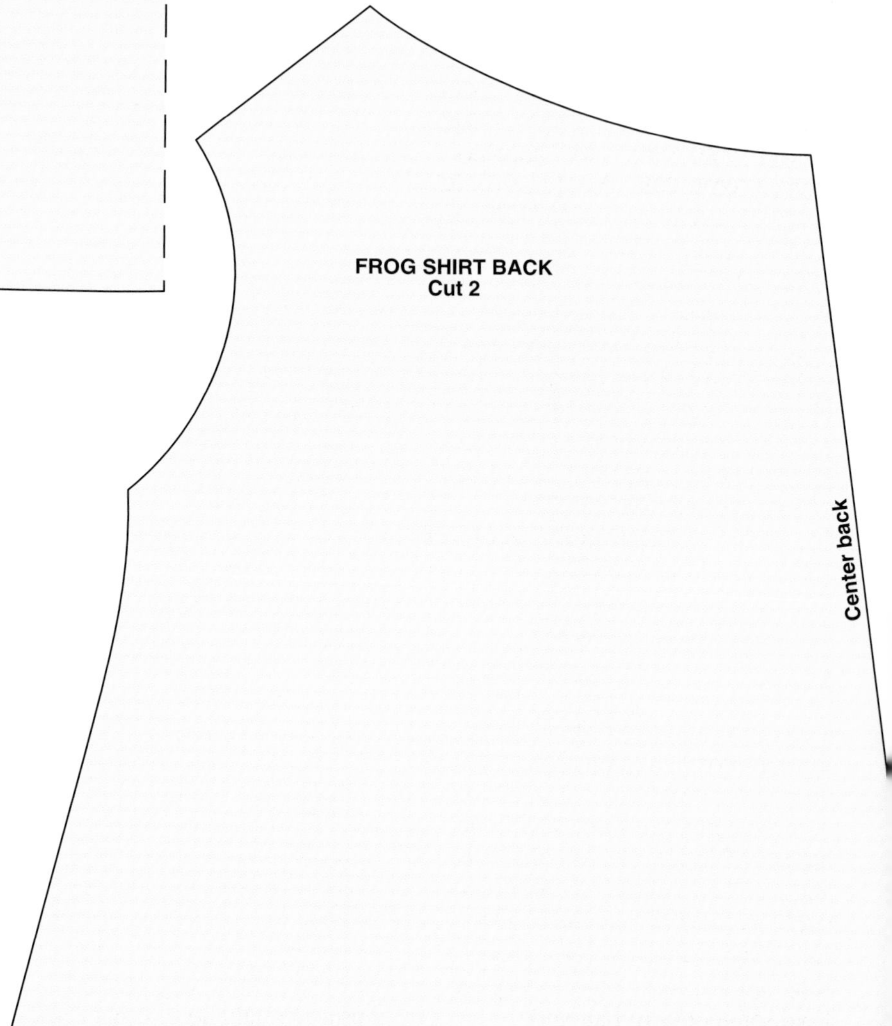

extending beyond sleeves. Sew the side seams.

Press under ¼ inch along lining side seam raw edges. With right sides facing, sew lining to jacket around all edges. Turn jacket right side out through side openings in lining. Press seams with lining side up. Hand-stitch lining side openings closed. Sew one button to each side of jacket front.

For hat, sew short ends of hatband together. Press hatband in half lengthwise with wrong sides facing. Position lining circle atop hat circle with wrong sides facing. Gather edge of doubled layer to fit hatband. Sew gathered hat top to outer raw edge of hatband. Turn under ¼ inch along remaining hatband edge and whipstitch to inside of hat along seam line.

Dress frog; tie ribbon around neck of shirt with bow in front.

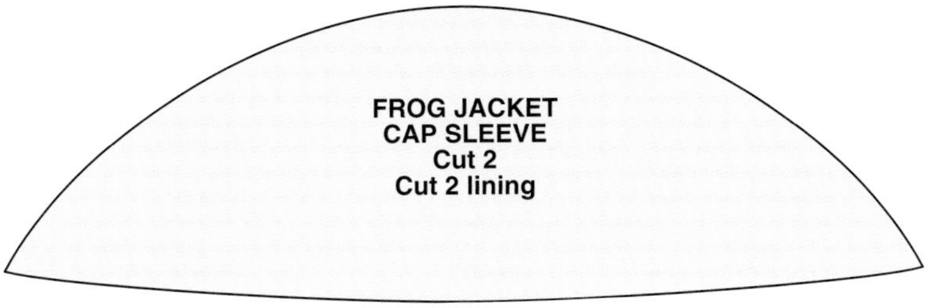

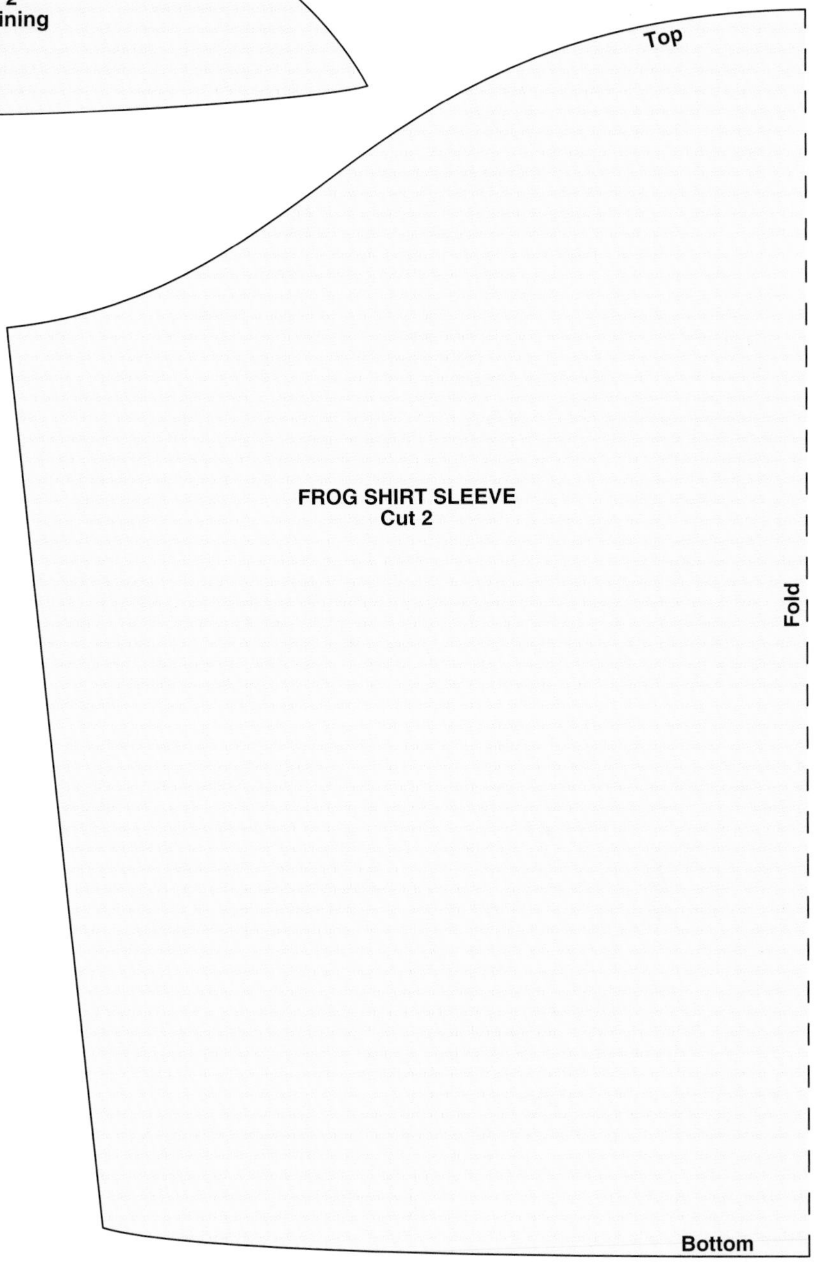

Tiny Carolers

As shown on page 130, carolers range in height from 2⅞ to 5¾ inches tall.

MATERIALS

Tracing paper
Heavyweight scrap paper; crafts glue
2 wood craft sticks; 12 craft picks
5 small and 4 large flat clothespins
Four ¾-inch-diameter wood craft circles (optional, for dolls to stand)
Acrylic paints: rose, white
Small artists' brushes
Ultra fine-tip markers: red, black
2 pipe cleaners
Black carpet thread (optional, for hanging)
Cotton embroidery floss: White, Medium mahogany (DMC 301), black (DMC 310), True pewter (DMC 317), Dark steel (DMC 414), Deep violet (DMC 550), Dark Christmas green (DMC 699), Pale topaz (DMC 727), Medium royal blue (DMC 796), Light royal blue (DMC 797), Medium coffee brown (DMC 801), True red copper (DMC 919), Dark electric blue (DMC 995), Deep dusty rose (DMC 3350), Deep antique mauve (DMC 3802), Dark mauve (DMC 3803), True celadon green (DMC 3816), True hazel (DMC 3828), and Deep old gold (DMC 3829)
Felt scraps: tan, kelly green, black, and maroon; cotton balls

INSTRUCTIONS

Trace skirt, bonnet, hat, and cap patterns, *page 144*; cut out. Cut two large skirts and three small skirts from heavyweight paper. Cut woman's bonnet from maroon felt and girls' bonnets from black felt. Cut large hat from black felt, and small hat and cap from tan felt. In addition, cut three ⅝×1¼-inch rectangular songbooks and three ½×⅞-inch songbooks from heavyweight paper. Fold songbooks in half and decorate, using fine-tip marker, as shown on pattern, *page 144*. Set all pieces aside.

If pieces are to stand, paint wood circles white to make bases for men and boys; set aside.

Select two large clothespins for men, two large clothespins for women, three small clothespins for girls, and two small clothespins for boys. Paint faces on top section of each clothespin accordingly, using photograph, *page 130*, as a guide. Paint eyes, lashes, eyebrows, mustaches, and noses using black marker. Paint mouths with red marker. Add rosy cheeks with dots of rose and highlight eyes with tiny dots of white.

For men's arms, cut 1¼-inch piece off each end of each craft pick. For boys' arms, cut ⅞-inch-long piece off rounded end of four craft picks. For women's arms, cut 1¼-inch-long piece off rounded end of two craft picks, and cut 3-inch-long piece of pipe cleaner. For girls' arms, cut four pieces as for boys, and also cut 2½-inch-long piece of pipe cleaner. Set arm pieces aside until needed.

To make all curly hair, wrap strand of floss tightly around craft pick. Wet

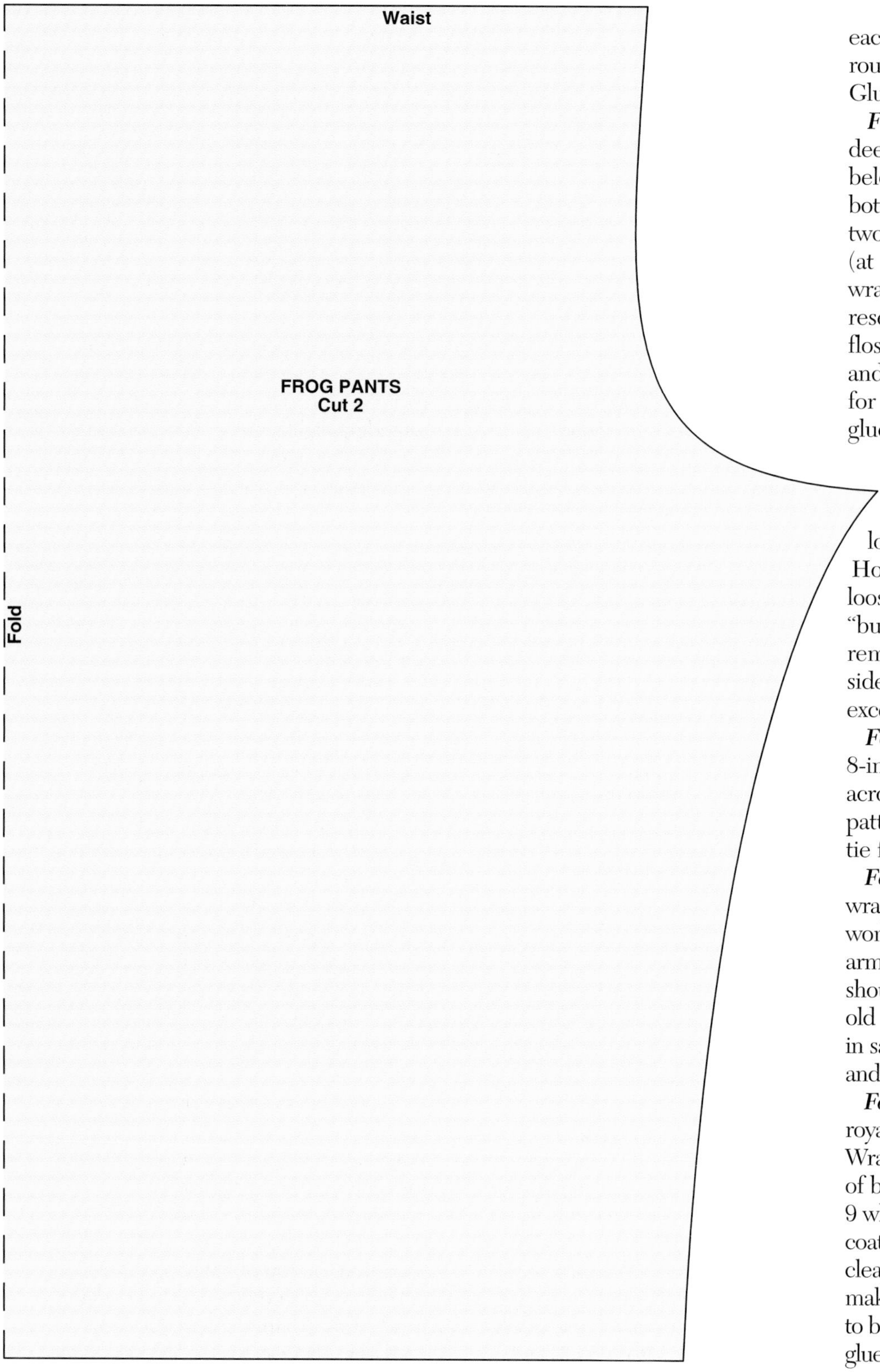

with hot water; let dry. Remove hair from pick. Glue curls to head; fluff.

To make all buttons, tie strand of floss in two knots, one atop the other; trim ends.

To wrap pieces with floss, use full strand. Secure floss at beginning with drop of glue. Wrap floss so each strand is directly below the other, covering the object completely with little or no overlapping. Add glue as necessary while wrapping.

Glue large skirts to women dolls and small skirts to girl dolls. Wrap each so top edge meets base of rounded middle section of clothespin. Glue edges together for back seam.

For woman with bonnet, wrap deep violet floss from neck to ½ inch below waist. Wrap dark mauve from bottom of deep violet to hem. Wrap two arms from approximate wrist (at rounded end) to top. Continue wrapping upper part of each arm to resemble puffy sleeve. Wrap black floss three times around each wrist and around base of jacket six times for trim. Make five black buttons; glue down jacket front. Glue arms to body at shoulders, with arms extending slightly forward.

For hair, make eight 6-inch loops with deep old gold floss. Holding loops all together, tie two loose knots in center. Glue knot "bun" to base of head at back. Wrap remaining floss around to top and side of head; glue to secure and trim excess.

For bonnet, glue center of 8-inch-long strand of black floss across maroon bonnet as shown on pattern. Glue bonnet on head and tie floss ends in bow at chin.

For matching girl with bonnet, wrap and create clothing as for woman, *above*. Wrap small craft pick arms in same manner and glue to shoulders. Make curly hair using deep old gold; glue to head. Make bonnet in same manner using black bonnet A and dark mauve floss tie; glue to head.

For woman with muff, wrap medium royal blue floss from neck to hem. Wrap white floss atop bottom ¼ inch of blue floss at hem for trim. Make 9 white buttons; glue down front of coat. Wrap 3-inch-long piece of pipe cleaner with medium blue floss to make arms. Glue center of pipe cleaner to back of neck to form arms. When glue is dry, rewrap upper part of arms several times to form puffy sleeves. Bend arms to curve down toward front.

Make curly hair using medium mahogany floss; glue to head.

For muff, glue cotton around paper label from floss skein. Insert hands into muff and glue to secure.

For hat, wrap cotton around fingers

and shape into hat; glue to head.

For matching girl with muff, wrap and create clothing as for woman, *above left*, using dark electric blue floss for coat and $2\frac{1}{2}$-inch-long piece of pipe cleaner for arms. Glue seven white buttons to coat.

For hair, wrap center of eight 2-inch loops of black floss with scrap of floss to make part. Glue part to head top. Coat head with glue and press loops to head to cover.

Make smaller versions of woman's muff and hat; glue pieces in place.

For girl with songbook, wrap true celadon green floss from neck to hem. Wrap small craft pick arms with green; glue arms to shoulders. Wrap black floss over celadon green from neck to $\frac{3}{8}$ inch below tops of arms to make cape. Wrap black floss once more around body under arms, beginning at base of previous black wrapping and ending at waist.

Cut three 2-inch-long pieces of true celadon green floss. Make two knots in each piece, $\frac{1}{2}$ inch apart. Cut away floss tails beyond knots, leaving $\frac{1}{2}$ inch of straight floss between knots. Glue knotted pieces down front of cape for closures, as shown in cape closure diagram, *page 144*.

For bonnet, glue center of 8-inch-long strand of true celadon green floss across black bonnet B as shown on pattern. Glue bonnet on head and tie floss ends in bow at chin.

For man in long topcoat, wrap each "leg" of clothespin with medium coffee brown floss. Wrap true hazel floss from neck to $1\frac{1}{8}$ inch above bottom of clothespin. Wrap hazel floss all the way back up to neck in order to give coat bulk. Make nine medium coffee brown floss buttons; glue down front of coat. Wrap craft stick arms with true hazel floss, stopping $\frac{3}{16}$ inch above bottom curve. Glue arms to body at shoulders, extending slightly forward. To make coat collar, wrap medium coffee brown floss loosely around neck and shoulders 12 times. Using scissors, clip collar partway up front so edges separate below neck; secure ends with glue.

For hair, apply glue to head. Press tiny pieces of floss to head to resemble hair with center part.

For hat, use tan felt hat pieces. Glue short ends of rectangle together to form ring, making sure circular opening fits hat top circle. Glue hat top circle to ring and opposite side of ring to hat brim to complete hat. Wrap floss twice around hat for hatband. Glue hat to head.

For matching boy in topcoat, wrap legs and topcoat as for man, *above*. Make 12 medium coffee brown buttons; glue in double row of six each down front of coat. Wrap small craft pick arms with true hazel floss. Glue arms to shoulders, extending slightly forward.

For hair, apply glue to head. Press tiny pieces of true red copper floss into glue to resemble hair.

For scarf, cut three 6-inch-long pieces of green floss; braid. Knot ends and trim. Tie around neck; glue.

For cap, glue cap top piece atop cap bottom; glue to top of head.

For earmuffs, wind and glue green floss into $\frac{3}{16}$-inch-diameter circle right below cap on each side of head. Cut snips of floss and glue "fuzz" to each earmuff.

For man in jacket with stovepipe hat, wrap each leg with dark steel floss. Wrap medium royal blue floss from neck to $\frac{3}{4}$ inch below waist. Wrap craft stick arms with medium royal blue floss. Glue arms to body at shoulders, extending slightly forward. Make black hair as for man in long topcoat, *left*.

For scarf, cut two 8-inch-long strands each of true hazel, dark steel, and deep antique mauve floss. Grouping like color strands together for each braid strand, braid floss and knot ends. Trim ends, making scarf about 5 inches long. Drape scarf over shoulders; glue to secure.

For hat, use black felt hat pieces and make as for man's hat, *above*.

For boy in stocking hat, wrap legs with dark steel floss. Wrap deep antique mauve floss from neck to $\frac{5}{8}$ inch below neck. Wrap small craft pick arms with deep antique mauve. Glue arms to shoulders, extending slightly forward. Make five black floss buttons; glue down front of jacket. Glue black hair to head as for boy in topcoat, *left*. Make scarf in same manner as for boy in topcoat, using medium royal blue floss.

For stocking hat, cut six 8-inch-long pieces of medium royal blue floss. Grouping two strands together for each braid strand, braid loosely and knot ends. Trim one end to $\frac{1}{4}$ inch; fluff ends to become pom-pom on top of hat. Beginning at back, wind and glue braid around head, ending with pom-pom on top.

Glue songbooks to hands.

For dolls to stand, glue white wood circle to bottom of each man and boy.

For dolls to hang, thread 8-inch-long piece of black carpet thread through strand of floss at back of neck. Knot thread ends to make loop.

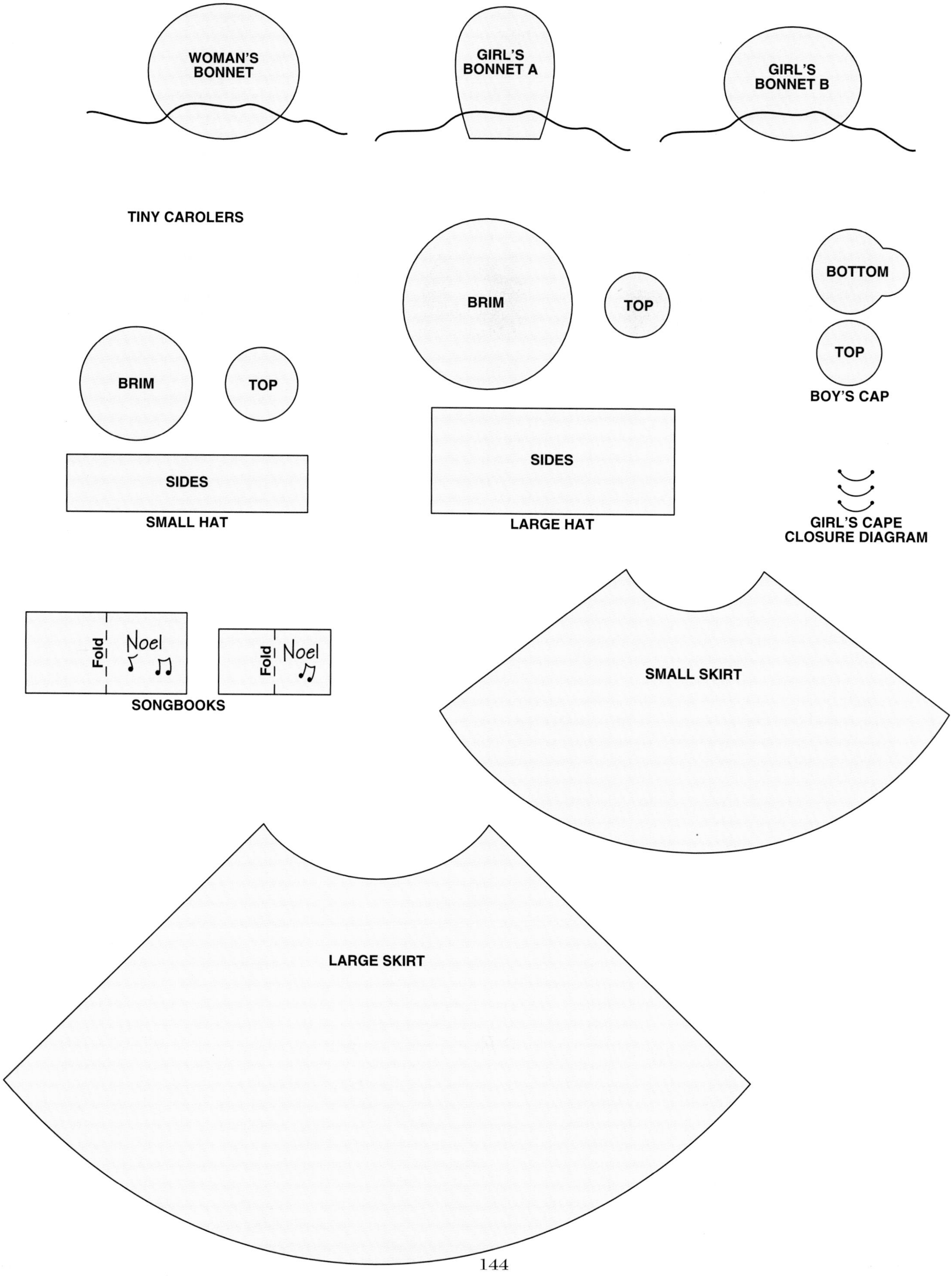
WOMAN'S BONNET
GIRL'S BONNET A
GIRL'S BONNET B
TINY CAROLERS
BRIM
TOP
BOTTOM
TOP
BOY'S CAP
BRIM
TOP
SIDES
SMALL HAT
SIDES
LARGE HAT
GIRL'S CAPE CLOSURE DIAGRAM
Fold
Noel
Fold
Noel
SONGBOOKS
SMALL SKIRT
LARGE SKIRT

The Glorious Evergreen

The Christmas tree is the centerpiece of our holiday decorating and the inspiration for the festive crafts in this chapter. We've touched every room of the house with tree trims, wrappings, decorations, even goodies to eat—all inspired by that wonderful and stately symbol of the season, the glorious evergreen.

Button-Tree *Trims*

Buttons and Christmas-colored fabrics combine to make our easy-to-craft tree ornaments. The pieces are lightly stuffed and trimmed using the blanket stitch. Instructions and patterns are on page 152.

Design: Jeff Julseth

Gift-Giving *Mittens*

What a clever way to give that most popular gift of fun money! Our little felt mittens are handing out what many people on your list like best. Instructions and patterns for these clever gift-giving mittens begin on page 152.

Designs: Susan Cage-Knoch

Flannel *Tree Quilt*

Simple and stunning, our country Christmas tree quilt is made using warm and cozy flannel. We've used favorite (yet ready to be recycled) flannel shirts for many of the blocks in this quilt. The colorful pieces are sewn into tree blocks, then connected with sashing strips of red and gold. *Instructions and patterns for this dynamic piece begin on page 153.*

Design: Margaret Sindelar

Vintage *Hankie Tree*

Vintage poinsettia handkerchiefs (or brand-new ones) are displayed on a covered cork board, creating a three-dimensional fabric tree. We've used pins and favorite buttons to attach the hankies to the board. Instructions for making our clever tree are on page 154.

Design: Anna Hansen

Holiday *Yule Log*

Welcome your guests with the spirit of Christmas by serving our delightful and delicious yule log cake. Made jelly-roll style, this cake is filled with Coffee Cream Filling and topped with Rich Chocolate Frosting. Turn to page 155 for the recipe for this traditional dessert.

Country Homespun Trims

Simple symbols of the season are used as the inspiration for these Christmas tree trims. Made from plaid and solid fabrics, each of these country motifs is highlighted with blanket stitches in colorful embroidery floss. Instructions and patterns begin on page 155.

Designs: Phyllis Dobbs

Christmas Collection Tree

What better way to share your favorite collectibles than on our wooden Christmas tree display shelf. The piece is designed with four shelves for showing off any collection—from Santas to teacups. Made from plywood, the piece is painted with acrylic paint. Instructions and pattern for this handsome piece are on page 157.

Design: Gaylen and Donna Chesnut and Carol Dahlstrom

Button-Tree Trims

As shown on page 146, finished ornaments measure $4\frac{1}{2}$×7 inches.

MATERIALS *for one tree*

Tracing paper
$5\frac{1}{2}$x9-inch piece of green solid or plaid quilted fabric
15-inch-long piece of brown twisted paper wire
Ecru embroidery floss
Tapestry needle
Polyester fiberfill
10 assorted buttons
Two $\frac{3}{4}$x6-inch strips of fabric in different red, green, or gold prints
$\frac{3}{8}$-inch-diameter gold jingle bell

INSTRUCTIONS

Trace pattern, *below*, flopping pattern along dotted line to complete; cut out. Cut two trees from quilted fabric.

Bend twisted paper wire to form a three-quarter circle. Bend a small loop into each end. Pin the quilted trees together with the wrong sides facing. At each X as shown on pattern, insert one end of the twisted paper wire and pin in place. Thread the tapestry needle with six plies of embroidery floss. Begin working blanket stitches around perimeter, spacing stitches $\frac{1}{4}$ inch apart and $\frac{1}{4}$ inch deep, and securing ends of wire. Before completing stitching, stuff tree shape lightly with polyester fiberfill. Hide the floss ends between the layers.

Use floss to sew eight buttons to ornament front, referring to photograph, *page 146*, as a guide. Using a half knot, tie fabric strips onto handle, one atop the other. Sew a button to knot leaving a 6-inch-long floss tail. Thread jingle bell onto floss end and knot in place, $1\frac{1}{4}$ inches from button.

Gift-Giving Mittens

As shown on page 146, each mitten measures $4\frac{3}{4}$×3 inches.

MATERIALS

Tracing paper
8x10-inch piece of white felt
4x6-inch piece of red felt
2x2-inch piece of green felt
Cotton embroidery floss: red and green
Embroidery needle
$\frac{1}{2}$-inch green star sequin
$\frac{1}{2}$-inch gold star sequin
Two 2-mm pearl beads
White sewing thread
3 inches of $\frac{1}{4}$-inch-wide white satin ribbon

INSTRUCTIONS

Trace patterns, *below*, onto tracing paper and cut out. Cut four mittens from white felt, tree from green felt, and heart from red felt. In addition,

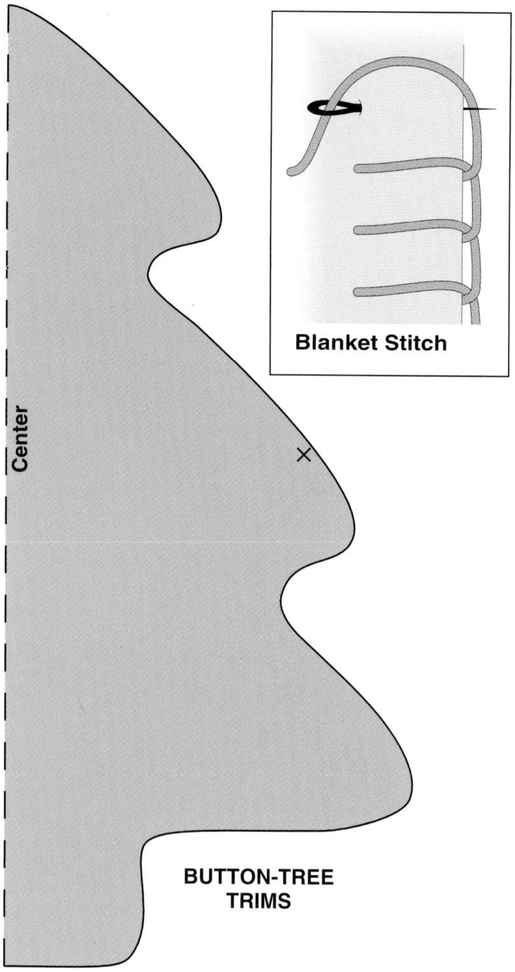

Blanket Stitch

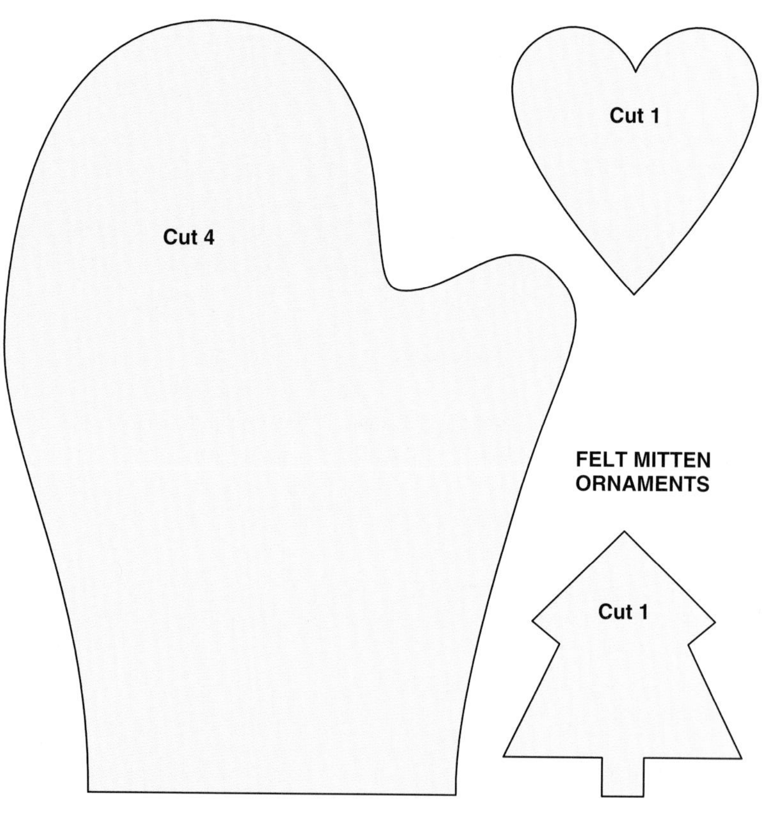

cut two 3¾×1½-inch mitten cuffs from red felt. Pattern and measurements include ⅛-inch seam allowances. Sew all seams with right sides facing.

Determine front piece of each mitten. Center tree on one mitten front; whipstitch in place using a three-ply strand of green floss. Repeat for heart on remaining mitten front, using red floss. Using pearl bead to anchor star, sew gold star to tree top. In same manner, sew green star to center of heart.

Sew mitten fronts to backs, leaving wrist edge open; turn. For each mitten, fold cuff in half lengthwise, matching edges. Sew doubled long edge of cuff to wrist edge of mitten, matching edges. Turn cuff up. Fold 1½-inch-long piece of ribbon in half. Insert the ribbon ends into open edges of cuff opening; tack in place. Whipstitch open edges closed.

Flannel Tree Quilt

As shown on page 147, quilt measures 90×78 inches.

MATERIALS

- **Graph paper**
- **Quilters' template material**
- **6 yards of 45-inch-wide green and red plaid flannel backing fabric**
- **4 yards of 45-inch-wide solid cream flannel**
- **3 yards of 45-inch-wide solid green flannel**
- **3 yards of 45-inch-wide solid red flannel**
- **1½ yards of 45-inch-wide gold cotton fabric**
- **½ yard of 45-inch-wide brown plaid flannel**
- **¼ yard each of sixteen 45-inch-wide different plaid flannel fabrics, in blues, reds, and greens**
- **Polyester batting**
- **#3 pearl cotton: gold and green to match fabrics**

INSTRUCTIONS

Enlarge quilt patterns, *page 154*, onto graph paper; cut apart on solid lines. Draw around pieces on template material, adding ¼-inch seam allowances. From solid green flannel, cut 16 As. Using blue, red, and green plaids at random, cut 16 Bs, 16 Cs, 16 Ds, and 16 Es. From cream flannel, cut 16 Fs. Turn template over and cut 16 more Fs. Also from cream, cut 32 Hs. From brown plaid, cut 16 Gs. From gold cotton fabric, cut 25 Is and 100 Js. Turn template over and cut 100 more Js. From solid red flannel, cut 20 Ks, 20 Ls, and 20 Ms.

In addition, cut eight 6½×12½-inch top and bottom row rectangles, eight 15½×6½-inch side edge rectangles, and four 6½×6½-inch-square corner blocks from cream flannel. From remaining solid green flannel, cut 3½-inch-wide binding strips to fit around outside edge of quilt. Measurements include ¼-inch seam allowances.

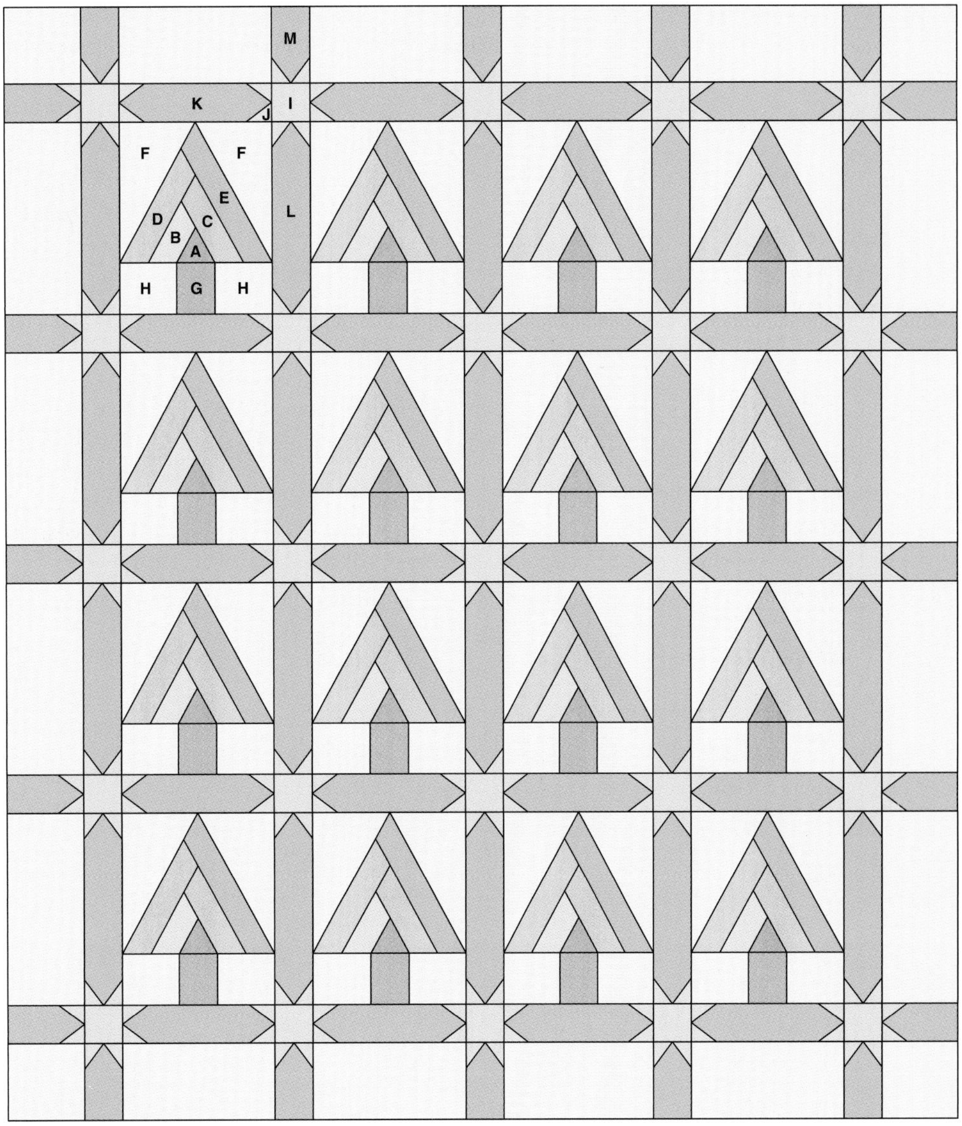

ASSEMBLY DIAGRAM

For each block, referring to pattern diagram, *page 154*, sew B to A, C to AB, D to BC, and E to CD. Sew F to each side of plaid tree triangle. Next, sew H to each long side of G. To finish block, sew HGH strip to bottom edge of plaid tree triangle. Make 16 blocks.

For sashing, sew diagonal side of J to each angled edge of M. Repeat for 20 pieces. In same manner, sew Js to all Ks and Ls.

For top row, sew a 6½×6½-inch cream corner block to left side of MJ piece with point down. Working left to right, sew short side of 6½×12½-inch rectangle to right side of MJ, add another MJ, a second rectangle, third MJ, third rectangle, fourth MJ, fourth rectangle, fifth MJ, and finally a corner block. Repeat and turn upside down for bottom row.

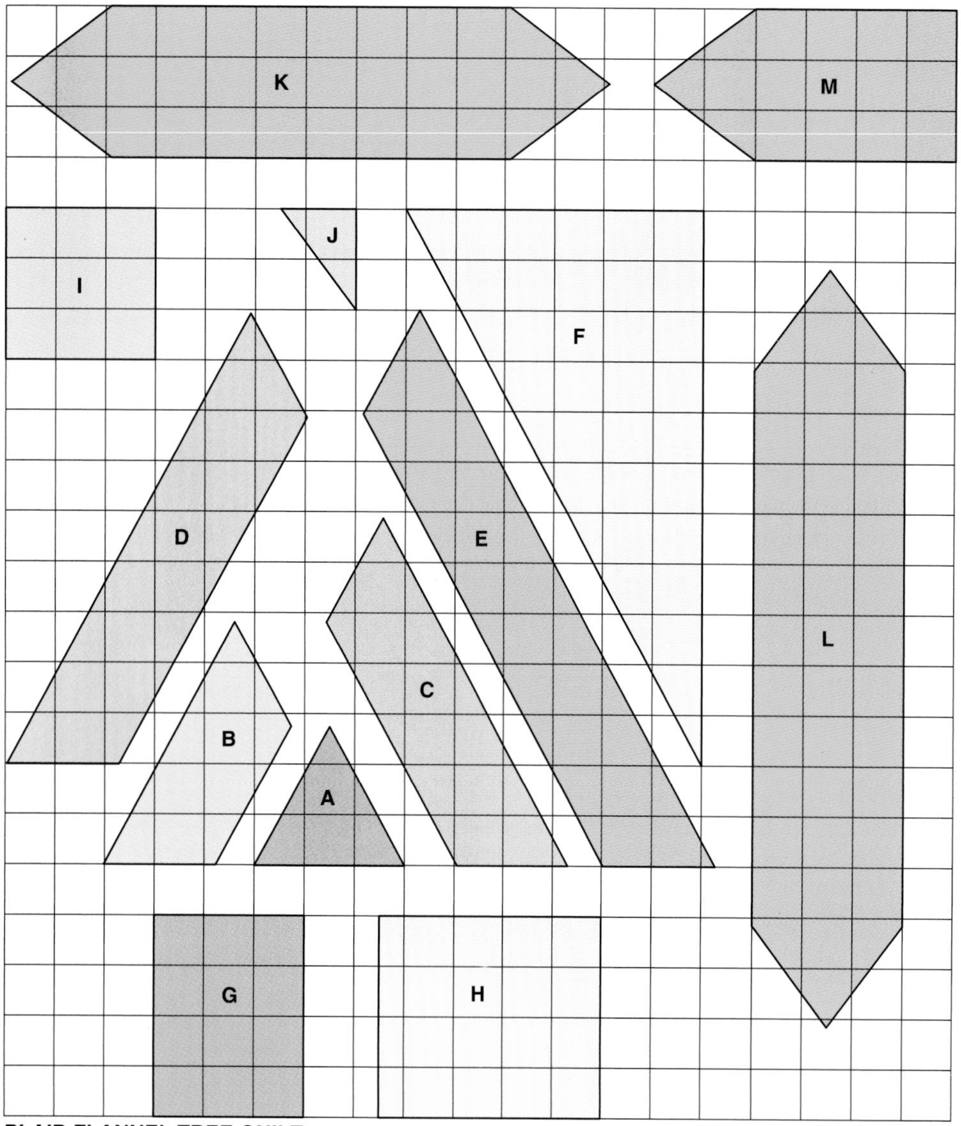

PLAID FLANNEL TREE QUILT

1 Square = 1 Inch

Arrange trees in four rows of four blocks each. For each tree row, sew long side of 15½×6½-inch rectangle to long edge of LJ, tree block to right side, LJ to right side of tree block, continuing left to right in same manner, ending with a 15½×6½-inch rectangle sewn to right side of fourth tree block. Repeat for all four tree rows.

For horizontal sashing, sew gold end of MJ to gold block. Working from left to right, sew KJ to right side of gold block, second gold block to KJ, and so forth, using four KJ pieces and ending with MJ piece, all separated by gold blocks. Make five horizontal sashing strips.

Sew horizontal sashing between all rows, as shown on assembly diagram, *page 153,* matching seam lines. Layer quilt top, batting, and back (pieced as necessary). Baste. Tie the corners of the gold blocks using gold pearl cotton. Using green pearl cotton, tie the trees at the top point and at the two center points below.

Trim batting and back pieces 1 inch beyond quilt top. Sew enough 3½-inch-wide strips together to fit around edge of quilt. Pin the binding to the quilt top, right sides together; stitch through all layers, using a ¼-inch seam and mitering the corners. Turn the binding to the back of the quilt and turn under ¼ inch along raw edge. Blindstitch in place.

Vintage Hankie Tree

As shown on page 148, framed tree measures 36×24 inches.

MATERIALS

36x24-inch framed cork bulletin board
Gold metallic spray paint
40x28-inch piece of green cotton fabric
Staple gun
10 handkerchiefs
Pins
White facial tissues
16 assorted 1-inch-diameter brass buttons
6 assorted colored buttons
2-inch-diameter gold plastic star
Hot-glue gun
Hot-glue stick

INSTRUCTIONS

Remove frame from corkboard. Spraypaint frame gold and allow it to dry.

Stretch the green cotton fabric over the front of the corkboard; staple the edges down in back. Replace the covered corkboard in frame.

To pin each handkerchief in place, pinch center between fingers, shake handkerchief, and then pin center to the bulletin board. Beginning 12 inches above the bottom edge of the green fabric, center four handkerchiefs with pins approximately 3 inches apart. For the next row, center three handkerchiefs about 6½ inches above the first, using the same spacing. In the same manner, center two handkerchiefs above the row of three with the final handkerchief at the top.

Insert a facial tissue under each handkerchief to add dimension if desired.

Hot-glue brass buttons in a square pattern, four across and four down, to fabric under tree to resemble a Christmas tree trunk. Hot-glue colored buttons to handkerchiefs at random. Glue the star to top of the tree.

Holiday Yule Log

As shown on page 149.

INGREDIENTS

- **1 cup all-purpose flour**
- **¼ teaspoon salt**
- **5 egg yolks**
- **2 tablespoons dry or cream sherry**
- **1 cup granulated sugar**
- **5 egg whites**
- **¼ teaspoon cream of tartar**
- **Powdered sugar**
- **Coffee Cream Filling**
- **Rich Chocolate Frosting**

METHOD

Grease and lightly flour a 15×10×1-inch jelly-roll pan; set aside. Stir together flour and salt in a small bowl. Beat egg yolks and sherry in a large bowl with an electric mixer on high speed about 5 minutes or till thick and lemon-colored. Gradually add ½ cup of the granulated sugar, beating till the sugar is almost dissolved.

Wash beaters. Beat egg whites and cream of tartar in a very large bowl on medium to high speed till soft peaks form (tips curl). Gradually add remaining granulated sugar, 2 tablespoons at a time, beating on medium to high speed till stiff peaks form (tips stand straight). Fold 1 cup of the egg white mixture into egg yolk mixture. Fold egg yolk mixture into remaining egg white mixture. Fold in flour mixture; spread in the prepared pan.

Bake in a 375° oven for 12 to 15 minutes or till top springs back. Immediately loosen cake from pan. Invert cake onto a towel sprinkled with powdered sugar. Roll up warm cake and towel jelly-roll style, starting from a short side. Cool on a wire rack.

Gently unroll cake. Spread filling onto cake to within 1 inch of the edges. Roll up cake without towel, jelly-roll style, starting from one of the short sides. Cut a 2-inch slice from one end of cake. Place the slice at the side of the log to form a branch. Frost with Rich Chocolate Frosting. Using the tines of a fork, score the cake lengthwise to resemble tree bark. Makes 10 servings.

Coffee Cream Filling: Beat 1 cup *whipping cream,* ¼ cup *sifted powdered sugar,* and 1½ teaspoons *instant coffee crystals* in a mixing bowl till soft peaks form. Makes about 2 cups.

Rich Chocolate Frosting: Heat and stir 2 ounces *unsweetened chocolate* and 2 tablespoons *margarine or butter* in a saucepan till chocolate melts. Remove from heat; stir in 2 cups *sifted powdered sugar,* ½ teaspoon *vanilla,* and 2 to 3 tablespoons *milk* to make a frosting of spreading consistency. Makes 1¼ cups.

Country Trims

As shown on page 150, each ornament measures 4×5 inches.

MATERIALS

For one of each design

- **Tracing paper**
- **Paper-backed iron-on adhesive**
- **4½x11-inch piece each of two different forest green plaid fabrics**
- **4½x11-inch piece of maroon plaid fabric**
- **8x10-inch piece of maroon solid fabric**
- **4x5-inch piece of forest green solid fabric**
- **Cotton embroidery floss: maroon, forest green, and country blue**
- **Embroidery needle**
- **Straight pins**
- **Three 5½x6½-inch pieces of quilt batting**
- **Three 5½x½-inch pieces of muslin**
- **Christmas green quilting thread**
- **Assorted ivory, dark green, and maroon buttons**
- **1 yard of ⅛-inch-wide forest green satin ribbon**
- **Hot-glue gun**
- **Hot-glue stick**
- **Sewing threads to match fabrics**
- **Polyester fiberfill**

INSTRUCTIONS

Cut each 4½×11-inch piece of plaid fabric into two 4½×5½-inch rectangles. Set aside one piece of each plaid fabric for the back of the ornament.

Trace the patterns, *page 156,* onto the iron-on adhesive. Following the manufacturer's directions, fuse the angel and rocking horse adhesive to the maroon fabric and star adhesive to the green fabric; cut out. Remove the paper backing; fuse the horse and angel to the green plaids and the star to the maroon plaid, centering the designs on rectangles.

Blanket stitch around each fused cutout using three plies of green embroidery floss for the angel and horse and three plies of maroon embroidery floss for the star. Using three plies of blue embroidery floss, make French knot eyes on the angel, using the photograph, *page 150,* as a guide.

For each ornament, layer the batting rectangle atop the muslin rectangle. Center the ornament front atop the batting. Pin all three layers together, so ½ inch of batting and muslin extends all around. Using green thread, machine quilt around the perimeter of the appliqué, ⅛ inch beyond the edges.

Using photograph, *page 150,* as a guide, sew buttons to ornaments as desired.

Cut three 4-inch-long pieces of green satin ribbon; tie each into small bow. Hot-glue one bow to the horse's neck, one at the angel's neck, and one to button in the center of the star.

Cut three 8-inch lengths of green ribbon to make hanging loops for the ornaments. For each hanging loop, fold the ribbon in half, stack the ends, and pin to the center top of the ornament front with the raw edges matching.

Sew each ornament front to back, using ¼-inch seam allowance and leaving an opening for turning. Turn ornaments right side out and stuff with polyester fiberfill; sew the openings closed.

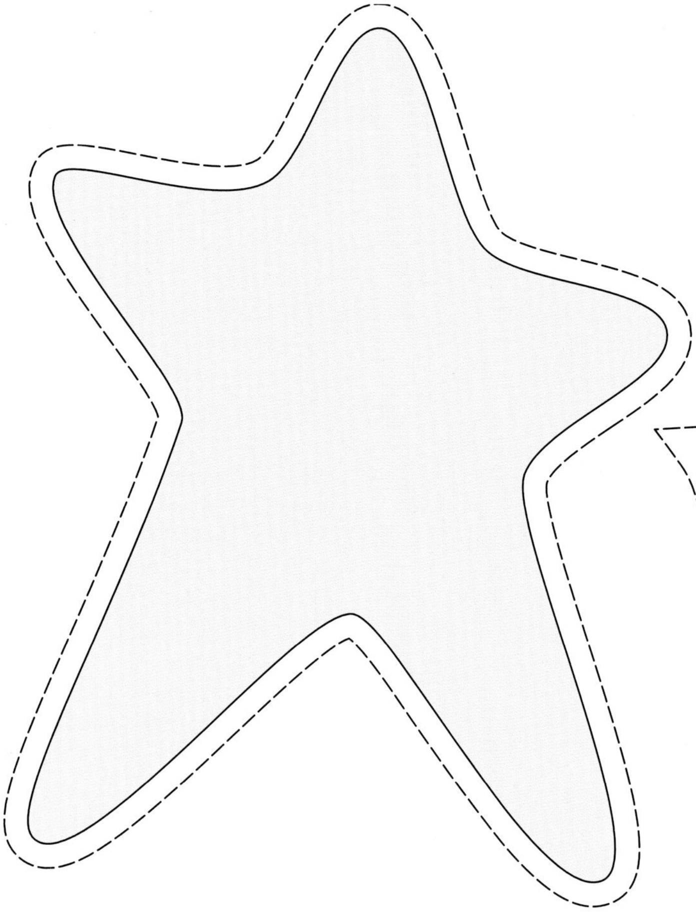

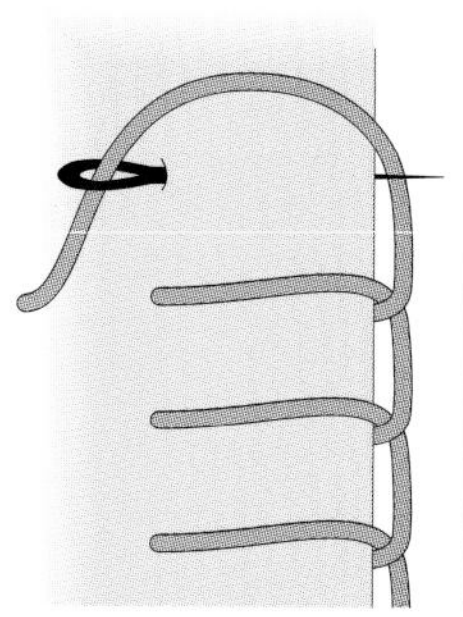

Blanket Stitch

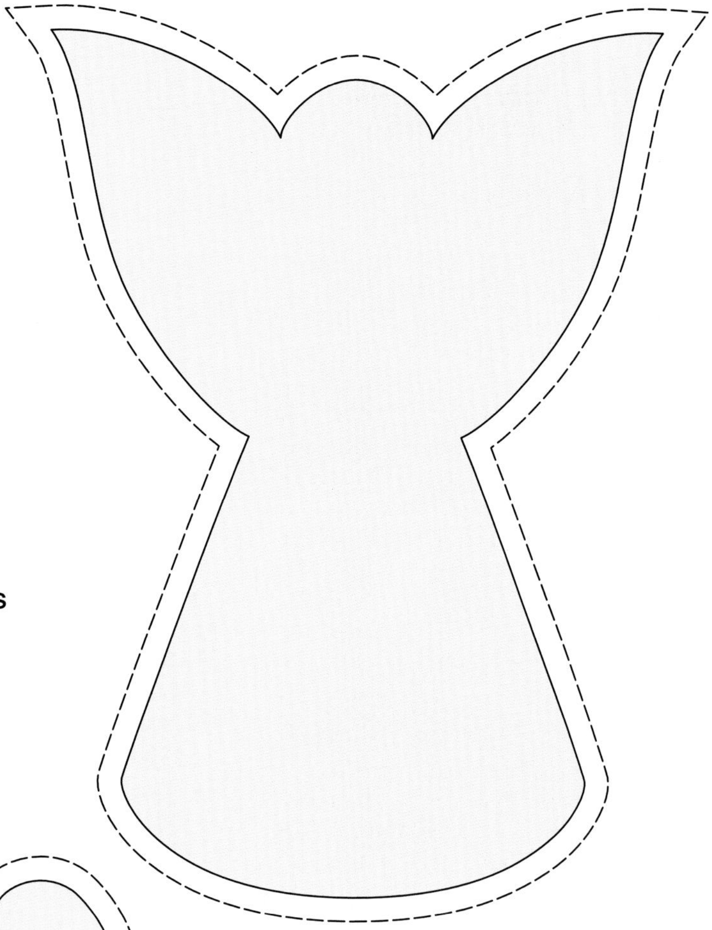

COUNTRY HOMESPUN TRIMS

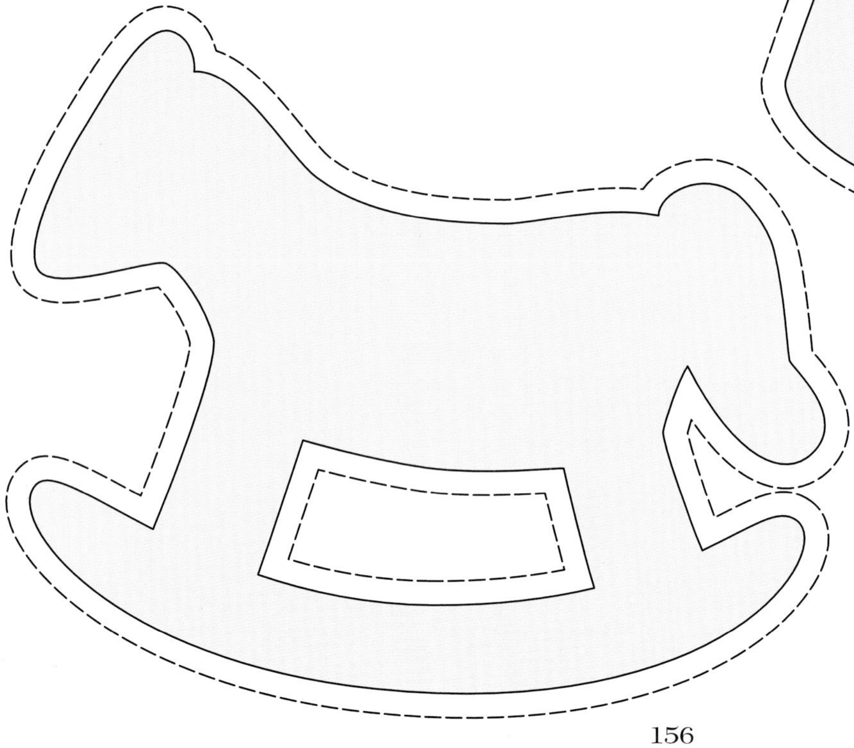

Christmas Collection Tree

As shown on page 151, tree measures 59 inches tall.

MATERIALS

Several sheets of 1-inch-grid graph paper
4x8-foot sheet of ½-inch AC plywood
9-foot strip of dentil trim
Jigsaw
Medium grit sandpaper
Wood glue
Fourteen 1¾-inch wood screws
Twelve 1½-inch finish nails
Three ¾-inch brads
Folkart acrylic paint: shamrock green, brown, and harvest gold

INSTRUCTIONS

Enlarge patterns, *right and below*, onto graph paper and cut out. Trace tree and star outlines onto plywood; cut out with jigsaw. From remaining wood, rip one 5×36-inch shelf, one 4½×30-inch shelf, one 4×24-inch shelf, and one 3½×18-inch shelf. Cut strips of dentil trim to measure 36, 30, 24, and 18 inches in length. Lightly sand all cut edges.

Attach shelves to tree using wood glue and screws. Beginning with longest shelf at bottom of tree, attach shelves in descending length from bottom to top, affixing each across the widest part of the branch shape. Attach trim to front of each shelf using wood glue and finish nails.

Paint tree green and trunk portion brown. Paint stars gold. Attach large star to tree top using wood glue and brads. Glue small star atop large star.

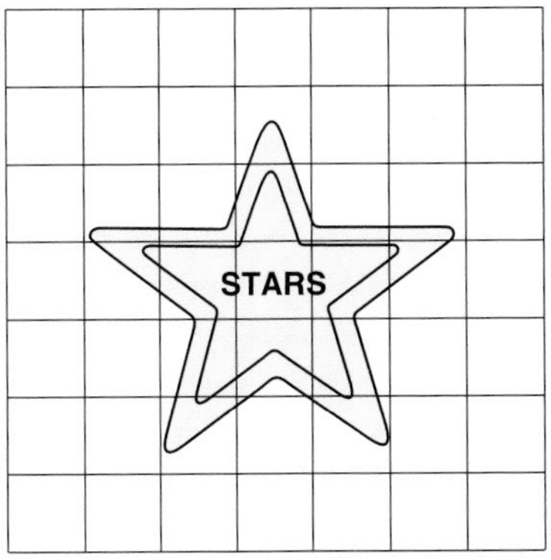

1 Square = 2 Inches

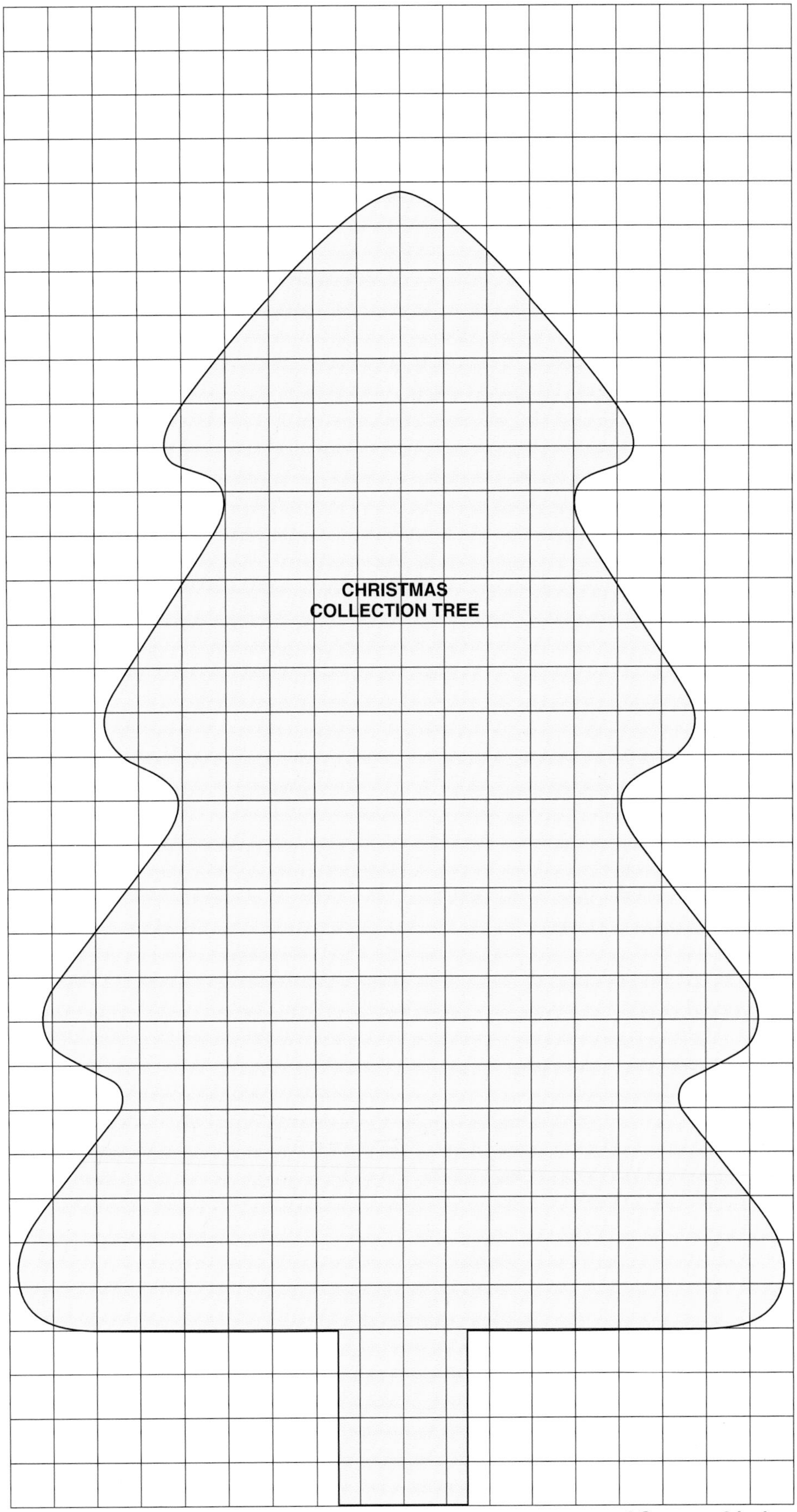

1 Square = 2 Inches

Index

A
A Child Is Born Bookmark 93
A Child Is Born Card 93

B
Bear-Paw Quilt 11
Beribboned and Beautiful
  Holiday Ribbon Tree 68–69
Bird Napkin Ring 28
Butterscotch Lollipops 126–127
Button-Tree Trims 146

C
Candle and Heart Garland 26–27
Candy-Cane Wreaths 12
Cardinal Door Decoration 8–9
Chenille Snowflake Afghan 29
Christmas Collection Tree 151
Christmas Twins 128
Clever Candy-Cane Containers 74
Clever Cut-Up Santa Cake 49
Cookies and Eggnog 12
Country Homespun Trims 150
Country Patchwork Stocking 107
Cranberry-Nut Pinwheels 12
Crazy Patchwork Jacket 13
Creamy White Gardenia Wreath 32
Crochet Abbreviations 159
Crocheted Candy-Cane Stocking 110
Crocheted Snowflakes 26–27
Crocheted Stockings 126–127
Cross-Stitched Nativity 88–89
Cross-Stitch Pillows 15
Crystal Candies 126–127

D–E
Dear St. Nick Pin 45
Elegant Hardanger Doily 33
Eucalyptus Tree Topper 26

F
Faux Gingerbread Friends 128
Festive Hardanger Stocking 108
Festive Holiday Eggnog 12
Flannel Tree Quilt 147
Flower Ribbon Prisms 68–69
Folk Art Pillow 90
Freddy the Frog Prince 129
Friendly Frosty Hot Pad 46

G–H
Gift-Giving Mittens 146
Grandma's Fudge 75
Happy Snowmen Banner and Doll 48
Holiday Pfeffernüesse 12
Holiday Yule Log 140
Honey Sand Balls 12
Hydrangea Topiary 28

I–M
Jewelry
  Dear St. Nick Pin 45
  Snow Family Pin 46
  12-Days Necklace 14
Knitting Abbreviations 159
Lace-Framed Ornaments 68–69
Marbled Bark 75
Mirrored Star Ornaments 68–69

N
Naturally White-on-White
  Holiday Evergreen 26–27
Nature Lover's Candles
  and Leaves 30–31
Nutcracker Ballet Stocking 109

O
Old West Cactus Bread 76–77
Ornaments
  Advent Angel Ornament 91
  Button-Tree Trims 146
  Country Homespun Trims 150
  Crocheted Snowflakes 26–27
  Crocheted Stockings 126–127
  Faux Gingerbread Friends 128
  Flower Ribbon Prisms 68–69
  Lace-Framed Ornaments 68–69
  Mirrored Star Ornaments 68–69
  Ribbon Cocarde Ornaments 68–69
  Sachet Pillowettes 68–69
  Sparkling Chrismons 92
  Sweet Advent Angel 91

P–Q
Painted Santa Doorstop 47
Personalized Festive Bows 72

R
Recipes
  Butterscotch Lollipops 126–127
  Candy-Cane Wreaths 12
  Clever Cut-Up Santa Cake 49
  Cranberry-Nut Pinwheels 12
  Crystal Candies 126–127
  Festive Holiday Eggnog 12
  Grandma's Fudge 75
  Holiday Pfeffernüesse 12
  Holiday Yule Log 140
  Honey Sand Balls 12
  Marbled Bark 75
  Old West Cactus Bread 76–77
  Spicy Pecans 74
  Sweet Spiced Walnuts 74
  White-as-Snow Cookies 26–27
  Yummy Caramel Corn 126–127
Ribbon Cocarde Ornament 68–69
Ribbon Rose Tree Skirt 69

S
Sachet Pillowettes 68–69
Santas
  Clever Cut-Up Santa Cake 49
  Dear St. Nick Pin 45
  Felt St. Nick Stocking 106
  Painted Santa Doorstop 47
  Santa Wall Quilt 50
  Welcoming Banister Santa 44
Santa Wall Quilt 50
Silver Pinecone Garland 26–27
Simply Wrapped Gifts 70
Snow Family Pin 46
Snowmen
  Friendly Frosty Hot Pad 46
  Happy Snowmen Banner
    and Doll 48
  Snow Family Pin 46
Sparkling Chrismons 92
Spicy Pecans 74
St. Nick Stocking 106
Stockings
  Country Patchwork Stocking 107
  Crocheted Candy-Cane Stocking 110
  Felt St. Nick Stocking 106
  Hardanger Stocking 108
  Nutcracker Ballet Stocking 109
  St. Nick Stocking 106
  Tiny Felt Stockings 110
Sweet Advent Angel 91
Sweet Candy-Cane Dress 10
Sweet Holiday Gift Bags 75
Sweet Spiced Walnuts 74

T–V
Tiny Carolers 130
Tiny Clever Package 71
Tiny Felt Stockings 110
12-Days Sampler and Necklace 14
Vintage Hankie Tree 148

W–Z
Wearables
  Crazy Patchwork Jacket 13
  Sweet Candy-Cane Dress 10
Welcoming Banister Santa 44–45
Western Clay Pots 76–77
White-as-Snow Cookies 26–27
Yummy Caramel Corn 126–127

Sources

Chapter 1
Crazy Patchwork Jacket, page 13: Pattern—FOLKWEAR, The Tauton Press, 63 S. Main Street, P.O. Box 5506, Newtown, CT 06470–5506; buttons and charms—JHB International, Inc., 1955 S. Quince Street, Denver, CO 80231; 303/751-8100.

Chapter 2
Chenille Snowflake Afghan, page 29: Yarn—Monsanto Co., 320 Interstate N. Parkway, Suite 400, Atlanta, GA 30339; 404/951-7600; http://www.thesmartyarns.com

Chapter 3
Dear St. Nick Pin, page 45: Paints—Delta Technical Coatings, Inc.; 800/423-4135.

Painted Santa Doorstop, page 47: Paints—Delta Technical Coatings, Inc., 800/423-4135.

Chapter 4
Ribbon Rose Tree Skirt, page 69: Ribbon—C.M. Offray & Sons, Inc., Route 24, Box 601, Chester, NJ 07930–0601.

Lace-Framed Father Christmas Ornaments, pages 68–69: Lace—St. Louis Trimming, Inc., 5040 Arsenal Street, St. Louis, MO 63139; 314/771-8388.

Mirrored Star Ornaments, pages 68–69: Beads and mirrors—The Beadery, 105 Canonchet Road, Hope Valley, RI 02832; 401/539-2432.

Chapter 5
Advent Angel Ornament, page 91: Paints—Delta Technical Coatings, Inc.; 800/423-4135.

Sparkling Chrismons, page 92: Threads—Rainbow Gallery, 7412 Fulton Avenue #5, North Hollywood, CA 91605.

Chapter 7
Faux Gingerbread Friends, page 128: Paints—Delta Technical Coatings, Inc.; 800/423-4135.

Freddy the Frog Prince, page 129: Paints, Fabric Color, and Fabric Dye Brush—Delta Technical Coatings, Inc.; 800/423-4135.

Tiny Carolers, page 130: Embroidery floss—DMC, Port Kearney Building 10, South Kearney, NJ 07032–0650.

Needlework Projects
Fabrics
• Charles Craft, P.O. Box 1049, Laurinberg, NC 28353; 800/277-0980. • Wichelt Imports, Inc., R.R. 1, Stoddard, WI 54658. • Zweigert, 2 Riverview Dr., Somerset, NJ 08873–1139; 908/271-1949.

Threads
• Anchor, Consumer Service Dept., P.O. Box 27067, Greenville, SC 29616. • DMC, Port Kearney Building 10, South Kearney, NJ 07032–0650. • Kreinik Manufacturing, 800/537-2166.

Photographers

Hopkins Associates: Front cover and pages 6–7, 10–11, 15, 25–28, 30–31, 33, 43, 46, 48, 67–69, 74–77, 87–89, 92–93, 102–103, 106–108, 125–128, 145–148, 151.

Scott Little: Pages 8–9, 12–14, 29, 32, 44–45, 47, 49–50, 70–73, 90–91, 109–110, 129–130, 149, 150.

Crochet Abbreviations

bch—bead chain
bsc—bead single crochet
ch(s)—chain(s)
cl—cluster
cont—continue
dc—double crochet
est—established
fpdc—front post double crochet
fpsc—front post single crochet
hdc—half double crochet
inc—increase
lp(s)—loop(s)
pch—pearl chain
psc—pearl single crochet
rep—repeat
rnd(s)—round(s)
RS—right side
RT—right
sc—single crochet
sk—skip
sl—slip
sp(s)—space(s)
st(s)—stitch(es)
trc—triple crochet
WS—wrong side

Knitting Abbreviations

beg—beginning
cont—continue
dec—decrease
est—establish
k—knit
p—purl
pat—pattern
psso—pass slipped stitch over
rem—remaining
rep—repeat
RS—right side
sl—slip
sl st—slip stitch
ssk—slip slip knit
st st— stockinette stitch
sts—stitches
tog—together
WS—wrong side
yo—yarn over